90 004

D1756592

This book is to be returned on
or before the date stamped below

POLYTECHNIC SOUTH WEST

ACADEMIC SERVICES
Plymouth Library
Tel: (0752) 232323
This book is subject to recall if required by another reader
Books may be renewed by phone
CHARGES WILL BE MADE FOR OVERDUE BOOKS

PSYCHOLINGUISTIC IMPLICATIONS FOR LINGUISTIC RELATIVITY:

A CASE STUDY OF CHINESE

Rumjahn Hoosain

University of Hong Kong

LEA LAWRENCE ERLBAUM ASSOCIATES, PUBLISHERS
1991   Hillsdale, New Jersey   Hove and London

Lawrence Erlbaum Associates, Inc., Publishers
365 Broadway
Hillsdale, New Jersey 07642

Library of Congress Cataloging-in-Publication Data

Hoosain, R. (Rumjahn)
    Psycholinguistic implications for linguistic relativity : a case study of Chinese / Rumjahn Hoosain
      p. cm.
    Includes bibliographical references and index.
    ISBN 0-8058-0898-1
    1. Chinese language--Psychological aspects.   I. Title.
PL1035. H66   1991
495.1'01'9--dc20   91-3357
                                                                              CIP

Printed in the United States of America
10 9 8 7 6 5 4 3 2 1

Contents

PREFACE

In the last dozen years, there have been five conferences on the psychological aspects of the Chinese language; the first was held in Taiwan and the subsequent ones in Hong Kong. I helped organize three of those conferences and eventually recognized that some systematic review of the topic was appropriate. The result is this book, the drift of which reveals a new aspect of the linguistic relativity hypothesis. I have to thank all the participants of the earlier conferences for much of the substance of this book.

I gratefully acknowledge a few people more specifically. My teacher Charles E. Osgood showed me the vista of psycholinguistics. He had planned to write a *Method and Theory in Psycholinguistics* as a sequel to his *Method and Theory in Experimental Psychology*. Alas, his health does not make this possible. I have intended this book to be a kind of *Method and Theory in Chinese Psycholinguistics*, as a small token of my indebtedness. It will be apparent to the reader that the work of Dr. Ovid Tzeng and Dr. Daisy Hung has been important for the development of some of the ideas here, although our conclusions may not always be the same. I owe to them the idea of linguistic relativity in terms of facility of information processing rather than in terms of world view. An anonymous reviewer made valuable suggestions. Finally, I wish to thank my wife, Dr. Farideh Salili, for her encouragement.

1 Introduction

This book proposes that unique linguistic properties of the Chinese language, particularly its orthography, have implications for cognitive processing, but not in the conventional sense of the Sapir-Whorf hypothesis of linguistic relativity (see Hoosain, 1986a; O. J. L. Tzeng & Hung, 1981). In the original hypothesis, it was suggested that language influences thought, and in such a way that the use of different languages can lead to different conceptualizations or thought structures. Also, attention to language differences was focused on vocabulary or grammatical structure. One example of the effect of language structure on thought was that the Hopi Indian's notion of time was different from that of the Westerner, since among other things the language did not have the three-tense system of Standard Average European (Whorf, 1956). Some ideas, such as that of absolute simultaneity, were supposed to be very difficult or impossible for the Hopi and had to be replaced by operational concepts. In this manner, conceptualizations or world views of different peoples were said to differ as a result of linguistic differences.

Introductory books on the linguistic relativity hypothesis usually refer to the many Eskimo words for snow, the various Arab words for camels, or the many words for types of rice in Southeast Asian languages, and dwell on the possible effects the words have on the ability of the respective language speakers to perceive the corresponding physical differences. We might note that in classical Chinese, there were a dozen distinct characters for varieties of cattle, although most of them are no longer used in modern Chinese (Ma, 1970). These included, for example, a separate character for a cow with a very long back, all in one morpheme. One could therefore speculate on the propensity of the earlier Chinese to be able to see the bovine distinctions depicted by the richer vocabulary. It does not have to be physical attributes either — perhaps abstract concepts are more interesting. Thus, social psychologists might wish to look at the implications of the absence of a concept corresponding to *privacy* in Chinese usage.

However, particularly with the work of Berlin and Kay (1969) and Rosch (1974) on basic color terms, people are more disinclined to think that language determines perception or thought, in the strong sense of linguistic determinism. Diverse languages all over the world show an orderly sequence of expansion of the vocabulary for basic color terms. Furthermore, whether a language has the full complement of 11 basic color terms like English or only 2 like Dani, the respective native speakers have been shown to perceive and remember color variations similarly[1]. Kay and Kempton (1984) demonstrated, in a study comparing English and Tarahumara (a Uto-Aztecan language of northern Mexico), that a color discrimination difference, based on the lack of a basic lexical distinction of "green" and "blue" in Tarahumara, disappeared when the strategy of using lexical labels was blocked. It could be that the way human beings come to see and encode colors has a physiological basis (Hurvich & Jameson, 1974; MacNichol, 1964), and so we would be less likely to find language effects on the cognition of color (Kay & McDaniel, 1978). In any case, it seems reasonable to accept that language provisions can direct a speaker's attention to certain physical or abstract attributes, and in this manner function to facilitate certain perceptions, but not necessarily "fully determine" them.

There has been some recent interest on an aspect of Chinese language structure and the effects it might have on thought processes. Bloom (1981) pointed out that Chinese does not have the subjunctive construction which acts as a marker for the counterfactual conditional in English (e.g., *If the government were to pass a law, then . . .*). Bloom had the impression that the Chinese found it difficult "to reason about things that they knew could not be the case" (p. 13). He hypothesized that the absence of the subjunctive structure predisposes the Chinese not to appreciate counterfactual import. His studies in Taiwan and Hong Kong, compared with those in the United States, appeared to support this hypothesis. When presented with sentences of the form "X was not the case, but if X was, then Y, then Z, etc.," Chinese subjects were reported to be less able to realize that the consequents were considerations of what might have been but wasn't. However, subsequent findings are inconsistent with Bloom's conclusions. The subjunctive was

---

[1] It might be noted that Chinese has only 10 basic color terms. The equivalent for *pink* (a basic English color term) is made up of two characters or morphemes and translates as 'powder red', which therefore is not a basic color term.

shown to be not necessary for counterfactual thought (Au, 1984). Rather, developmental factors were significant (L. G. Liu, 1985). Apart from empirical verification, one could perhaps note that Chinese does not need a subjunctive construction mirroring that of English to express a counterfactual thought. Chao (1955) noted a popular expression in Chinese that could embody this spirit, namely, "If p is true, my name is not Wang" (with the name of the speaker being Wang, of course).

These examples demonstrate how vocabulary and language structure could possibly influence the way we perceive or think about things. In this book though, we concentrate more on the orthography of the Chinese language and its cognitive implications. The influence of orthography on cognition, particularly the influence of the manner in which the script represents sound and meaning, was not originally recognized in the work of Sapir and Whorf. In his discussion of the interaction between language and cultural experience, Sapir stated that, "It is the constant interplay between language and experience which removes language from the cold status of such purely and simply symbolic systems as mathematical symbolism or flag signaling" (Mandelbaum, 1951, p. 11). But the history of mathematics has amply demonstrated that cold symbolism, just as much as culture- embedded language, influences cognitive processes. We only have to contrast the ease of calculating with Arabic numerals instead of Roman numerals or the use of the Leibnitz's notations for calculus instead of Newton's (see O. J. L. Tzeng & Hung, 1981). The important point to note is that the effects of orthography or symbol systems are more in terms of the manner or facility with which information is processed, rather than different categorizations of information, such as relating to time, snow, or counterfactual conditional.

The psycholinguistic implications of the Chinese orthography examined in this book are more in terms of the facility with which language users process information, and the manner of information processing. No categorically different perceptions need result from such language distinctions. It has been suggested that such language effects matter more in data-driven or bottom-up processes rather than in conceptually driven or top-down processes (Hung & Tzeng, 1981). The former are initiated and largely determined by sensory information, but the latter are dominated by experience and knowledge of possible interpretations of the sensory information (Lindsay & Norman, 1977). For example, in reading, factors like size and clarity of the print affect bottom-up processes, but command of the language and the subject matter affects top-down processes. In any given situation, the two types of processes interact to eventually determine perception. Thus, whereas all those who can read will be able to read what is printed clearly, good readers are more able to read bad handwriting. For them, top-down processes compensate for the degraded or ambiguous sensory information. We shall see if the effects of the Chinese orthography are mainly confined to bottom-up processes.

We review Chinese studies in the three areas of perception, memory, and neurolinguistics to see how language or orthography differences could affect the manner in which we process information. Before that, we review linguistic aspects of Chinese that have some bearing on cognitive processes. In this book, we are more concerned with the written language. We are also more often concerned with the comprehension rather than the production of language, that is, reading more than writing.

Two sets of notes are used in this book. Those indicated by superscripts are ordinary footnotes for each chapter. Those indicated within brackets [ ] refer to illustrations with Chinese characters listed in the Appendix.

2 Aspects of the Chinese Language

A unit of written Chinese is the character, and the distinctiveness of a character lies in its being simultaneously a visual whole, a syllabic unit, and the unit of meaning. This script–sound–meaning convergence provides the character with a salience and versatility that is absent in units of other languages, even though a character is not quite a word. Chinese characters are labeled variously as pictographs, ideographs, or logographs. These labels are sometimes applied inappropriately, and a clarification would help our understanding of the orthography. Acquaintance with the manner in which characters are used to make up words and larger linguistic units would also be useful in appreciating the cognitive implications of the language.

2.1 SCRIPT

To start with, Chinese characters are made up of configurations of eight major types of strokes, each with a label of its own [1]. Finer discrimination can produce about 20 distinct strokes (see W. S.-Y. Wang, 1973). The number of strokes in a character can vary from 1 to well over 20. In the simplified script adopted on the mainland after the establishment of the People's Republic of China — as distinct from the traditional script used in Taiwan, Hong Kong, and other overseas communities — the number of strokes is often significantly smaller (see Table 2.1).

The average number of strokes of the 14 most frequently occurring characters written in the traditional script, according to a corpus of more

5

TABLE 2.1
Examples of Simplification of Traditional Characters

1. *Delete Component*		
Traditional:	兒	務
Simplified:	儿	务
2. *Delete Repeated Component*		
Traditional:	篔	齒
Simplified:	貟	齿
3. *Replace with Simpler Component*		
Traditional:	傷	劉
Simplified:	伤	刘
4. *Substitute Phonetic*		
Traditional:	癢	劇
Simplified:	痒	剧
5. *Substitute Radical*		
Traditional:	颿	跡
Simplified:	刮	迹
6. *Alter Phonetic Compound to Other Compounds*		
Traditional:	巖	陰
Simplified:	岩	阴
7. *Change Nonphonetic Compounds to Phonetic Compounds*		
Traditional:	郵	態
Simplified:	邮	态
8. *Substitute with Homophone*		
Traditional:	穀	纔 才
Simplified:	谷	髟 須
9. *Revive Archaic Character*		
Traditional:	禮	
Simplified:	礼	

Adapted from So (1979).

than a million characters surveyed by C. M. Cheng (1982), is 6.5. In a corpus of simplified script of more than 50,000 characters, with 3,317 different characters identified, M. Y. Chan (1982) found that the 14 characters with the highest frequency of occurrence had an average of 5.6 strokes. Also, the average stroke number of 2,000 commonly used characters was reduced from 11.2 to 9.0. There is an inverse relationship between frequency of usage and number of strokes in characters (M. Y. Chan, 1982). This would correspond to a similar relationship between frequency and word length in alphabetic languages, and both can be taken as indication of the principle of least effort expounded by Zipf (1949).

At the level of sensory integration, it is the character that is the unit, constituting sensory wholes in the Gestalt sense. This sensory closure is achieved by the configuration and proximity of component strokes to each other, and the segregation of these strokes from those of other characters. The constituents of each character have a common fate, coming and going together as wholes, and meeting the requirement for sensory integration as a closure mechanism (Osgood & Hoosain, 1974).

Component strokes of characters are formed within a more or less square space allocated to each character, and they are usually written in the order of left to right as well as from top down. Stroke sequence is prescribed by convention (which has probably evolved according to psycho-motor principles), and correct stroke sequence is emphasized in learning to write.

Traditionally, characters are written in vertical columns from top down, and columns proceed from right to left. However, in modern times, particularly with the establishment of the People's Republic of China, texts are written or printed horizontally, with characters proceeding from left to right. In the case of shorter sequences of only a few characters, such as headlines and logos, characters can also be written horizontally in the order of right to left. This flexibility in direction-of-character sequence can result in the phenomenon that, in some newspapers in Hong Kong for example, lines of characters are printed in all three directions on the same page, with each direction marking a different article or headline.

2.2 SOUND

Nearly all characters are pronounced monosyllabically in Chinese. But a small number sometimes can be pronounced subsyllabically. A frequently used one is the character [2], pronounced as /-r/ in Putonghua (the Mandarin dialect),[1] which is attached to other nouns to indicate the diminutive or as a form of endearment, although it can also be pronounced as /er/, a full syllable, to mean 'son'. R. L. Cheng (1985) reviewed subsyllabic units in the Taiwanese dialect and was able to suggest some generalizations. For example, the negative marker is often realized as a voiced bilabial nasal initial rather than as a full syllable. These are considered historically to be reductions of full syllables.

In view of the predominance of the syllable in Chinese, we might note that although there are smaller sound units in linguistic analysis, notably the phoneme (the smallest unit of sound that makes a difference to meaning),

---

[1] While *Putonghua* is the term used for the official dialect in the People's Republic of China, *Mandarin*, an older name for the same dialect, remains the term used in Taiwan and some overseas communities. In this book, when reference is made to a particular study, whichever term is adopted in that study is the one used in the relevant part of the text.

there is evidence that human awareness of phonemes is not as good as awareness of syllables (e.g., Bryant & Bradley, 1985). This is particularly so in the case of children. There is also evidence that segmentation of speech sounds within the syllable is not a native human ability (Read, Zhang, Nie, & Ding, 1986).

Parallel to the segments of the syllable are the suprasegmental features of tones. These features are not lined up in sequence with phonemes but are superimposed on them. In Chinese, tonal difference affects meaning just as change in consonants and vowels does. There are four tones in Putonghua although other dialects may have more. The Cantonese dialect, spoken in Hong Kong, Guangzhou (Canton), and elsewhere, for example, is generally taken to have nine tones, exploring the upper and lower registers more fully. Of the six tonal variations of /ji/ in Cantonese [3], the high level tone means 'clothing', the high rising tone means 'chair', the mid level tone means 'meaning', the low falling tone means 'child', the low rising tone means 'ear', and the low level tone means 'two' (Ching, 1988).

There are supposed to be nearly 420 different syllables in Chinese. In his survey of a corpus of more than a million characters, C. M. Cheng (1982) identified 401 syllables. With these 400-odd syllables, the permutation of tonal variation in Putonghua in effect results in more than a thousand different pronunciations, with some syllables not realizing all the tonal permutations. This number is to correspond with tens of thousands of characters. Naturally, homophones abound. C. M. Cheng (1982) found that the 12 highest frequency syllables and their tonal variations made up 25% of the distribution of sounds in his corpus of characters, and the 45 highest frequency syllables made up 50%.

As changing the tone of syllables alters meaning as much as changing a consonant or a vowel, it makes sense to ask which variation is more noticeable to the native speaker. There seems to be agreement that tones are acquired earlier than segmentals in young children, both for Mandarin (C. N. Li & Thompson, 1977) and Cantonese (Tse, 1978). However, Tsang and Hoosain (1979) found that with adult Cantonese speakers in an auditory task, differences in segmental phonemes were easier to discriminate than differences in tones. Tonal variations are signaled primarily by pitch variation. A lipreader would not be able to discriminate characters differing in tones (see Ching, 1988).

2.3 PICTOGRAPHS AND IDEOGRAPHS

A small percentage of characters convey meaning by pictographic representation, either iconic or abstract. The former are more direct, such as the character for *bird* (see Fig. 2.1). Whereas these pictographic characters have

FIG. 2.1. Derivation of the pictograph meaning 'bird'. The character for *bird*, second from the right, is derived from earlier versions on the left of varying likeness to the object depicted. The character on the right is the simplified form used in the People's Republic of China.

an etymology related to pictures, this relation is unlikely to have psychological reality in present day usage. It is not possible for the uninitiated Chinese reader or indeed the nonreader of Chinese to discern or guess at the meaning of such symbols. The confusion between having a pictographic etymology and having psychologically real pictographic function can lead to misunderstanding (see subsection 5.1.4).

Some representations are more abstract rather than iconic. An example would be the character meaning *a wood* [4], made up of a repetition of the pictograph for *tree* (an iconic representation of a wood would require many more trees). Such characters need not always represent concrete things. For example, the character meaning 'to trust' or 'letter' [5] is made up of the characters for *man* and for *word*. Such abstract representations have been called ideographs. Only relatively few characters fit the label in this sense. But the label "ideograph" is also being loosely applied to all Chinese characters (e.g., Besner, Daniels, & Slade, 1982; Huang & Jones, 1980) as graphic symbols representing meaning directly. This usage is similar to that of calling Arabic numerals ideographs, because each Arabic numeral represents a number directly without doing so through a more primary representation of sound, as in the case of English number names. It is sometimes useful to distinguish which usage is intended when the label "ideograph" is applied.

2.4 PHONETIC COMPOUNDS

Some components of characters are derivatives of other characters and have no independent existence of their own, such as the three dots depicting water being part of characters having to do with liquids [6]. Whether these constituents are themselves characters, or are derivations of characters, such groupings of strokes are referred to as radicals when they form parts of more complex characters. Without the aid of an alphabet, Chinese dictionaries usually order their listings according to radicals and list radicals according to their number of strokes. There are 200-odd radicals listed in an ordinary dictionary. The same radicals can occur in different locations in the square space of resultant characters, although many radicals have habitual locations. Also, the same radical can be written in different sizes as components of different characters, depending on the relative complexity of the remaining components of each character (see Fig. 2.2).

About 90% of Chinese characters are phonetic compounds, and this percentage has been increasing over the centuries (Y. P. Zhu, 1987). These compounds are made up of a phonemic radical (often referred to as a *phonetic*), which can contribute some aspect of its sound to the character, and a semantic radical (often simply referred to as a *radical*), which contributes some aspect of its meaning to the resultant character. There are approximately 800 phonetics in Chinese. Both phonetics and radicals can be characters on their own. Currently, when the need arises, new characters are created as phonetic compounds rather than as pictographs or ideographs. This eliminates the need to create genuinely novel graphic elements. Although the phonetic and the radical may be related in sound and meaning to the emergent character, the exact sound or meaning of each phonetic compound has to be learned individually. Distinct from alphabetic or syllabic languages, there are no grapheme-to-phoneme rules to guide the reader.

In modern-day usage, 26.3% of phonetic compounds share identical pronunciation with their phonetics. If frequency of usage is taken into consideration, in 18.5% of encounters with phonetic compounds, the pronunciations of the phonetic and the whole compound are identical (Y. P. Zhu, 1987). The relationship between phonetic compounds sharing the same phonetic is described as belonging to the same group in traditional Chinese rhyme classification (Leong, 1986). When there is a large discrepancy between the pronunciation of the phonetic and the phonetic compound, it is often the result of sound change over the years. But, quite often, the frequency of usage of the phonetic compound as a whole can be higher than that of the independent existence of its phonetic [7]. Actually, I have seen children mistakenly adopt the pronunciation of a high frequency

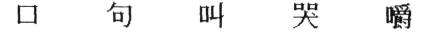

FIG 2.2. Radicals as components of characters. The radical which can also exist on its own, meaning 'mouth', is on the left. It occurs in different locations of other characters in different relative sizes depending on the complexity and configuration of the rest of the characters. The four characters, starting second from the left, mean 'sentence', 'to call', 'to cry', and 'to chew', respectively.

phonetic compound for that of its lower frequency constituent phonetic when the two have different pronunciations [8]. In effect, they reverse the role of the phonetic compound and its constituent phonetic.

The important thing to note is that the phonetic cuing function of phonetics is not rule governed, and the pronunciation of the phonetic itself, afterall, has to be learned individually. This is quite distinct from the situation with the representation of sound by letters of the alphabet. The role of the phonetic in phonetic compounds has sometimes been overplayed and needs to be put in perspective. The semantic cuing function of the radical is estimated to be greater than the phonemic cuing function of the phonetic (Y. P. Zhu, 1987). In desperation, of course, such as when faced with a new character, a reader might adopt the pronunciation of the phonetic to be that of the whole character until clarification is obtained.

The relative importance of the cuing functions of the phonetic and the radical can be indicated by their locations in the space of the character. Radicals tend to be located at the top or the left of characters, and phonetics tend to occupy a right hand side or bottom location. In a check of the major Chinese radicals that were a component of at least 20 different characters listed in a small dictionary, I identified 67 such radicals. Most tend to be located on the left half of characters. There are also more occurrences on top than at the bottom (see Table 2.2). Yau (1982) analyzed over 8,000 relevant characters in a classical dictionary and found that only 16% were exceptions to his schema that the "semantic category" should be written before the "graphic differentiator or phonic indicator."

Another indication of the differential information value of various parts of the character is in their cognitive complexity. R. X. Peng (1982) analyzed 3,000 Chinee characters in terms of the complexity of the four constituent quandrants. In comparisons between the top-left quadrant and the bottom-right quadrant, the former was found to have more complex subpatterns and more junctions of component strokes. Because character strokes tend to be written left to right and top down, the beginning strokes therefore are more discriminative. A corresponding situation exists with other scripts. The left halves of English words, for example, tend to convey more psychological information than the right halves. This can be verified simply by covering the left versus right halves of words in a text and trying to read the two versions. Similarly, top halves of lines of print convey more information than bottom halves.

TABLE 2.2
Frequency of Location of Radicals Within a Character

Top	Bottom	Left	Right	Peripheral	Total
11	3	41	10	2	67

2.5 LOGOGRAPHS

Logograph is usually defined as a graphic symbol representing a spoken word. This is not quite accurate in describing Chinese characters in modern usage, because many characters do not function as linguistic words by themselves. They are more like bound morphemes, being parts of bimorphemic or other multimorphemic words. Logograph would be a more apt description of characters in classical Chinese where words were usually monomorphemic. Chinese characters are representations of morphemes as well as monosyllables. But the meaning of a character is represented by the character directly, not mediated by sound symbols, and a syllable is indicated as a whole rather than spelled out, as in alphabetic languages. The theoretical contrast in the script–sound–meaning relations of Chinese and alphabetic or syllabic languages is represented in Fig. 2.3.

Letters of alphabetic languages and syllabaries of syllabic languages primarily represent sounds. Characters, on the other hand, represent meaning directly; they also have a one-to-one relationship with their pronunciation. This distinction is sometimes described as the contrast between script mapping onto the sound of language and script mapping onto meaning. Of course, the psychological reality of this distinction still has to be demonstrated with empirical data. For example, it could be that with repeated experience (that is, for highly familiar words) the sign-meaning route becomes more direct, bypassing sound, as represented by the dotted arrow in Fig. 2.3. In any case, the distinguished linguist Chao (1968b) made the following intuitive observation: "In looking for something in a page of English you have to look for *it*, but in doing the same on a page

FIG. 2.3. Script–sound–meaning relations.

of characters the thing looked for, if it is on the page, will stare *you* in the face" (p. 112).

One advantage of a direct script–sound plus direct script–meaning relation is that written characters, pronounced differently in various Chinese dialects, can still be understood all over the country. This advantange would be of even greater significance before the days of the modern media and greater mutual awareness. With an alphabetic or syllabic orthography, the mutually unintelligible dialects of China would have to be spelled out in graphic forms that are just as mutually unintelligible. In fact, this is a major consideration in the decision against the romanization of Chinese that has been suggested from time to time in modern history.

The labels "ideograph" and "logograph", when applied to Chinese characters in a somewhat loose manner, attempt to depict the two (script-meaning and script-sound) complementary sides of the unit of Chinese writing. To be more precise, the label "morpheme-syllable" is perhaps preferable. Otherwise, the neutral term "character" is generally accepted.

2.6 MEANING AND MORPHOLOGY

Although nearly all Chinese characters are morphemes, the units of meaning in language, a few two-character words have constituent characters with no independent meaning. They are therefore not morphemes, such as the two characters together meaning *grape* [9]. These two-character words usually refer to objects introduced a long time ago from remote corners of the Chinese empire. However, with repeated usage, one of the characters tends to assume the meaning of the combination, amounting to a kind of morpheme in restricted contexts [10]. This supports Chao's (1968a) observation that "completely meaningless monosyllables in Chinese are always felt as something of an anomaly" (p. 139).

In both alphabetic and syllabic scripts, the units of writing (letters and syllabic signs, respectively) indicate sounds only and have no dovetailed relation with meaning. To illustrate the mismatch between sound and meaning, we can note that *tables*, for example, is divided into the morphemes *table* and *s* (indicating plurality), but then into the syllables *ta* and *bles*. Successive syllables in English are often not morphemic units. But the Chinese character provides a dovetailed unit, simultaneously representing the smallest unit of meaning as well as the smallest salient unit of sound at the psychological level. When reading Chinese, the reader looks at a sequence of sensory wholes, each corresponding to a monosyllable, as well as conveying meaning. One benefit of this is that it becomes easier to grasp and remember meanings of multicharacter words when they are made up of more or less familiar component morphemes. For example, remembering the meaning of *eclectic* in English could be a hit-or-miss matter, but there are usually some meaningful cues from components of multicharacter Chinese words to make the corresponding process less chancy.

Largely because of the salience of the character derived from the convergence of script–sound–meaning features, the word in Chinese is not as intuitively obvious as in the case of English. What delineates a word in English, for example, a group of letters that appears in print bounded by space on its sides, would not be appropriate to Chinese. This delineation would apply to all single characters, including those that are only parts of multimorphemic words (i.e., as bound morphemes, although in Chinese they are not spatially bound with other morphemes). In classical Chinese, words were usually monosyllabic. But, in modern Chinese, words are often two characters long, although they can be more or less than two characters. There is no spatial separation between words over and above that between characters. Many component characters of multisyllabic words are also words on their own.

In Figure 2.4, the three characters together mean 'Wednesday'. Each can occur as an unbound morpheme meaning, respectively, 'star', 'period', and 'three' (the first two characters by themselves also form the word for 'week'). The first character is an example of a phonetic compound. The top half is a radical and also a character by itself with pictographic origin meaning 'sun'. The bottom half is the phonetic, a character by itself pronounced as /sheng/. The character as a whole is pronounced as /xing/, in the same tone as the phonetic. The middle character is also a phonetic compound. The left half is the phonetic, pronounced as /qi/. The compound as a whole is also pronounced as /qi/ but in a different tone. The right half of the compound is a radical that is a pictographic symbol of the moon. The third character is an example of an iconic representation.

Some of the ways in which multisyllabic words are fashioned out of otherwise free monosyllabic words include: (a) combining words that have overlapping or redundant meanings, where each component character as well as the resultant two-character word mean more or less the same thing (apart from redudancy, a richer tone of meaning is achieved); (b) combining opposites that then come to mean the underlying entity, like the characters for 'active' and 'passive' together meaning 'movement' or 'happening'; and

星期三　WEDNESDAY

FIG. 2.4. Chinese and English translaton equivalents. The two scripts are reproduced in the exact proportion of their sizes as they appear in a bilingual calendar.

(c) combining words to depict a new entity in their emergent meaning, like the characters for 'star' and 'period' together meaning 'week', or 'sky' and 'hall' together meaning 'heaven' [11]. The last method is the most common.

It makes sense if we adopt the definition of a word as the linguistic item that allows unlimited insertions at its boundaries and hence combines as a free syntactic form with other words to form an infinite variety of sentences (see Greenberg, 1957). Words do not allow insertions *within* their boundaries (between constituent characters in the case of Chinese) without alterations in their own meanings, whereas insertions *at* word boundaries preserve the original meaning. For example, inserting the character for 'new' in front of the two-character word meaning 'exit' does not alter the meaning of the word for 'exit'. But inserting 'new' between the two component characters results in a phrase meaning 'out to new road' [12]. In other words, a multimorphemic Chinese word is more than just a linking of the meanings of the constituent characters (see Weinreich, 1966). This contrasts with genuine linking in the case of some noun phrases, such as the two characters meaning 'long road', where the meaning is not altered if we insert, say, characters meaning 'asphalt' between the two characters to mean 'long asphalt road' [13].

That multimorphemic words do not allow insertions within their boundaries without losing their integrity indicates that they are meaningful wholes. On the other hand, the Chinese orthography allows their bound morphemes to be spatially separate and thus retain that extent of perceptual individuality. One example of this individuality is the possibility of printing the constituent characters of some words far apart, with other visual materials in between. Fig. 2.5 shows two versions of a bilingual exit sign which are actually found on the same floor housing the Psychology Department at the University of Hong Kong. The insertion of the English in between the two component characters, of course, is not the same thing as insertion of other Chinese characters within the boundaries of the bimorphemic word. But the fact that extraneous visual materials can

出　EXIT　路

EXIT　出路

FIG 2.5. Bilingual exit sign showing visual separability of bound morphemes. The two characters, meaning 'but' and 'road', can be used singly as independent words. They can be ordered in any direction except bottom-to-top.

separate the bound morphemes without destroying their semantic togetherness demonstrates very well some individuality for the constituent characters.

In the case of some idioms, the constituent characters of bimorphemic words can actually be separated by other characters without affecting the meaning of the words [14]. (These bimorphemic words themselves tend to be formed by combining morphemes with overlapping meanings.) Although such idioms are special constructions, they serve to demonstrate the individuality of characters in multicharacter words in Chinese, while generally conforming to Greenberg's (1957) definition of a word.

Multimorphemic Chinese words are similar to some English nominal compounds. The constituents of, for example, *oil well* are each an unbound morpheme. There are no spatial or other orthographic cues to identify the constituents of nominal compounds as belonging together. But they do form meaningful wholes, as demonstrated by the fact that lexical insertions can only be made at their boundaries and not within them (*big oil well* is fine, but *oil big well* would alter the meaning of *oil well*). But one important difference between multisyllabic Chinese words and English nominal compounds is that the latter, as a category of linguistic units, are much less productive. There are relatively few of them in English and they are predominantly noun equivalents. But Chinese multimorphemic words span the range of the entire vocabulary, and they are the primary way of coining words into the language.

In fact, the versatility of the character as the building block for multimorphemic words can be indicated by the morphemic network shown in Fig. 2.6. Each character shown is the initial part of some bimorphemic word as well as the end of another, leading to an interlocking chain of morphemes that form words in overlapping segments. Each segment of such a chain needs not always be bimorphemic, although they are so in Fig. 2.6 for simplicity. This interspersing of characters in a diversity of multimorphemic words indicates that characters weave an intricate fabric of semantic interrelations in the Chinese vocabulary. In contrast, in English for example, bound morphemes like *pre-* or *-ish* have one habitual location in words and serve only one function.

Wu and Liu (1988) reported on a data base system for Chinese characters and words that includes an associative value for each character, defined as the number of different double- or multiple-character words including that character. The mean value for the 120 highest frequency characters is 126 words, although this value drops to 77 words for the next 120 highest frequency characters. This means that the more common characters exist as constituents of about 100 different words in Chinese.

Much has been said about the large number of characters or words that a Chinese person has to learn to be literate. Actually, with the character as

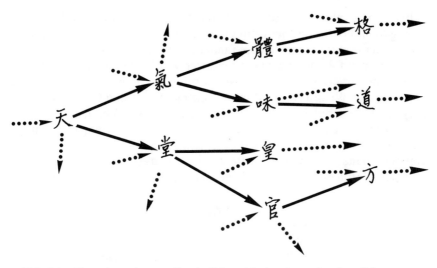

FIG 2.6. The character as the building block of words. A solid arrow indicated an actual combination of charaters forming a word, listed below with their English translations. A dotted arrow indicates that an indeterminate number of other combinations is possible, involving characters preceding or following the charater in question. The characters, independently, can usually function as liguistic words, as follows:

'sky'	天		'weather'	天 氣
'gas'	氣		'heaven'	天 堂
'hall'	堂		'gas'	氣 體
'body'	體		'smell'	氣 味
'taste'	味		'grand'	堂 皇
'king'	皇		'waiter'	堂 官
'official'	官		'physique'	體 格
'matrix'	格		'taste'	味 道
'road'	道		'official'	官 方
'square'	方			

the building block of many multimorphemic words, the situation is not as extreme as sometimes assumed (see Leong, 1986). M. Y. Chan (1982) estimated that in modern Chinese usage in the People's Republic, the most frequently occurring 10 characters account for 11% of frequency counts, and the most frequently occurring 3,800 characters account for 99.9%. Thus, most words are generated by less than 4,000 characters, and knowledge of them would be quite sufficient for reading ordinary texts.

In Chinese, there is actually a name for *word* in the linguistic sense discussed earlier, as distinct from the name for *character* [15]. However, it is the latter that is the much more familiar term. The computed frequencies of occurrence for the two single-character words are 36 and 359, respectively, out of about one million words sampled, according to I. M. Liu, Chuang, and Wang (1975). Multimorphemic words like those for 'dictionary' and 'vocabulary' all have the character for 'character' as their component instead of the character for 'word'. It also appears that the underlying linguistic meaning of the character for 'word' is not often apparent to many ordinary Chinese speakers. I have found that some junior high school students are not completely able to segment a text that had been assigned for detailed study into the constituent units of words. Also, the character for 'word' has another usage which is common; referring to a form of poetry or words set to music.

The predominance of the word for 'character' over the word for 'word' in Chinese usage again testifies to the salience of the character, embodying the visual, auditory, and semantic unit of language. However, it might be of interest to note that whereas the ordinary language user is more familiar with the morpheme for 'character' than that for 'word', when it comes to the time for grammarians to coin names for parts of speech, the latter is used. Thus in Chinese, we have literally 'naming word' for nouns, 'describing word' for adjectives, and 'moving word' for verbs, and so on. The grammarian, of course, is more exacting.

2.7 THE BISYLLABIC WORD
IN MODERN CHINESE

Modern Chinese is written in what is called the colloquial style, largely based on the Mandarin or Putonghua dialect. It is less terse than the literary style used in classical Chinese and even currently in more formal domains. Although the literary style was by no means uniform over the ages (see Ma, 1970), one dominant feature was that the character was usually a free form, that is, words were usually monomorphemic. It is only in modern colloquial style Chinese, advocated in such historical events as the May 4th Movement of 1919, that written words are made to reflect speech more closely. Whereas ordinary people in their everyday lives would find it awkward to converse in monomorphemic words, the written language has also become free of this yoke.

For example, Lee (1976) surveyed a large corpus of verbs being used in writing between 1903 and 1934 and documented a shift away from monosyllables to multisyllables around the time of the May 4th Movement. Similar trends can be found with other parts of speech. For example, a single character was used as a word in classical Chinese to mean 'teacher'. But the same character is now used together with another meaning 'old' to mean 'teacher' [16]. It should be noted though that the written language has not just become more redundant, it has equipped itself with a means of productive combination of characters to form a richer vocabulary of words, just as the productive combination of radicals has been used to form new characters.

Although words in modern Chinese tend to be two characters long, the most frequently used ones tend to be monosyllabic.[2] Of the 60 words ranked highest in usage (Suen, 1986) only 2 are two characters long. Many of the single-character words are function words or auxiliaries. As a result, in the corpus of 1,177,984 characters in the word count by I. M. Liu, Chuang, and Wang (1975), a total of 982,110 word occurrences was identified. This yields an "isolation ratio" of 1.2 (see Aaronson & Ferres, 1986). This ratio is closer to 1 than 2, but we ought to realize that it is based on word tokens and not word types. This pattern of usage simply reflects the principle of least effort where more frequently used words tend to be shorter.

The difference in the frequency distribution pattern of individual characters, compared with the frequency distribution of words (which can be of one, two, or more characters), is demonstrated by statistical data produced by C. M. Cheng (1982). Frequency of occurrence of Chinese words shows a lognormal distribution similar to that of English words. Higher frequency words tend to constitute a more unevenly large cumulative percentage of occurrence. But frequency distribution for individual Chinese characters shows less of such a pattern, because "common" characters can occur in common as well as rare multicharacter words. In this way, they are like English morphemes. C. M. Cheng (1982) also found the same extent of variety of Chinese words in his sample as was found in the corpus of English words by Kucera and Francis (1967), both with a type–token ratio of about 1:20. This means that each word occurs an average of 20 times in the samples surveyed. Thus, Chinese words (but not characters) have distribution patterns like that of English words.

But characters used to function mostly as words in classical Chinese. The difference between characters as free forms in classical Chinese and as bound morphemes in modern Chinese is blurred by the fact that an educated Chinese person is familiar with classical literature and literary style usage. Classical Chinese texts are commonly assigned in high school, and therefore the usage is much more familiar than, say, the language of

---

[2] Kennedy and De Francis (e.g., De Francis, 1950) referred to the "monosyllabic myth", but Chao (1968b) noted that "the monosyllabic myth is one of the truest myths in Chinese mythology" (p. 103), as far as Classical Chinese is concerned. Again, one has to always bear in mind that classical literature is familiar to the present-day educated.

Chaucer would be to the average English speaker. Hence, it is at times difficult to determine whether a certain character in isolation is a free form (i.e., a word) or just a bound morpheme waiting to be combined with other characters to form words. It could function as one or the other depending on context, usage, and the user's facility with the language.

The shift to multisyllabicity in modern Chinese is indicated by comparing English translations of the classics with translations of modern Chinese. English translations of the classics require two or more times the number of syllables in English than in Chinese. On the other hand, the number of syllables in modern Chinese and their English translations is usually comparable. This tendency for multisyllabicity goes hand in hand with the attrition of the repertoire of sounds in the history of Chinese (see Kalgren, 1949). In any natural language, there are always many more meanings to be conveyed than there are units of sounds. Without the general device of having multisyllabic morphemes, as in alphabetic or syllabic languages, the remaining means for disambiguation would be to have multimorphemic words. In this context, two is the smallest number and therefore the most economical. Hence, the tendency for bisyllabic words in modern Chinese. The need for disambiguation is of greater importance in oral language. Otherwise, the visual nature of the written script tolerates more homophones, because homophonic characters have more freedom to assume different visual shapes than homophones in alphabetic languages. In the latter case, homophones tend more to look alike.

The gravitation to bisyllabic words in modern Chinese can also be seen in the adaptation of loanwords. The problem of adaptability of loanwords lies in the discrepancy between the orthographies of Chinese and other, mostly alphabetic, languages. It has been suggested that linguistic factors, more than social ones, account for the relative indisposition of Chinese for lexical borrowing. Novotna (1967) estimated that there were about 650 loans (not counting geographic names) from European languages in modern Chinese and 800 hybrid words. In this context, it is possible to distinguish loanwords assimilated into modern Chinese from those that remain as unassimilated foreignisms in the language. The former acquires the ability to form new words in Chinese with additional characters, but the latter remain unproductive. Novotna (1967) found that the average length of assimilated loanwords in Chinese was 2.52 characters, whereas that of unassimilated loanwords was 3.27 characters.

The gravitation to bisyllabic words avoids the problem of homophones. When people talk of homophones in Chinese, they usually refer to individual characters that have the same pronunciation. It is usually considered that about 60% of Chinese characters have homophones and almost a quarter of them have six or more homophones. But in a few cases even two-character words can have homophones, such as the Cantonese pronunciation for 'finish' or 'pencil' [17]. This is simply the result of the great number of homophonic characters.

2.8 SYNTAX

Chinese is usually classified as a subject–verb–object (SVO) language. It has been suggested that the direction of word order change in Mandarin is from SVO to SOV (C. N. Li & Thompson, 1974), although this suggestion is being challenged (S. F. Huang, 1978; Light, 1979). Other aspects of word order, such as that of prepositional phrases, also appear to have experienced diachronic change (Light, 1979). Diachronic change of any language is nothing unusual, but we have to bear in mind that classical Chinese is always well known to educated Chinese speakers, and never far from their consciousness.

Another element that makes the Chinese speaker more exposed to variations in word order is dialect difference. Speakers of other dialects have to learn to write in standard written Chinese based on Putonghua, and some variations in word order could be involved. For example, in colloquial Cantonese, the preferred word ordering is for the direct object of bitransitive sentences to precede the indirect object (e.g., *I gave an apple (to) him*). But in standard written Chinese, the preferred (unmarked) ordering is for the indirect object to precede the direct object (*I gave him an apple*) [18].

Word order, or rather character order, is an important aspect of meaning at the sentence level and also at the lexical level. As an example of the former, a change in the ordering of one character in the Cantonese sentence meaning 'He/she has not given [Chinese new year lucky money] red packets' results in 'He/she has no red packets' [19]. As examples of the latter, there are some bisyllabic words where the constituent characters form different words if their order is reversed. For example, 'story' becomes 'incident' when the two constituent characters are reversed [20]. There are also some names of places in China which refer to a different place if the characters are reversed. A Cantonese newscaster once read the sentence 'America has taken action' as 'all of America's action' [21]. In this case, the newscaster read the more frequently used ordering of the crucial two characters instead of the actual ordering. This illustrates the importance of paying attention to ordering and the interrelation of characters in reading Chinese.

The net effect of all of these elements is that Chinese speakers are exposed to a greater variety of character/word ordering in their various language activities. Attention to form-class classification, though, is of less relevance in Chinese usage (L. Wang, 1959). As a matter of fact, many dictionaries do not bother to mention the form-class of their listings, and there are debates about the form-class of some of the most familiar characters, such as the character with the highest frequency of usage [22]. Grammar as such is not taught in Chinese schools. Instead, what is attended to are the interrelations of meanings of individual characters and the emergent meanings derived from their combinations. For example, Kalgren (1949) wrote: "A Chinese grammar in actual fact becomes very meager; mainly rules for the relative position of the words in the sentence, and, in addition, the functions of a number of auxiliary grammatical words" (p. 68).

Of course, we do not imply that there are no rules of grammar in the Chinese language; there are good analyses of Chinese grammar (e.g., Chao, 1968a). But the legacy of the structure of Chinese is that the reader has to monitor the semantic relations of character sequence, more so than in alphabetic languages, particularly in the absence of word boundaries. The lack of inflections in Chinese is another reason to pay attention to semantic relations. One needs to figure out, for example, the intended tense of verbs and whether nouns are in the singular or plural. In the extreme case of some classical texts, there were no punctuations to mark phrase or sentence boundaries. Segmentation depends on the only available cue of meaning and semantic relations between characters.

To conclude this chapter, we note again that the unit of Chinese orthography, the character, has a special status as the locus of visual, auditory, and semantic features. Although many Chinese words are bimorphemic, the character retains its individuality, versatility, and salience as a unit of language. In the case of Chinese texts, the interrelations among and the ordering of characters are important indicators of lexical and grammatical relations.

3 Perceptual Aspects of the Chinese Language

This chapter examines some perceptual implications of an orthography made up of individual visual forms representing morpheme-syllables, that is, writing units that are simultaneously meaning units and sound units. The topics covered include visual acuity and scanning direction, the perceptual unit, speed of getting at the sound versus that of getting at the meaning of Chinese characters, phonological recoding, as well as eye movement and reading. Some of the phenomena we look at are related to the physical layout and appearance of the Chinese script itself, whereas others have more to do with relations between the script and sound or meaning. In looking at cognitive effects of language differences, we bear in mind the question of whether they play a greater role in bottom-up or top-down processes (see Hung & Tzeng, 1981).

3.1 VISUAL ACUITY AND DIRECTIONAL SCANNING

3.1.1 Visual Acuity

The visual field within which objects can be detected by humans is not circular but has a greater horizontal extent than vertical. This makes sense, of course, because as dwellers on the surface of the earth, or rather, more on floors of buildings these days, things happening in front of us tend to be extended sideways rather than upward or into the ground. However, foveal vision which allows us to identify details is more circular, and it has been suggested that the more or less square shape of Chinese characters might be better adapted to make use of the circular fovea more so than elongated English words (Woodworth, 1938).

With regard to native English speakers, Freeman (l980) reported that random letters presented in horizontal rows were better seen than if they were arranged in vertical columns. The letters were printed so small that only about 75% correct identification was generally achieved. Also, similar horizontal-vertical difference was found when subjects were asked to identify the letters in the order of right to left versus bottom to top. In other words, the acuity effect was selective for orientation but not for direction. The horizontal-vertical difference was limited to language materials. When subjects were tested for acuity with grating test targets, there was no difference between horizontal and vertical orientations. When they were presented with Landolt rings, with circles having gaps at the top, bottom, left, or right, the difference between horizontal and vertical arrays also disappeared.

However, Freeman (1980) found that when native Chinese were presented with Chinese characters in horizontal versus vertical arrays, there was no corresponding acuity difference for horizontal and vertical orientation. The difference in the acuity performance for English and Chinese was linked to language experience rather than national origin. American children who knew the alphabet but had not yet learned to read did not show the horizontal–vertical acuity difference when trying to identify random letter arrays. Chinese-Americans who had not learned to read and write Chinese showed the same pattern of horizontal–vertical acuity difference for letters as other American subjects. Freeman also found that for Chinese-English bilinguals, their performance pattern with English letters appeared to be influenced by their Chinese learning experience: Although there was a tendency for an increased number of errors for column arrays, the trend was not significant. It seems that the experience of reading Chinese does have some effect on a fundamental visual process that would normally be expected to be largely data driven or bottom up. Freeman attributed the effect to the possibility of reading and writing Chinese text vertically as well as horizontally, unlike English.

3.1.2 Directional Scanning

Freeman (1980) did not find significant difference for left to right versus right to left, or top down versus bottom up direction in the test for acuity, but another procedure showed something else. The human visual system appears in some cases to have a built-in preference for a certain direction of visual scanning, although this also can be modified by language experience. It has been generally reported, in studies with different types of visual materials, that people prefer to scan from left to right or from top down (e.g., Aaron & Handley, 1975). With regard to readers of Hebrew, which is written from right to left, it has been reported that younger readers show a scanning preference of right to left, including on non-Hebrew materials. But this tendency was reversed with mature Hebrew readers (see Braine, 1968; Kugelmass & Lieblich, 1970). It was suggested that the left-to-right preference was the result of a universal maturational mechanism, but older Hebrew readers would tend to have come across more left-to-right reading materials of other languages.

In section 2.4, we saw that different sides or quadrants of the Chinese character do not convey the same kind or amount of information. This could be a language factor that is related to preferred directions of scan for Chinese, in addition to any possible built-in preference in the human visual system. I. M. Liu (1983) compared reading performance when different quadrants of individual Chinese characters in a text or in a random list were erased. Deletion of upper quadrants of characters resulted in significantly more reading errors, and the deletion of left quadrants also produced more errors, although not significantly so. I.M. Liu (1983) also compared reading times for characters with different quadrants missing. Again, the greater cuing power of those parts in the top and left locations was demonstrated with longer times required to read characters having these parts missing.[1]

From the contrast in the informational content of different sides of Chinese characters, we should have some expectations about the preferred scanning direction in reading Chinese, assuming that attention should be paid to more informative parts first. A further consideration is that Chinese text can be written in the direction of left to right or top down. L. K. Chen and Carr (1926) used various procedures, including reading, recall, and symbol detection, to compare reading in horizontal and vertical directions. Chinese was written predominantly vertically at that time, and subjects performed better with vertical texts. The same subjects did better with English printed horizontally rather than vertically. Shen (1927) and Tu (1930) found similar preference for vertically printed texts.

More recently, M. J. Chen (1981) compared Chinese eighth graders in Taiwan, with one year of experience learning English, and undergraduates with more exposure to English. Presented with familiar shapes, colors, Chinese characters, Arabic numerals, and English letters, the students were asked to report verbally all the items on display in each trial (the items were

---

[1] This finding throws some light on the extent to which the phonetic on its own, as a component of phonetic compounds, provides cues for pronunciation. Whereas the phonetic tends to be found on the right side of such characters (see section 2.4), it takes more time to pronounce characters with the top and left quadrants missing. It would appear that access to the pronunciation of phonetic compounds is not through identification of the phonetic as a separate entity.

presented in different orientations). Scanpath analysis was used to examine the order of report in each trial, as an indication of preferred direction of scan. There was not much difference in the scan patterns of the two groups, although the eighth graders usually took longer to report the items. There was high consistency in the scan patterns for the different types of materials, both linguistic and nonlinguistic. The students preferred starting at the top and on the left, starting at the top when the two were in conflict. They preferred top-to-bottom as well as left-to-right directions, similar to those reported for English readers elsewhere. These results are consistent with the possibility that there are built-in preferences for direction of scan. But investigation covering a greater range of age and language experience is needed to clarify the role played by various factors.

H. C. Chen and M. J. Chen (1988) provided such clarification. Three groups were used, each differing in their language experience. They included the following students in Hong Kong: (a) first-grade children who already had two years of Chinese learning but little experience with English, (b) fifth-grade children from a Chinese school who had a few years of learning English, and (c) Chinese-English bilingual undergraduates. The students were asked to perform a naming task in which color patches, Arabic numerals, and Chinese characters, respectively, were presented in a square matrix. They were to name the presented items either in left-to-right order for each row, from the top row down, or in top-to-bottom order for each column, from the right hand column on. Response time results showed that reading experience indeed affected performance.

The first-grade students with little experience with horizontal print showed faster times for vertical reading (elementary Chinese reading materials used in Hong Kong are printed vertically, in right-to-left columns). Their advantage for the vertical direction was strongest for Chinese characters, when compared with color patches or Arabic numerals. But no difference between vertical and horizontal directions was found in the other two groups of students, who had more experience with horizontal print, both in English texts and in Chinese materials (which are now printed and written horizontally as well as vertically).

H. C. Chen and M. J. Chen (1988) also tested undergraduates with a Chinese prose passage, using different speeds of presentation. Characters forming each passage were displayed on a screen in a matrix form, and the text proceeded either from top down in columns from right to left, or left to right in rows from top down. The students were allowed either a normal or a shorter time duration to read the passages, and they then had to answer comprehension questions. Comprehension scores showed no difference between vertical and horizontal reading direction at normal reading speed, but there was an advantage for the horizontal direction in speeded reading.

These studies on directional scanning in Chinese indicate that language experience is a significant variable. The inherently flexible direction of flow for the Chinese script, the unique historical change from a traditionally vertical to a modern predominantly horizontal direction of print, as well as the difference in direction of print in elementary and advanced texts enable us to obtain convincing evidence that preferred scanning direction changes with reading experience and habit.

L. K. Chen and Carr (1926) found an advantage for the vertical when this was the predominant direction of print more than 60 years ago. H. C. Chen and M. J. Chen (1988) found that even in present times, young children who were not yet exposed to the hoizontal direction still showed an advantage for the vertical. In the case of the more advanced Chinese reader (just as in the case of the more mature Hebrew reader), it is not clear how much the advantage for left-to-right horizontal scan is influenced by experience with European languages. If there is a universal preference for horizontal scan, it is probably related to the shape of the human visual field, with greater horizontal than vertical extent, as well as to the anatomy of eye muscles, which are more adept at making sideways eye movements than vertical ones.

This section shows that both visual acuity and directional scanning can be influenced by language experience. The former, in particular, indicates a language effect on a very basic aspect of perception. Acuity would normally be expected to be largely determined by the quality of the sensory information alone (assuming, of course, that there is no defect in the visual system). Freeman (1980) has shown that language experience can make a difference.

3.2 PERCEPTUAL UNITS

After the discussions of visual acuity and directional scanning, we proceed to see what are the perceptual units in Chinese. Chinese text is a sequence of graphic signs that can be divided up in different manners, such as strokes, radicals, characters, words, and so forth. The versatile character can occur as a part of another word (as a kind of bound morpheme) or as a word on its own. The crucial question becomes whether it is (a) the character, whether as a word or only part of a word, or (b) the word, which can consist of different numbers of characters, that is the more salient unit of language perception.

The question of perceptual units is dominated by the consideration that the notion of what is a word is not entirely clear to many Chinese readers. On the other hand, it still makes sense to ask whether, in specific situations, the character or the word has greater salience. In some ways, the question amounts to whether it is sensory integration factors alone or linguistic (mainly meaning) factors that determine perceptual salience. With a two-character word, for example, we want to know if it is perceived as one Gestalt whole according to its meaning or as merely a juxtaposition of two visual units. Somewhat related questions about the salient unit of perception in English have been asked (e.g., Osgood & Hoosain, 1974). For alphabetic languages, some of the procedures used to investigate perceptual units look at illusory conjunction, word superiority and inferiority, as well as perceptual thresholds. We look at some studies of Chinese using these procedures.

3.2.1 Illusory Conjunction

Findings from English illusory conjunction studies implicate perceptual units bigger than letters. For example, when subjects looked at a string of letters of different colors, they sometimes saw letters and colors in wrong combinations, and such illusory conjunctions were more likely to occur between letters within the same syllable rather than between letters of different syllables (Prinzmetal, Treiman, & Rho, 1986). This indicates that items at least as big as the syllable are the perceptual units. Because elements of Chinese characters are laid out in spatial configurations rather than in sequential strings, illusory conjunction would involve confusion and recombination of components of different characters presented in close proximity.

This has been reported by Lai and Huang (1988). Three characters were presented in each trial, such that illusory conjunction involving components of two of these characters could occur, and subjects might report having seen a new, recombinant character [1]. The third character in the display provided a contextual cue to facilitate component migration to form the new character. A priming character was presented just prior to the display of the three characters, providing either a phonetically similar character, a semantically related character, or an irrelevant character as a prompt for the formation of the illusory conjunction target. Finally, subjects were shown the target and asked to indicate if they did or did not see it in the three-character display. Subjects sometimes reported having seen the recombinant target characters, and hence illusory conjunction occurred. However, Lai and Huang (1988) found that the effects of priming and context were not significant. This was taken to mean that illusory conjunction was automatic and bottom up, independent of top-down constraints. The finding of illusory conjunction between components of different characters suggests that items at least as large as the character are the more salient perceptual units in Chinese.

3.2.2 Word Superiority Effect

An indication that the word is the unit of visual perception comes from the word superiority as well as word inferiority effects. However, a study of the voicing version of the word superiority effect demonstrates the ambivalent status of the character in multisyllabic words. For the word superiority effect, it has been shown that the letter *k*, for example, is easier seen as part of the word *work* than when standing alone. Subjects in such studies were given a forced choice; to report either that they saw *k* or *d* in the example (Reicher, 1969). The superior identification of a letter as part of a word suggests that perception of the word cannot be based on identification of independent component letters. This would entail no difference between identification of single letters standing alone and letters occuring within the context of words.

The word superiority effect has been reported for both monosyllabic and bisyllabic Chinese words (C. M. Cheng, 1981). A target radical was embedded: (a) in a character (monosyllabic word) forming part of the character, (b) in a pseudocharacter with radicals occupying the relative locations that they normally do, which resulted in a reasonably possible "character" not actually in use; and also (c) in a noncharacter with radicals occupying impossible locations, which resulted in a nonexistent "character" [2]. Subjects were shown one of these items for a short period of time. In a forced-choice task, the presented item was shown together with a distractor, and subjects were asked to identify which one they saw. Radicals were identified better when they occurred in characters than in pseudocharacters. Pseudocharacter contexts were, in turn, better than noncharacter contexts. (In this study, most of the radicals did not have independent existence as characters on their own. Also, both pseudocharacters and noncharacters cannot be pronounced, unlike their counterparts in alphabetic languages.)

The single-character word superiority effect shows that components of characters are not detected independently of or prior to the perception of each whole character. Otherwise, detection of components in pseudocharacters and noncharacters should not be more difficult than components in ordinary characters. This should be particularly so as, in the forced-choice procedure, subjects were provided with two alternative responses, whether the item was a character, a pseudocharacter, or a noncharacter. This removes any advantage from guessing based on knowledge of Chinese writing, in the case of ordinary characters. Unfortunately, the single characters used by C. M. Cheng also happened to be words on their own. It is therefore not possible to clarify whether individual non-word characters (bound morphemes) might have the same kind of perceptual salience enjoyed by single-character words.

In an accompanying experiment, C. M. Cheng (1981) found that an individual target character was identified better as part of a two-character word rather than a two-character nonword. The two-character word/nonword was shown briefly and subjects were given a forced-choice task. Faced with the presented two-character item and also a distractor item, they had to report which item contained the target character during the previous brief presentation. It was found that target characters embedded in two-character words were identified better in most conditions of high/low stroke number, high/low frequency of usage, and whether the first or the second character was the target. The only exception was for high frequency characters with low stroke number in the second-character position, in which case there was little difference between word and nonword contexts.

The Chinese word superiority effect for two-character words indicates that, generally, they are not perceived as juxtapositions of two separate units. If it were so, identification of characters in nonword contexts should not be inferior to identification in two-character word contexts. On the other hand, the absence of the word superiority effect for targets in the second position of simple, high frequency words requires attention. This phenomenon is not found in English. The target letter of *k* in *work*, for example, is at the end of a short, high frequency word, and the word superiority effect was found. This contrast between the two languages suggests that components of two-character words could have some individual salience, particularly if they are easier to see. Assuming that these are also words that are learned earlier in life, it could also reflect the manner in which young children's attention in vocabulary learning is more directed to the character rather than to the linguistic word.

In the voicing version of the word superiority effect, I. M. Liu (1988) found another difference between Chinese and English. Subjects were asked to pronounce as quickly as possible a character that was: (a) a constituent of a two-character word (with an indicator pointing at the character to be pronounced), (b) a constituent of a two-character nonword created by recombining constituents of the two-character words, and (c) a character standing alone. Characters were pronounced faster in the first position than in the second position, for words and particularly so for nonwords. Characters embedded in two-character words, whether in first or second position, as well as those standing alone were pronounced faster than those embedded in nonwords, whereas there was no significant difference between the first two types of items.

In a second experiment, three-character words and nonwords as well as characters in isolation were used. Pronunciation times were slower for characters in the first position of nonwords, compared with characters in the first position of words as well as characters in isolation. There was not significant difference between the latter two. For characters in the middle position as well as characters in the third position, there was no significant difference between those in words and those in nonwords, but both were pronounced slower than characters in isolation.

In a third experiment, Chinese-English bilingual undergraduates were asked to do a corresponding pronunciation task with English words. Bimorphemic items were used (e.g., *base-ball* and *gold-mine*, with a hyphen separating the two morphemes when presented. Nonwords were created by random combinations of the morphemes. The students were asked to pronounce one of the constituent morphemes (which was underlined) as quickly as possible. Irrespective of being the first or second constituent, words in the bimorphemic compounds were pronounced faster than those in nonword compounds or those standing on their own as words.

The interesting finding of this study was the absence of facilitative effect on voicing of constituent characters in Chinese words, compared with characters in isolation. This contrasted with the bilingual students' performance on English words, where constituent words in compounds were pronounced faster than in isolation. This suggests that constituent characters of Chinese words are handled somewhat independently, rather than as integral parts of words, particularly when phonological processes are required.

I. M. Liu (1988) proposed a "component decidability model of spelling-sound correspondences" to account for the data. Voicing of a word is the outcome of a process of finding the right pronunciation. In the case of English, pronunciation indicated by components of words (letters) is facilitated by the sequence of other letters providing disambiguating clues (e.g., whereas *t* can be pronounced variously, as in *take*, *thin*, or *tsar*, if it is followed by *a*, there can be only one pronunciation). But for Chinese, the absence of grapheme–phoneme conversion rules means that there is little such within-character disambiguation (component decidability), and a large number of character-sound associations has to be learned. The result is that naming of a character is more likely to be disrupted in the context of other characters, each with its own possible character–sound associations to contend with.

There was a variety of English items used in I. M. Liu's study. There were bimorphemic words like *baseball* as well as two-word noun phrases like *gold mine*, although all were presented with a hyphen inserted in the middle. The majority appear to be of the former type. Hence, in previous experience with such items the students would have seen them as bimorphemic words with no space or other marking separating the two constituent words. In this manner, these English items were not strictly comparable to two-character Chinese words.

The lack of the word superiority effect in pronunciation latency reported by I. M. Liu (1988), as well as the finding that word superiority effect disappears for the visual identification of some characters within two-character words (C. M. Cheng, 1981), together suggest that the character could have an ambivalent role as the unit of perception in Chinese. Whereas it could fuse its identity into a whole within two-character words, there are times when it retains its individual salience as a result of its status as a sensory unit.

3.2.3 Word Inferiority Effect

In the case of the word inferiority effect, it has been reported that, for example, while searching for the letter *t* in a text, subjects are more likely to make mistakes and miss the target embedded in correctly spelled words compared with misspelled words (Healy, 1976; Healy & Drewnowski, 1983). Mistakes were particularly more likely with familiar words like *the*. Using a prose passage, H. C. Chen (1986) showed that the word inferiorty effect could also be found in Chinese. Subjects were asked to detect a radical anywhere it existed. When it was embedded in a single-character word, it was not detected as well as when it was embedded in a noncharacter [3]. This word inferiority effect was found whether subjects were asked to detect the radical while reading an ordinary printed text at their own speed for comprehension, reading the same text presented on a display monitor for about a quarter of a second for each character, or reading characters of the same text in scrambled order on a monitor.

The apparent contradiction between the word superiority effect and the word inferiority effect, originally discovered for English, has been explained in a set of hypotheses about unitization at the word level when reading (e.g., Healy & Drewnowski, 1983). It appears that the hypotheses are applicable to Chinese as well. Word inferiority is found in situations where continuous texts or at least a few items together are presented. It is hypothesized that processing at different levels proceeds in parallel, including that for words and individual components such as letters. Thus, subjects will process both *the* and *t* simultaneously (or characters and their constituent radicals simultaneously). They are able to complete processing highly familiar words like *the* quickly. Once the larger unit is identified, processing of its components stops and attention is directed to the following item. Hence, detection errors tend to be greatest for highly familiar words (or Chinese characters) and lowest for nonwords (or noncharacters). In the latter case, identification of larger units (the nonwords and noncharacters) is not facilitated by any degree of familiarity, and the parallel processing of both the larger units themselves and their components persists longer, providing a better chance for detection of the components.

The word superiority effect, on the other hand, is found in conditions where only single words are presented. After the identification of the word (like *work*), with nothing else around, subjects proceed to identify its components (including *k*), which is facilitated by the prior identification of the word carried out in parallel. The result is faster identification of components embedded in words, compared with those alone or embedded in nonwords (and similarly faster identification of radicals embedded in characters compared with those in non-characters).

Further evidence for the applicability of the unitization model to Chinese was found by H. C. Chen (1986). Subjects were asked to read a passage, comprehend its meaning, and look for the occurrence of a certain radical. Accuracy for detection of the radical was compared when characters were displayed one by one and when they were in groups of 10 characters at a time. The word inferiority effect was found only in the 10-character display format and not when characters were displayed one after another. A similar result was obtained when the passage was scrambled and subjects were asked to look for the radical, with characters displayed one at a time or 10 at a time. Such results are consistent with the unitization hypothesis that, with a larger display size, once a character was identified, subjects did not proceed to identify its constituent elements but went on to succeeding characters. On the other hand, in the single-word display format, with no other items around, subjects could proceed to identify components after a character was identified (provided of course that there was still time), thus reducing detection errors. The word inferiority effect hence disappears.

The word superiority and inferiority effects indicate that the linguistic word is generally the salient unit in the perception of Chinese, although there are situations in which component characters show some degree of individual salience.

3.2.4 Perceptual Threshold

Perceptual threshold studies in English provide some hints for Chinese, although only indirect evidence on thresholds for various Chinese language units is available. Evidence from nominal compounds like *stumbling block* indicates that it is meaning rather than sensory integration that is more crucial in delineating salient units of perception. Osgood and Hoosain (1974) found that the minimal exposure times required to see nominal compounds and ordinary words matched for familiarity and length as well as physical shape (like *stumbling block* vs. *acknowledgement*) are comparable. On the other hand, nominal compounds had lower perceptual thresholds than noun phrases like *copper block* (which allows insertions without destroying its linkage of meanings, e.g., *copper and lead block*). The emergent meaning of *stumbling* plus *block* functions to tie the two constituent words together as one unit of meaning, which is not the case with *copper block*.[2] Given that two-character words in Chinese are like

---

[2] Murphy (1988) pointed out that noun modification resulting in complex concepts, such as *corporate clothing*, can be "productive." (Note that *corporate clothing* still accepts insertions, such as *corporate and personal clothing*, and is therefore different from nominal compounds

nominal compounds, in that a couple of sensory wholes (characters) together create an emergent meaning in the lexicon (and are listed in dictionaries, for example), it might be expected that they also form some kind of salient unit of perception.

One problem makes it impossible to compare perceptual thresholds of multicharacter and single-character words without confounding the two. There is no way to match "word length," as can be done with alphabetic languages, because multicharacter words are bound to be longer than single-character words (whereas we can match the length of single English words and nominal compounds, like *acknowledgement* and *stumbling block*). On the other hand, there is some indication from English that salient units of language can have lower perceptual thresholds than shorter items that are not salient units. Osgood and Hoosain (1974) showed that multisyllabic English words like *provoke* actually had lower perceptual thresholds than monosyllabic bound morphemes like *voke*, with no independent existence.

There is a study that indirectly indicated that perceptual thresholds are higher for two-character words than for single characters (although this was under special conditions). O. J. L. Tzeng, Hung, Cotton, and Wang (1979) showed subjects single- and two-character words either in the left or right visual field and found that single characters were perceived better in the left visual field, whereas two-character words were perceived better in the right visual field. This difference is discussed in subsection 5.1.3, but the point of interest for the present discussion is that exposure time for the two types of items were determined in preliminary trials, so that each subject achieved a certain level of accuracy of identification for both types of items. The mean exposure time found suitable for single-character words was 40 milliseconds, with a range from 20 to 75 milliseconds for the entire group of subjects. The mean for two-character words was not reported, but a subsequent publication (Hasuike, Tzeng, & Hung, 1986) indicated this to be more than 100 milliseconds. Thus, much longer exposure times were required for two-character words rather than for single characters in order to achieve comparable levels of accuracy of identification.

The higher perceptual thresholds for two-character words compared with single-character words do not necessarily mean that they are processed as juxtapositions of two separate perceptual units, because word length is

---

like *attorney general*.) *Corporate clothing* involves novel modification of *clothing*, which is created and understood. Murphy showed that the conceptual complexity of such noun phrases depends on the nature of the modifier, and reference to knowledge of the world is required to understand many such combinations. However, Murphy (in press) also thought that idioms and familiar phrases such as *apple pie* may already have representations in the lexicon. This would be the case with nominal compounds like *attorney general* or *stumbling block* — and multimorphemic Chinese words.

confounded. We have seen that for English, bimorphemic words have lower perceptual thresholds than their bound morphemes (e.g., *provoke* compared with *voke*). In the case of English, the bound morphemes do not have salience as individual sensory wholes. Perhaps more importantly, they cannot function as linguistic words, which is not the case with single characters.

3.2.5 Segmentation of Text

There is an apparent self-contradiction in the view that two-character words could be salient units of perception in reading of text. There are no space boundaries in Chinese beyond the spacing between individual characters, and there is no physical indication of word boundaries. In fact, I. M. Liu, Yeh, Wang, and Chang (1974) showed that there was no advantage for reading performance when multicharacter word boundaries were marked with additional spacing. In such a text, the regular between-character spacing was augmented by additional space between linguistic words. Of course, it could be that the lack of facilitation effect was mainly because subjects could not get used to the novel format, having been exposed to the traditional regular spacing all their lives.

The segmentation of a string of characters into words of varying numbers of characters requires some kind of lexical access that gets at the meaning of characters. But how is this segmentation possible before the identification of each constituent character? How do we determine what constitute meaning wholes without prior identification of sensory wholes? The answer probably lies in some kind of parallel processing, similar to those suggested in the unitization hypothesis.

It can be hypothesized that segmentation of strings of individual characters into linguistic words proceeds simultaneously with identification of individual characters. The former, just as the latter, is assisted by knowledge of the language, the preceding text or context, as well as the subject matter. It can be assumed that the purpose of such a cognitive process is to determine the meaning of the passage, and the reader's task is to identify progressively larger and hence more meaningful units of the text (see Healy, Oliver, & McNamara, 1987). The word, whether single-character or multicharacter, is the smallest meaningful unit that accepts almost unlimited insertions at its boundaries and therefore can combine with other words to form an infinite variety of sentences. In this manner, words are psycholinguistic units, and the parallel process of identification of individual characters is in this sense subordinate to the identification of words. At any stage during the parallel processing, if it is felt that there is enough information, both from bottom-up and top-down processes, to decide on a segmentation and its meaning, the reader proceeds to the next segmentation.

To summarize this section on perceptual units, it would appear that the linguistic word, even if it consists of two characters, can be a unit of visual perception. The two-character word superiority effect found by C. M. Cheng (1981) would suggest that such words do have some unitary characteristics rather than function as juxtapositions of two items. However, particularly in cases where component characters are simple and highly familiar, or when individual characters have to be pronounced, there is some degree of individual salience for these characters that is not likely to be found in the case of bound morphemes in English. This individual salience has to do with the character as sensory unit.

3.3 GETTING AT THE SOUND OF WORDS

There are two related questions in connection with sounds of words. One is how does the reader get at the sound of the visual word, sometimes referred to as activation of the phonological code or phonological access? The other is what role does this sound code play in getting at the meaning of the word, or what is the need for phonological recoding in lexical access and reading? These questions are in turn tied to the nature of script–sound–meaning relations in Chinese, referred to in Chapter 1.

3.3.1 Phonological Access

Getting at the sound of words can proceed in at least two different manners. One is by access to lexical information that includes all the individual characteristics and meanings of a word as a whole, stored in memory for each word. The other is through grapheme-phoneme conversion rules, getting at sound from how a word is spelled. In the case of Chinese, with the absence of grapheme-phoneme conversion rules, getting at the pronunciation of characters would have to be through lexical information alone. We have noted that about one-quarter of phonetic compounds have pronunciations identical with their phonetics. But it should be borne in mind that the phonetics are characters on their own, and their own pronunciations have to be learned on a character-as-a-whole-to-sound-as-a-whole basis and not through grapheme-phoneme conversion rules. In other words, the only way to get at the sound of Chinese characters is through lexical information, whether directly or indirectly (through the phonetic of each phonetic compound). If this indirect route is still referred to a grapheme-phoneme conversion route, it should be realized that there is some fundamental difference compared with grapheme–phoneme conversion in alphabetic or syllabic languages.

One effect of the difference in arriving at the sound of Chinese words is noted in a study by Stevenson (1984). It was found that, generally, Chinese first graders surpassed American first graders in reading skills, and the reasons appeared to be unrelated to orthography and had more to do with effort. But American children who were good readers surpassed their Chinese counterparts. The explanation this time was related to orthography, that it was possible to "sound out" new words in English but not in Chinese. Good readers who caught on to the system of grapheme–phoneme conversions in English had an advantage over the Chinese children who had to rely on lexical information, that is, learn characters one by one.

In studies of the nature of phonological access, naming latencies are compared for different language items. These are measures of the time it takes the reader to start to pronounce words, counting from the moment a word appears to the moment some pronounced sound stops the timing equipment. Such measurements can be affected by distortions due to articulation times as well as acoustic characteristics of sounds that stop the timer at different points in time after onset. If we could ignore these variables, naming latency would be the most readily available indicator of the speed of getting at the sound of words.

There is a study specifically looking at naming latencies for Chinese and English words (Seidenberg, 1985). For Chinese, Seidenberg compared the naming times for phonetic compounds whose pronunciation was similar or identical to that of their phonetics, and naming times for nonphonetic compounds without components providing possible clues to their pronunciation. Both types of characters could have high or low frequencies of usage. Naming times were faster for phonetic compounds compared with nonphonetic compounds, but only for low familiarity characters and not for high familiarity characters. Seidenberg took this to mean that for familiar characters, getting at the sound is through character-as-a-whole-to-sound-as-a-whole lexical information. But with less familiar words, getting at the sound is by a kind of "grapheme-to-phoneme conversion" which is conducted through the phonetic. Seidenberg's finding had been replicated by Zhu (1987) who compared naming latency of phonetic compounds having pronunciations identical to those of their phonetics, and phonetic compounds with pronunciations different from those of their phonetics. Naming times were faster for phonetic compounds with identical pronunciation as their phonetics, but again only for low familiarity characters and not for high familiarity characters.

Seidenberg (1985) conducted a parallel study with English words, and the naming latency pattern was very similar to that obtained for Chinese. Items used were high and low familiarity words that had regular or exceptional pronunciations, such as *luck* and *said*, respectively. (One of the criteria to distinguish if a word has regular or exceptional pronunciation is to see if all words with similar spelling patterns are rhymes.) Again, there was no difference in naming times between regular and exceptional words of high familiarity. But, for those with low familiarity, regular words were named faster than exceptional words. Seidenberg took this similiarity in the pattern of results for Chinese and English words to mean that in both cases, readers used lexical information to get at the sound of familiar words but used grapheme–phoneme rules for unfamiliar words. Seidenberg also used this finding to support a time-course model of visual word recognition, which is taken to apply to both Chinese and English. With familiar words, visual information from the word results in recognition, which in turn activates their phonological representation. But with less familiar words, the slower recognition allows enough time for phonological information to accrue through means such as grapheme–phoneme rules (in the case of Chinese, this means reading the phonetic).

In evaluating the results for the low familiarity items in these two studies, it is useful to bear in mind that some subjects might not know immediately the pronunciation of some of the unfamiliar Chinese characters. In section 2.4, we noted that, if necessary, the reader can simply adopt the pronunciation of the phonetic as that for the whole character. The reader would not know if he or she is right, but in the experiment just discussed, would end up doing quite well anyway. The error rates for pronunciation of the low familiarity Chinese words were quite high in Seidenberg's study, nearly twice as high as error rates in the parallel study of English words. This would suggest that a substantial number of correct naming could be the result of guessing. There is a difference between naming a character when a subject actually knows the character and naming the character when he or she is unfamiliar with the character itself but only reading off the phonetic. What happens in the latter case of lucky guessing is of less theoretical interest for the present discussion. Nevertheless, it could explain the difference in both naming latency and accuracy between low frequency characters with helpful phonetics and low frequency characters without such clues.

Fang, Horng, and Tzeng, (1986) looked at the consistency effect in naming characters as well as pseudocharacters. Consistency was defined in terms of the extent to which the pronunciation of a character was shared by other characters having the same phonetic. For phonetic compounds that sounded the same as their phonetics, high consistency was found to facilitate naming latency. Also, simple characters that could act as phonetics had slower naming latencies if compounds in which they occurred had lower consistency values. The consistency effect was also found in pseudocharacters. Because consistent words (e.g., *wade*) in English also have faster naming latencies than inconsistent words (e.g., *wave*; see Glushko, 1979), the authors took the results to suggest that similar processes could be involved in getting at the sound of Chinese and English words. Some light on this point could be shed by comparing naming latencies for different languages.

3.3.2 Naming Latencies for Different Languages

If the nature of phonological access for Chinese is different from that for alphabetic or syllabic languages, naming latencies for words in the different orthographies could be different. Seidenberg's (1985) suggestion that orthography differences does not matter (for familiar words) is contradicted by findings comparing kana and kanji in Japanese. Naming latencies for color names written in kana are faster than the same color names written in kanji (Feldman & Turvey, 1980).[3] The kanji color names actually have higher frequencies of usage than kana names. Also, identical pronunciations are used for the kanji and kana names (this removes the variables of articulation time difference and acoustic characteristics difference that could distort measurements of naming latencies, referred to earlier). Subjects were used as their own controls, and the only difference involved was that they had to access the same phonological codes either through symbols that indicated sounds by grapheme-phoneme rules apart from possible lexical information (i.e., kana), or through symbols that indicated sounds only through the latter, direct one-to-one relations (kanji). The results showed that phonological access is facilitated when the script provides grapheme-phoneme conversion information. It is also possible that in naming kana words, processing of their meaning is less involved than is the case with naming kanji words. With a more direct script-meaning relation, awareness of meaning of kanji or Chinese words is more unavoidable and could result in added information processing and hence increased naming latency (see also subsection 3.4.1).

Seidenberg (1985) reported that frequency of words made a greater difference in naming latencies for Chinese than for English. Also, for low frequency words, the difference between exception and regular words was greater for Chinese. Thus, there seems to be some distinction between getting at the sound of Chinese words, which rely on lexical information, and English words, which embody some degree of grapheme-phoneme

---

[3] Kanji are characters borrowed from the Chinese script, whereas kana are the more simplified syllabic script. The two scripts are intertwined in ordinary text, each used to represent different types of words. Detailed comparison of these two scripts and the psychological relevance of their distinctions are available in Paradis, Hagiwara, and Hildebrandt (1985).

correspondence. We should note that even for English words with exceptional pronunciation (e.g., *said* in the Seidenberg study), there is still some amount of graphemic indication of pronunciation, and the subject does not have to rely completely on lexical information. In fact, the clue to pronunciation provided by the graphemes in the so-called exception words in English can be actually more than provided by the phonetics of those Chinese phonetic compounds that do not have identical pronunciation as their phonetics. For example, in the case of both examples of phonetic compounds given in the article by Seidenberg (1985), the phonetics have different tones compared with their respective phonetic compounds [4]. Access to whatever phonological information that is provided by the phonetic cannot be compared to grapheme–phoneme conversion in alphabetic languages.

A strong support for this point is that some nonphonetic compounds, such as the two reported in Seidenberg (1985), could themselves function as phonetics in other phonetic compounds [5]. How can it be argued that access to the sound of such nonphonetic compounds (when they stand alone) is through lexical information, but access to the sound of phonetic compounds (which are actually made up of these same nonphonetic compounds now acting as phonetics) is through grapheme-to-phoneme conversion? Afterall, how is the sound of these phonetics arrived at in the first place?

In further analyses of his English data, Seidenberg (1985) showed that the difference between low frequency regular and exception words was due to slower subjects. There was negligible difference between these two categories of words for fast subjects. No such distinction between slow and fast subjects was reported for the Chinese data. It is only with English that subjects have the alternative of getting at the sound of words through grapheme–phoneme rules besides lexical information. We have seen how, even with exceptional words like *said*, the graphemic information still provides some clue.

There is another report comparing the naming latencies for English and Chinese words. So, Potter, and Friedman (1978) compared naming latencies of Chinese and English words that were names of the same set of pictures, and therefore presumably translation equivalents. Naming times for the words were significantly faster than latencies for naming the pictures themselves. There was also a nonsignificant difference between the times for the Chinese and English words, although the average response times for English words were about 100 milliseconds faster than those for Chinese words. It would appear that there were sizable variances in the subjects' naming latencies for such a difference to be nonsignificant. In the case of Seidenberg's (1985) study, the naming latencies for the Chinese words were two or three hundred milliseconds slower than those for the English words.

Although the author cautioned that the English and Chinese stimuli were not equated for variables such as frequency, it should be noted that the latencies for all the categories of Chinese items were longer than even the most difficult category of English items (low frequency exception words).

Given the difference in latency levels found in independent studies for Chinese and English words, it is difficult to hold the view that similar processes of getting at the sound of words take place in the two languages. In this regard, we might note the idea of languages varying in orthographical depth (see Frost, Katz, & Bentin, 1987). In shallow orthographies, such as Serbo-Croatian, the phonemic and graphemic codes are isomorphic. In deeper othographies, such as Hebrew, the relation between spelling and sound is more opaque. Chinese orthography, in this regard, would be one of the deepest.

3.3.3 Phonological Mediation in Lexical Tasks

Although the manner of phonological access may be different for Chinese, there is little doubt that phonological mediation plays a role in lexical decision for Chinese words. In lexical decision tasks, subjects are asked to indicate if a presented item is an actual ("legal") word or not. Variation of this task includes presentation of pairs of words sharing some visual, phonological, or semantic relatedness to see the effect of these factors on lexical decision. The relevance of visual, phonological, or semantic processing in the task is then inferred. These words can be presented simultaneously or separated by some time interval. Some reports have used variations of this procedure, and shown that similar patterns of results are obtainable with Chinese as with English words.

When subjects are shown pairs of English words and asked to indicate *yes* if both are legal words and *no* if either one or both are illegal, response times are faster if they share both visual and phonological similarity (e.g., BRIBE–TRIBE compared with BRIBE–HENCE). However, Meyer, Schvaneveldt, and Ruddy (1974) found that when the words shared only visual similarity (e.g., FREAK–BREAK), response times were slower than control (unrelated) word pairs. According to C. M. Cheng and Shih (1988), Hsieh (1982) also found that visually similar and phonologically dissimilar Chinese character pairs required longer decision times. Also, the fastest times were recorded for visually dissimilar but phonologically identical character pairs. It would appear that phonological mediation is similarly involved for English and Chinese in this task.

C. M. Cheng and Shih (1988) produced further evidence that phonological processes were involved in lexical decision. They used one character as a prime, preceding another character that could have related visual shape or pronunciation. Decision times, that the target character was legal, were faster when preceded by a homophonic cue. Visual cues were not helpful. In another procedure, subjects had to decide if both presented characters were legal, and again phonological identity facilitated response time but visual similarity did not. These results were taken to show that prelexical phonological recoding occurred for Chinese characters, that is, sound-related processing of characters took place before lexical decision. However, it should be noted that the comparison between the visual and phonological factors was not quite fairly made. Whereas visual *similarity* was involved on the one hand, with shared radicals in the character pairs,[4] phonological *identity* was maintained as a comparison. It is thus not possible to weigh the relative roles played by visual and phonological factors in such a situation.

Yeung (1989) also demonstrated that phonological mediation takes place in the perception of single-character Chinese words. A single-character prime was shown for half a second before a single-character target that could: (a) be opposite in meaning to the prime, (b) simply sound the same as what the opposite would be (homophone pseudo-opposite), or (c) unrelated to the prime. Targets were shown only at around threshold levels, averaging a little more than 50 milliseconds. Subjects were asked to indicate if the target was opppposite in meaning to the prime or not. There was a significantly higher rate of misidentifying the homophone pseudo-opposites as genuine opposites, compared to control words. Although the task was to decide if a target was opposite in meaning to the prime, some activation of the sound of the target must have occurred to produce the misidentification. Furthermore, for high frequency words the effect was similarly found for both characters that had high consistency pronunciations and those that had low consistency pronunciations (see subsection 3.3.1). It was only for low frequency words that those with low consistency pronunciations showed a lower rate of misidentification than those with high consistency pronunciations. It would seem that phonological activation involving unfamiliar characters with exceptional pronunciations was slower, and therefore reduced error rates.

To summarize this section, we can say that getting at the sound of Chinese words involves somewhat different processes than those of English. It appears that speed of getting at the sound of words with means for

---

[4] In the use of visually similar characters in Hsieh (1982) as well as in C. M. Cheng and Shih (1988), there is some indication that components within characters do not have much individual visual salience in the quick lexical decision tasks. Visual similarity did not facilitate processing. This could happen if the shared common radicals lost their individual salience when they were embedded as parts of whole characters. In other words, characters were seen as visual Gestalt wholes and the common radicals were not attended to individually. To the extent that this was the case, visual similarity between the prime and the target would have less effect.

grapheme-phoneme conversion can be faster than for words without such a possibility. Nevertheless, there is evidence that phonological mediation does take place in the perception of Chinese words.

3.4 GETTING AT THE MEANING OF WORDS

Reading models usually postulate two distinct routes for getting at the meaning of what is written. One is a phonological route, in which some form of speech recoding, deriving some sound-related code from the written symbol, is carried out (according to grapheme–phoneme rules or by direct lexical information) as a preliminary to arriving at the meaning. The other is the visual route, in which meaning is accessed directly from the visual information. It is also often assumed that because the visual route is more direct it results in faster reading (see McCusker, Hillinger, & Bias, 1981). To appreciate the postulation of the phonological route, it is helpful to remind ourselves that spoken language is prior to written language. This is true in the historical development of human languages as well as in the language development of most individuals. Therefore sound–meaning relation is prior to script–meaning relation, giving rise to the question of the need for phonological recoding before access to meaning. Another question then follows as to whether phonological recoding is involved to a different extent depending on the nature of the orthography. If the script primarily represents sounds of the language, script–meaning relation may not be so direct, and getting at the meaning more likely may be mediated by phonological recoding.

Before we proceed, it has to be recognized that understanding the meaning of printed words without phonological recoding in the conventional sense is possible, in any language. For example, people who are congenitally deaf and mute can come to learn to read. On the other hand, it is equally obvious that in many situations, whether it is for a child or an adult, reading (e.g., of verse) simply doesn't feel the same without pronouncing aloud or silently – the reader's feel for the meaning is different without phonological recoding. However, apart from these situations, it still makes sense to ask how much phonological recoding is involved in reading Chinese compared with other languages.

For English, there is some suggestion that more skilled readers tend to be visual readers, that is, those who get at the meaning of words through direct lexical information. But children or less skilled readers have to rely more on the phonological route to get at meaning (see Rozin & Gleitman, 1977). However, this view is challenged by the finding that visual distortion of print (such as mixing upper- and lower-case letters in WoRdS) hinders poor readers more than skilled readers (Mason, 1978). This finding contradicts the expectation that because mixed lettering destroys the overall visual shape of words, reading by those who recognize words and access their meanings as wholes would suffer more than those who proceed through individual component letters.

Similar findings with visually distorted Chinese characters have also been reported (Hung, Tzeng, Salzman, & Dreher, 1984). Subjects were asked to judge whether the two-character items they were shown were meaningful words or not. These items were either presented in regular print or in distorted print, produced by writing the components of the characters disproportionately to each other so that they lost their conventional configuration. Reaction times showed that better readers were affected by the distortion less than poor readers. The implication of such studies with English as well as Chinese has to be that better readers have greater resources (top-down processes) to employ in any given situation, and they exploit whatever route is more available at any time.

Conceivably, depending on the circumstance and purpose of the reading task, there could be a greater tendency to rely more on one route or the other, and indeed the two can proceed in a "horse racing" model (see Hung et al., 1984). This is why different studies could lead to different conclusions, varying from phonological recoding is necessary for accessing meaning of words, to it plays no essential part in reading, possibly occurring post lexical access, after getting at the meaning of words, or even only as an epiphenomenon.

So, what is really in question is when phonological recoding is involved, in which type or stage of processing. After their comprehensive review of the literature, McCusker et al. (1981) summarized that: "Phonological mediation is clearly used with difficult, infrequent, or unfamiliar material, in tasks that emphasize storage and processing in depth, and with subjects of low fluency" (p. 241). Two of the crucial terms in the above quotation, difficulty and depth of processing, denote relative attributes, and therefore the need for phonological recoding could not be established in absolute terms. In our present discussions though, we would wish to see if the need for phonological recoding might be different in corresponding and comparable situations with different orthographies. It is also helpful to distinguish between situations where single words are involved under more controlled situations and situations where sentences or continuous texts are read, with the reader having more freedom to proceed. As far as the former is concerned, quite a few phenomena clearly indicate that meaning of Chinese words can be accessed more directly. This is despite evidence in the last section showing that phonological mediation definitely occurs in the perception of single Chinese words. The phenomena reviewed in the following sections include the Stroop and size incongruity effects, affective meaning response times, speed of similarity judgments, translation asymmetry for number names, and cross-language priming.

3.4.1 Stroop and Size Incongruity Effects

The difference in the size of the Stroop effect between Chinese and alphabetic languages is a well established phenomenon and can be taken as strong evidence that meaning of Chinese characters is more manifest and more directly available visually. In the Stroop phenomenon (Stroop, 1935), subjects are asked to name the color of patches of ink as well as the color of the ink of printed color names. When a color name is inconsistent with its ink color (such as if the word *RED* is printed in blue ink), it takes subjects longer to name the color of the ink than to name the color of ink patches or the color names with consistent ink color (*RED* printed in red ink). The explanation for this phenomenon is that even though subjects are asked to attend to the color of the ink of printed words, it is to some extent unavoidable to process the meaning of the printed word. When this meaning is inconsistent with the physical ink color, the interference results in longer response latencies.

Biederman and Tsao (1979) reported that the Stroop effect for Chinese color names was greater than that for English. The implication was that it was even more unavoidable to process the meaning of the Chinese color names. This implies that meaning of Chinese words is more manifest. This is, of course, consistent with the view that the script-meaning relationship of Chinese is more direct. Morikawa (1981) found that the Stroop effect for Japanese subjects was greater when color names were printed in kanji than in kana. This further strengthens the view that the size of the Chinese Stroop effect is related to the orthography. Because the pronunciations were the same for the two scripts in Japanese, the result also indicated that the locus of the interference effect was in perceptual processes rather than in response processes such as pronunciation of the color names. Morikawa (1986), however, cautioned that the greater effect for kanji could be related to the higher frequency of usage of color names in kanji than in kana. But common color names are very frequently used words in both English and Chinese, and frequency difference is probably irrelevant in the Chinese–English Stroop effect difference. It could be hypothesized that difference in reading times for color names in Chinese and English might be relevant. However, we shall see that there is a parallel of the Stroop effect for number names in Chinese and English, and in that case we know that number names are read faster in Chinese than in English (see subsection 4.1.1).

Although the Stroop phenomenon concerns only a small domain of color words, there is a corresponding effect in another domain. This involves the inconsistency between physical size of number names and their numerical values, but it seems to obtain only for Chinese. O. J. L. Tzeng and Wang (1983) presented pairs of characters which are Chinese number names. One of the characters was printed physically larger than the other, and subjects were asked to indicate which was physically larger. Response times were slower if a name indicating a smaller number was printed physically larger, that is, if there was inconsistency between the meaning of such characters and their physical size. This again demonstrated that it was unavoidable to take note of the meaning of characters, even if the task at hand was only that of processing some physical attribute (printed size) of the characters.

O. J. L. Tzeng and Wang (1983) reported that this size incongruity effect disappeared for English number names (e.g., when *six* was printed larger than *nine*). However, the effect was also obtained with Arabic numerals, such as if *6* was printed larger than *9* (see Besner & Colheart, 1979). Arabic numerals represent meaning directly, rather than alphabetically, just as Chinese characters. These differential incongruity effects suggest that access to meaning of such "ideographic" symbols is more direct and that processing of such meaning can be actually unavoidable in some situations. O. J. L. Tzeng and Wang (1983) also found that Chinese-English bilinguals showed the size incongruity effect even for English number names, as if they had transferred their reading behaviors from Chinese to English words.

3.4.2 Affective Meaning Response Times

Another line of evidence for the greater ease of getting at the meaning of Chinese characters is provided by comparing the time needed to process affective meaning of Chinese and English words. Hoosain and Osgood (1983) compared the processing times for English words by a group of native speakers in the United States and processing times for their translation equivalents in Chinese by a group of Hong Kong subjects.[5] The words had comparable syllabic length in the two languages. The task was to look at the meaning of each presented word (e.g., *heaven*) and decide whether it meant something positive or negative. The time it took the subject to say either "positive" or "negative" [6] was recorded. Within the duration of each recorded response time, the subject would have to (a) look at the presented

---

[5] It should be noted that for the purpose of this study, respective native speakers are more preferable subjects than balanced bilinguals. The notion of balanced bilingualism usually assumes that the same language function is carried out with equal facility by native speakers of the two languages, which is precisely the possibility we wish to question. Using balanced bilinguals, if differential response times are obtained for the two languages, it would not be possible to distinguish whether the subjects are not balanced afterall or if there is a genuine language difference.

TABLE 3.1
Pronunciation Times (in msec.) for Saying "Positive" and "Negative"
and Response Times for Positive and Negative Words

	"Positive"	*"Negative"*	*Positive Words*	*Negative Words*
English	498	479	964	1,045
Chinese	486	503	806	923

From Hoosain and Osgood (1983). Reprinted with permission of Psychonommic Society, Inc.

item, (b) process its meaning, (c) decide on the affective polarity of the meaning, and (d) say "positive" or "negative" in the respective language. The first and last are peripheral processes, taking place between the eyes and the sensory cortex in one case and between the motor cortex and the vocal apparatus in the other. The two mediating processes are central meaning processes. Osgood's cross-cultural work (e.g., Osgood, May, & Miron, 1975) has shown very clearly that affective meaning, with the underlying dimensions of evaluation, potency, and activity, is a human universal, and subjects had no difficulty in deciding on affective meaning when they saw the presented words.

To obtain an estimation of the time required for only peripheral processes for English and Chinese, subjects were repeatedly shown the stimulus words *positive* and *negative* in random order (or the Chinese equivalents for the Chinese subjects). Their task was simply to pronounce what word they saw each time as quickly as possible. These random presentations required only the processes (a) and (d) given earlier, whereas the actual responses, saying "positive" or "negative", was identical with those of the experiment proper. Table 3.1 shows that it took less time to say "negative" than "positive" in English, but it was the reverse for the Chinese equivalents. The differences had to do with articulatory as well as acoustic aspects of the pronunciation of these words, which determine the speed at which the timer was stopped through a voice key. When the two naming latencies within each language were averaged, the cross-language times became comparable. (It might be noted that although *positive* and *negative* each has three syllables, the Chinese equivalents are both single syllables, but the naming latencies for the Chinese were not faster.)

When we look at the response times that involved processing word meanings in the two languages, the Chinese times were significantly faster.[6] This contrasted with the comparable times for the peripheral processes, (a)

---

[6] The faster times for positive rather than negative words reflect a different phenomenon, referred to as the Pollyanna effect (see Boucher & Osgood, 1969; Osgood & Hoosain, 1983), in which human beings are more ready to handle and talk about positive rather than negative things. This is not of particular relevance here.

and (d), and were therefore quite clear indication that meaning-processing times are faster for Chinese than for English. Given the universality of affective meaning, it is not likely that the slower meaning response times for English had to do with any difference in how the respective subjects handled this aspect of meaning. The words used were all common items in both languages. Therefore, the faster meaning response times for Chinese could be taken to mean that access to meaning was more direct. There is further indication that this quicker access to meaning is related to the possibility that phonological recoding is less implicated in the Chinese word meaning responses. This came from the pronunciation duration times for the Chinese and English words used in the study.

Native Cantonese speakers were asked to read the 60 Chinese words used in the study, and native English speakers were also asked to read the 60 English words. Both groups were asked to read at the rate of about a word every second. The recordings of the pronunciations of the two lists of words were analyzed with a mingograph. The mean sound durations were found to be significantly longer for the Chinese words. It should be noted that the 60 words in the two languages were matched in terms of mean number of syllables. In the original comparison of meaning response times, if the mediating process of phonological recoding had to occur similarly before the Chinese and American subjects could get at the meaning of the presented words in their respective languages, we would expect these recoding processes to require relative durations of time that were related to the actual pronunciation duration times of these words. This should be the case, because phonological recoding is supposed to be related to the sounds of the language concerned. Longer time durations for the Chinese words ought to mean, then, that phonological recoding took longer for Chinese words than for English words, if it was similarly involved in getting at the word meanings. This should further mean that response times for the Chinese words ought to be slower, which was not the case. It would then appear that phonological recoding was less involved for the Chinese words in this situation.

It might be argued that reading aloud and phonological recoding are different processes, and there is no specific evidence that longer reading aloud times reflect slower speed of phonological recoding. However, a close parallel of this situation can be found in the faster reading times for Chinese number names compared with those of other languages, and the corresponding bigger digit span for Chinese (see subsection 4.1.1). Digit span depends directly on the duration of the phonological code of the number names.

3.4.3 Speed of Similarity Judgments

Another way of comparing the extraction of graphemic, phonemic, or semantic information from words is to have subjects look at a group of words and decide which one shares some similarity in one of these aspects with a target. D. L. Peng, Orchard, and Stern (1983) conducted one such study, based on the English study by Condry, McMahon-Rideout, and Levy (1979). Groups of three characters were shown to the subject in a triangular location format. A target character was on top and two test items were on the bottom. Subjects had to indicate which test character was similar to the target, in either graphic, phonetic, or semantic aspects. The other test character was either a distractor, similar to the target in some irrelevant aspect, or a control, with no obvious similarity with the target. Grade 4 and undergraduate students were tested.

Both groups found the graphic comparison the easiest, although there was no significant difference between graphic and semantic comparisons. Phonetic distractors had no effect on semantic similarity judgments, for either the children or the adults (which was not the case in the English study by Condry et al., 1979). This indicates that access to meaning in Chinese is more direct than in English and involves less phonological mediation. Graphic distractors had significant effects on phonetic similarity judgments only for the children (whereas it had significant effects for both second- and fifth-grade children as well as adults in the English study). Chinese adults appeared to access the sound of characters more in a character-as-a-whole to sound-as-a-whole manner. For the undergraduate students, graphic distractors had greater effect than phonetic distractors for semantic similarity judgments.

M. J. Chen, Yung, and Ng (1988) employed a variation of the visual search task. They asked Chinese subjects to look at a row of nine characters that could be graphemically similar (sharing a common radical), phonemically similar, semantically similar, or dissimilar in all three aspects. The characters were preceded by a graphemic, phonemic, or semantic cue, and subjects had to indicate if all items contained the cued feature or if one of them was different from the rest in this regard. A corresponding task with English words was also designed for the bilingual subjects. Results showed that, for Chinese, graphemic and semantic processing times were equally fast and both significantly faster than phonemic processing times. This showed that getting at the meaning of Chinese was direct and did not involve significant phonological recoding, whereas getting at the sound could actually be slower.

3.4.4 Translation Asymmetry

Translation asymmetry here refers to the phenomenon that the speed of translating from one language to another is different from the reverse. This can be due to a difference in the level of achievement in the respective languages, of course, and it is often assumed that translating into the native or stronger language is easier than translating into the nonnative or weaker language. In the present case, however, a reversal of this pattern reveals the relative speed of getting at the meaning of different languages. This contrasts with the lack of difference in getting at the sound of the respective symbols.

Hoosain (1986b) used a translation-cum-reading task to again tease out the times required for peripheral versus central meaning processing for number names in English and in Chinese. Chinese-English bilingual undergraduates in Hong Kong were asked to (a) read a list of 200 random Arabic numerals, varying from 1 to 9, as fast as possible, in Cantonese and also in English; (b) read a similar list of random Chinese number names (in the native Cantonese dialect) and read a list of random English number names; and (c) translate a printed list of English number names orally into Cantonese, and translate a printed list of Chinese number names into English. The time each subject required to complete a task was divided by 200 to obtain the average time required for each condition. Table 3.2 shows the results for the six conditions.

The subjects pronounced Arabic numerals more quickly in Cantonese than in English. There are two possible reasons for this difference. The subjects could be Chinese-language dominant, having started to learn English only in school, although they had used English as the medium of instruction in school and at the university for at least 8 years. Furthermore, sound duration for digits pronounced in Cantonese is shorter than in English (see subsection 4.1.1). Subjects also read Chinese number names faster than English, and by about the same margin of difference as between reading Arabic numerals in the two languages. Identical motor responses were being made when the subjects read, for example, *seven* and *7* in English. The difference between reading number names in Chinese or English and reading Arabic numerals lies in the decoding of the stimulus and not in the encoding or production of the oral response. It is between having to get at the sounds of number names written in either of the languages and getting at the sounds of the neutral Arabic numerals. The magnitude of difference in pronouncing in English and pronouncing in Cantonese was comparable in the two sets of tasks. It would seem that getting at the sound of Chinese number names was about as fast as getting at the sound of English number names.

The translation results, on the other hand, indicated that getting at the meaning of Chinese number names was faster. Table 3.2 shows that Chinese-to-English translation was faster than English-to-Chinese translation. The faster Chinese-to-English translation involved producing oral responses in English, which had been shown to take more time in the reading trials. It also meant translating into the bilingual subjects' nonnative language. The explanation for faster Chinese-to-English times would have to be that the initial getting at the meaning of the Chinese number

TABLE 3.2
Reading and Translation Times (in msec.) for Number
Names and Arabic Numerals

Reading	
Chinese number names	273
English number names	370
Numerals in Chinese	267
Numerals in English	358
Translating	
English to Chinese	454
Chinese to English	399

From Hoosain (1986b).

names was faster than the corresponding task of getting at the meaning of English number names in the reversed English-to-Chinese translation. And this advantage in getting at the meaning of Chinese number names was big enough to overwhelm the slower times for pronunciation of responses in English for Chinese-to-English translation.

3.4.5 Cross-language Semantic Priming

Another indication of the more direct and therefore faster speed of getting at the meaning of Chinese words comes from a study of cross-language semantic priming. Keatley (1988) used a group of Chinese-English bilinguals in Hong Kong whose English-as-second-language performance was screened. They had reading speed and comprehension comparable to native English speakers. The materials used were Chinese words and English words that were translation equivalents. In the priming task, subjects were shown a single-character Chinese word or an English word as a prime, followed by a word or nonword in the other language as a target. Nonwords were created by substituting a portion of a character with other strokes, or a constituent letter of an English word with another letter. The task involved lexical decision, to push a button as quickly as possible after the target appeared, to indicate if it was a word or nonword. Semantic priming occurs if response time for a target is faster with a related prime (e.g., *doctor* as a prime and *pain* as a target) than with an unrelated prime (*doctor* as prime and *pine* as target). The prior processing of the prime has been found to facilitate targets with related sound or meaning (Posner, 1978). Cross-language priming occurs when such an effect occurs when the prime and target are in different languages. Keatley found significant cross-language priming with the prime being shown for a quarter of a second and another quarter of a second separated the prime and the target, but only when Chinese words were the primes and English words the targets, not when they were in reversed roles.

If we can accept that the bilingual subjects had native fluency for English, the explanation for the data would most likely be the greater ease of getting at the meaning of Chinese words than English. With the short time that each prime was being presented, the speed of arriving at the meaning of Chinese primes means that there was a greater opportunity for the semantic priming process to operate and facilitate lexical decision concerning the target. It appears that the priming effect obtained in this study was not the result of any deliberate reasoning that required relatively longer durations. The effect was not significant when the interval between the prime and the target became longer, 2 seconds instead of the quarter of a second. This indicated that the priming effect was automatic rather than strategic, and is consistent with the account that speed of getting at the meaning of the prime was crucial, to have to be more or less completed in time for the impending presentation of the target.

To summarize this section, getting at the meaning of Chinese words, across a wide variety of situations, is more direct and faster. This is consistent with the possibility that phonological recoding is less involved for processing individual words in the nonalphabetic script, although other studies reviewed in the last section showed that phonological recoding does occur. Phonological access for Chinese can be slower. It would appear that getting at the meaning of Chinese words and getting at the sound are two sides of the same coin, arising from the absence of grapheme–phoneme conversion rules in the orthography.

3.5 SENTENCE READING

In the case of the more bottom-up process of processing single words, we have seen that access to meaning can be more direct. On the other hand, the question of the need for phonological recoding often refers to reading of text rather than individual words. What goes on with reading individual words and reading texts could be different in some important ways. Reading of text involves more top-down processes, where the interpretation of context plays an important part in understanding. Working memory (see section 4.1) is more necessary in reading sentences, to follow the flow of meaning. This is not quite the case with getting at the meaning of single words. We have already noted that in the review by McCusker et al. (1981), it was held that phonological recoding is implicated when storage of information and processing to greater depth is required. Furthermore, it is also more difficult to control the situation in reading tasks with longer materials. Subjects can adapt themselves and use all their resources and ingenuity to exploit different available cues to accomplish their task. It is often not possible to tie them down to a predetermined mode of functioning, which is more possible in the case of processing single items in strictly controlled situations, as referred to in the last few sections. These reasons explain why, when we come to the reading of text, the findings are more mixed than the processing of individual words. However, some suggestions about what might be going on are provided by eye movement data recorded during reading.

3.5.1 Phonological Recoding During Reading

There are studies that show that phonological recoding takes place in the reading of Chinese. O. J. L. Tzeng, Hung, and Wang (1977) demonstrated the presence of phonological recoding in both a memory task and a sentence-judging task, but it is the second task that is relevant here. Subjects had to read a seven-character-long sentence and decide if it was grammatical or anomalous. Anomalous sentences were created simply by having the order of the verb of grammatical sentences placed in a wrong position. The two types of sentence strings consisted of characters that sounded either phonemically similar or dissimilar. There were nine sentences for each condition of grammaticality and phonemic similarity.

Mean response times were slower for sentences with phonemically similar constituents, which suggests that phonological recoding had taken place. Thus, the mediating similar sound codes of the constituents of these sentences produced interference among themselves, affecting access to the meaning of words in the sentences to decide on their grammaticality. An interaction effect also indicated that subjects used different strategies when judging phonemically similar sentences and phonemically dissimilar sentences. With sentences having phonemically similar characters, the subjects seemed to use a self-terminating strategy, which resulted in faster response times for identifying anomalous sentences than for identifying grammatical sentences. As soon as subjects detected that the verbs were in the wrong place in anomalous sentences, they made their judgment before getting to the end of the sentences. But with grammatical sentences, they got to the end to be sure that there was nothing anomalous. However, with sentences having phonemically dissimilar characters, subjects seemed to use an exhaustive strategy, getting to the end of both anomalous and grammatical sentences before making their judgments. This resulted in the same amount of time for identifying both anomalous and grammatical sentences.

In another study, O. J. L. Tzeng and Hung (1978) asked subjects to judge whether visually presented pairs of characters had the "same" visual shape (i.e., looked similar), the same vowel, or the same meaning, while they were simultaneously engaged in repeating numbers presented orally. Response times were longer when judging if presented pairs shared the same vowel than in the other two situations. The times for judging similarity of meanings of character pairs were comparable to those of judging similarity of visual shape. Again, this would mean that getting at the meaning of individual characters can be quite direct, with little if any phonological recoding.

However, an accompanying experiment in the same study showed that processing sentences involved significant phonological recoding. Subjects looked at sentences that were either well formed or nonsensical. They had to decide if each sentence was well formed or not, and for half the time they also had to simultaneously repeat orally presented numbers. Responses were slower in the latter case. This was taken to mean that a significant amount of phonological recoding was necessary in deciding on the grammaticality of the sentences, and this was interfered with by shadowing presented numbers. Thus, whereas semantic judgment for character pairs was not subject to interference by auditory-vocal activity, judgment of grammaticality of sentences was. This indicated that sentence processing in Chinese is mediated by phonological recoding. Why should processing individual words not necessarily involve phonological recoding but processing sentences does? O. J. L. Tzeng et al. (1977) suggested that phonological recoding is implicated in working memory, where information is stored temporarily in our immediate consciousness to keep track of sequential stimuli such as component words of sentences.

Given that phonological recoding is involved in Chinese sentence processing, just as in the case of English sentences, we still have the question of whether the need for phonological recoding could be relatively smaller for Chinese. This was investigated by Treiman, Baron, and Luk (1981) who compared the processing of English and Chinese sentences. Native speakers of the respective languages were asked to judge the truth/falsity of presented sentences that could be a "homophone" sentence, such that it sounded true when read out loud (e.g., *A pair is a fruit*). When compared with control sentences (*A pier is a fruit*), English homophone sentences required more response time and resulted in more errors, which suggested that even though they were presented visually phonological recoding must have taken place. Because a homophone sentence was a true-sounding sentence, it interfered with the appropriate response, which was that such a sentence was false. For Chinese sentences though [7], the corresponding homophone sentences resulted in significantly less impairment than the control sentences. Subjects still required longer time for the homophone sentences, but the difference was not as great as that for English sentences. Also, they actually made fewer errors on homophone sentences than on control sentences. As less interference was produced by true sounding Chinese sentences that were actually false, it showed that phonological recoding was less involved for Chinese sentence processing.

This finding seems to give us grounds to say that getting at the meaning of Chinese is really more direct, not only in the case of the more bottom-up situation of tasks involving individual words but also in sentence (albeit only single sentence) processing tasks. However, it is difficult to decide to what extent the task designed by Treiman et al. (1981) was really a sentence-judgment task. It was possible for subjects to simply compare the two crucial words or characters in each sentence (e.g., *pair* and *fruit*) and decide whether they had a category–member relationship, thereby deciding if the sentence as a whole was true or false. Thus, it would be possible to produce the required response more like doing a word-pair task such as that of O. J. L. Tzeng and Hung (1978), already mentioned, without really going through the whole sentence. This would be particularly so because the two crucial words would occupy the same relative positions in different presented sentences. As in the case of the task in O. J. L. Tzeng and Hung (1978), seeing if word-pairs had the same meaning, the finding was that phonological recoding was not much involved for Chinese. We still do not have conclusive evidence that phonological recoding is less involved in reading Chinese text.

3.5.2 Eye Movements and Reading

Further information regarding the role of pronunciation of words in reading tasks is provided by eye-movement studies. Eye movements take place in reading when there is more to see than can be covered in one fixation. Before we proceed to look at eye movements, we have to return to visual acuity for a moment. Foveal vision, within which we can see things clearly, covers only a small extent of about 2 degrees of visual angle, corresponding to about eight letters or nearly one and a half English words or a couple of Chinese characters, when viewed under normal reading conditions. Materials in parafoveal or peripheral vision beyond the immediate area around the fixation point are not seen so well, but it is still possible to discern crude shapes of things within another dozen or so letter spaces (see McConkie & Rayner, 1975). The two main variables in eye movement are the duration of fixation pauses of the eyes as well as the distance between eye fixations during reading. Together, the two determine reading speed. Normally, except for tracking a smooth moving target, actual eye movements do not sweep over a continuous smooth path but are usually in quick jumps called saccades in between fixation stops, each of a different duration. An eye camera can be used to record both the location and duration of fixations as well as the path and distance of saccades. In reading, saccades usually proceed along the line of print, but the direction can be occasionally regressed when the eyes revert to preceding words for clarification.

In the case of reading Chinese, another relevant factor to note is that modern printed Chinese (not to mention classical Chinese) is more dense than English, so that the same contents take up less space in print.[7] Generally, when we look at translation equivalent passages, in some bilingual publications for example, English versions are 50% or 60% longer than the corresponding Chinese passage, in terms of the total length of the printed lines. If we just consider this density, it would mean that the reader of Chinese is able to see more proportion of the text with any one fixation, that is, perceptual span in terms of content information covered is greater. This consideration alone, if there are no other relevant factors, should mean that a Chinese reader finishes reading the same message quicker than the reader of its English equivalent. However, there are other variables that make the picture more complicated.

It turns out that for the same physical length of text in a line of print, Chinese readers require more fixations, that is, have smaller saccades in terms of physical distance than do English readers (D. L. Peng et al., 1983; Sun, Morita, & Stark, 1985; Sun & Stark, 1986). The fixation times though are comparable, in the order of about a quarter of a second for ordinary text, which is the kind of time needed to complete quick cognitions or what Blumenthal (1977) referred to as rapid attentional integration. According to D. L. Peng et al. (1983) as well as Sun and Stark (1986), there is also no difference between Chinese and English readers in average durations associated with the different pause types, such as the first fixation pause on a line, the last fixation pause on a line, and fixation pause preceding a regression.

When saccades are measured in terms of number of linguistic words covered between fixations instead of length of the line of print, then

---

[7] There are a few aspects to this density. The syntax of Chinese, such as the absence of inflections, could be partly responsible. But the physical layout of the orthography is a significant factor (see Fig. 2.4). Because characters are not spelled out in letters, their generally square shape imposes mutual constraint between the height and width of characters. In horizontal text, for example, the limited height available between lines of print restricts the width of individual characters. Together with the fact that words do not tend to be more than two characters long, there is a limit to the physical length of written or printed Chinese words. In English, on the other hand, a given line height still allows variation in syllabic as well as word length. There is also more variation in overall word shape for English, in that letters like *l* and *j* extend above or below the line of print. Finally, the density of lines (strokes) in a given area of Chinese print is greater than that of corresponding English print, with more intersection of lines in the former case (the width of a stroke is also variable for Chinese). I have compared Chinese (printed horizontally) and English newspaper texts for their line density. Horizontally, half-way up the height of each line, the density of lines of Chinese is only 10% greater than English. But vertically, perpendicular to the line of print, the Chinese line density is roughly twice that of English (see, e.g., Fig. 2.4). One indication of the difference is that a 7 x 11 dot matrix is often used to print alphabetic letters, but a 50 x 40 matrix is used for Chinese (Taylor & Taylor, 1983). This means, of course, that Chinese generally has greater spatial frequency than English.

Chinese and English readers covered comparable ground. According to available information in D. L. Peng et al. (1983), each saccade covered about 1.9 words for both Chinese and English. In the study by Sun et al. (1985), the saccade was about 1.7 words for Chinese and 1.8 words for English. One explanation offered for this pattern of results is that there is a central processing mechanism that has a functional limit in terms of amount of information represented by words, so that the speed of eye movements has to be adjusted to accommodate this bottleneck higher up in the cognitive mechanism (Sun & Stark, 1986). Thus, even though a greater proportion of a Chinese message may be visually covered in each fixation, the eyes have to adjust their pace in moving across such a text to be commensurate with the speed at which sensory information can be handled higher up in the cognitive mechanism.

But there could be other explanations for the failure of eye movement in reading Chinese to be faster, taking advantage of its higher density. This is related to the visual shape of Chinese words. In the English situation, when the eyes are fixed at any point of the text, peripheral vision provides information about the general length and shape of the words to come, to the right of the fixation point. This crude information allows some kind of preliminary or preattentive processing of the information while focal attention is directed to the information in foveal vision. This preliminary information, together with what has been processed so far up to and including focal processing, enable the reader to decide where to fixate the eyes next. The availability of this word shape information has been found to be useful (e.g., Rayner, 1975).

Also, such peripheral information tends to be exploited by good readers more. Their experience and skill enable the information to be sufficiently identified through the interaction of bottom-up processes arising from the crude peripheral word shapes and top-down processes arising from understanding of the context of the message so far. But a good deal of such peripheral information is absent from Chinese text. There is no word-boundary spacing over and above regular boundary between individual characters. Characters are generally square, with less of the variation of ups and downs of some letters of the alphabet from the line of print. Also, there is nothing corresponding to printing the initial letter of a proper noun in the upper case.

As peripheral information in the form of varying word shapes is absent from Chinese, the high spatial frequency of Chinese text further renders peripheral vision less distinctive. Component strokes of Chinese characters are all packed within a square space rather than spelled out horizontally as in alphabetical languages. One effect is that, particularly with characters having large stroke numbers, the density of lines as well as the intersection of lines within any space of text would be greater for Chinese. This results in greater spatial frequency in the sensory information. In peripheral vision, the sensory information is more degraded, and with higher spatial frequency this information becomes even less distinctive (see Ho & Hoosain, 1989).

There is a suggestion based on studies on English that fluent readers ignore word shape (Paap, Newsome, & Noel, 1984), which would mean that the nature of peripheral word-shape information is immaterial. But it should be noted that this evidence is based on studies using individual words rather than continuous text. It is in the latter case that crude sensory information from peripheral vision can be exploited simultaneously with detailed sensory information from the fixation area. Haber, Haber, and Furlin (1983) showed that when subjects were stopped randomly in the middle of an English sentence, information about word length as well shape of the envelope of the next word were useful in guessing what it was.

Another possible explanation for eye-movement patterns for Chinese is related to its script–sound–meaning relationship. One suggestion of this is two reports of pursuitlike or smooth tracking rather than saccadic eye movements. When Shen (1927) compared the reading of Chinese printed horizontally and vertically, he found that fixation pauses had a tendency to glide into a continuous line when subjects read vertical script but not when they read horizontal script. At that time, vertical lines of text were the norm. (Eye-movements of modern Chinese subjects reading vertical text show fixation durations about 10% longer than for horizontal texts and only half the saccadic span [Sun et al., 1985]). Stern (1978) also reported one Chinese subject reading horizontal text and showed smooth pursuitlike eye movement with infrequent saccades and fixations. He attributed this pattern to the speed of access to meaning in Chinese. In contrast, it should be noted that in the case of English, only saccadic movements have been reported (see Carpenter & Just, 1981). The two reports of pursuit eye movement for Chinese are separated by more than half a century, and they are two out of only a very few reports of eye-movement studies in Chinese. They stand out like a sore thumb. It also appears that smooth eye movements can be found with both vertical and horizontal texts.

We therefore have two types of eye movements for Chinese, the regular saccadic movement, where physical distances covered by each saccade is smaller than for English, and the pursuitlike movement, which is found less often. I speculate that they indicate two different ways in which the reader proceeds with the reading task in Chinese, reflecting its unique script–sound–meaning relationship. With proficient readers, the pursuit-type movement is possible with Chinese text where meaning is more manifest and more directly available and the reader is reading for meaning. Because each character is a morpheme, lexical access proceeds in a steady manner through the continuous parade of uniformly paced meaning units, and eye movement can merge into a glide. In contrast, for English, varying word lengths and shapes would rule out evenly paced saccades. Of course, the evenly placed morphemic units can carry different amounts of information or vary in their conceptual complexity. This is common for any orthography, but evenly placed morphemic units are unique to orthographies like Chinese. This could provide some regularity of processing at certain levels.

With less proficient readers or when they decide to pay more attention to the phonological code, such as vocalizing or subvocalizing what is read, we have a different situation.[8] When the reader attends to the sounds of individual characters as well as to their meanings, the visual density of Chinese (with more words packed in the same length of text as compared with English) means that saccadic length measured in physical distance would be shorter than for English.[9] This is because whereas meanings of words in a sentence can merge, pronunciation of individual characters cannot and has to be treated one by one. Thus, the finding of the smooth-tracking type of eye movements in reading Chinese indicates proficient reading for meaning with minimal phonological recoding. And the more commonly found case of short saccades indicates the tendency to pay attention to sounds of individual characters in reading.

In this manner, the morpheme-syllable as the unit of writing in Chinese can be conducive to two alternative ways of reading, both paradoxically being facilitated by the orthography. The smooth tracking eye movement is facilitated by direct script-meaning relations. On the other hand, the small saccadic eye movement is the result of the one-to-one script-sound relation that does not involve grapheme-phoneme rules (hence, enticing some readers to pay extra attention to individual pronunciations). Which processing method the reader adopts depends on both individual differences and task demands, on the proficiency of the reader as well as the purpose of reading.

There is also some question of whether, for Chinese-English bilinguals, eye movement habits typical for Chinese texts might be carried over to the second language. We noted in subsection 3.1.1 that in the case of

---

[8] In this connection we should note that, traditionally, oral reading is emphasized in the learning of Chinese, and the ability to read every character aloud or recite a text can actually be taken to be a sign of having learned the text well. It is a common phenomenon in Chinese schools to see a whole class engaged in reading texts aloud in unison. This could be related to the lack of grapheme-phoneme conversion rules for Chinese characters, so that a premium is placed on the correct individual character-syllable association.

[9] We might note that the density difference appears to be in terms of visual-spatial density only. The density for the two languages in terms of number of syllables appears to be comparable. This comparison involves counting the number of the monosyllabic characters for a modern Chinese passage and comparing this with the number of syllables in a passage of English translation equivalent.

Chinese-English bilinguals, Freeman (1980) found some degree of transfer of visual acuity patterns from the native Chinese language to English. D. L. Peng et al. (1983) tested Chinese-English bilingual subjects who were graduate students or exchange scholars in the United States with reasonable proficiency in English. But their performance with English texts showed that all aspects of information processing were affected. Not only did they require more fixations per physical line of English text than native speakers, but they also made more regressive eye movements, read fewer lines without regressions, and spent more time per fixation. The small saccadic span could mean that they were transferring their habitual fixation patterns developed for Chinese to reading in the second language. But the implication of the other aspects of their results would be that their command of the second language was generally not that good, which would mean inferior results in all aspects of information processing revealed by eye movement.

3.6 CONCLUSION

The distinctive configuration of the Chinese script as well as its script-sound and script–meaning relations can differentially affect perceptual processes, compared with similar processes in English. These include: (a) lack of acuity difference for characters arranged in different orientations; (b) preference of direction of scan according to language experience; (c) the individuality of constitutent characters of bisyllabic words in some situations; (d) the more direct access to meaning of individual words, although access to sound could require a different effort due to the lack of grapheme–phoneme conversion rules;[10] and (e) the variation in eye movements in reading connected with different manners of reading.

Many of these phenomena would be considered as bottom-up processes. Perception in these situations is largely determined by the nature of the sensory information. Such bottom-up processes have been recognized where language differences could matter more to cognitive processes (Hung

---

[10] One question that has recently received attention is the possibility of a lack of phonological awareness, particularly with regard to submorphemic segments, in Chinese learners who have not been exposed to any alphabetic orthography. For example, monolingual Chinese who had no experience with pinyin (a phonetic script using letters of the alphabet as an aid to learning to read characters), adopted in China, were found to be inferior to Chinese-Dutch bilinguals in tasks such as involving deletion of initial consonants (Bertelson & de Gelder, in press). Awareness of sound segments is taken to indicate more advanced phonological awareness than mere awareness of syllables. The possibility that the use of pinyin facilitates reading instruction has also been investigated (Y. Wang & Taylor, 1990). In general, the question of confounding variables is very pertinent in such research. It is difficult to find comparable Chinese subjects who differ only in experience with alphabetic orthographies.

& Tzeng, 1981). As a contrast between bottom-up and top-down processes, we note that getting at the meaning of individual Chinese words is usually faster, but this is not reflected in the reading of sentences. In the latter case, more top-down processes are brought into play. It is suggested that the habit of paying attention to the pronunciation of individual characters might slow reading down. There is also a suggestion of a universal central processing mechanism that imposes a limit on how fast we can handle information at higher levels (Sun & Stark, 1986).

However, even though reading speed of Chinese text might be brought down to a level comparable to that of English, this does not mean that all aspects of reading are immune to language differences. We have noted independent reports of smooth tracking eye movements for Chinese, although their implications still require clarification. But perhaps more significantly, the Chinese orthography entails a different way of learning to read, which is examined in the next chapter.

4 Memory Aspects of the Chinese Language

The effects of language on cognitive processes need not be confined to processing the language itself but may extend to other cognitive functioning of people who have come to learn and use the language. In the case of Chinese, a very significant aspect of this functioning concerns what is called working memory (Baddeley & Hitch, 1974) and its role in problem solving. There is convincing evidence that the memory span for numbers in Chinese is significantly larger than for many other languages, and this facilitates mental operation with numbers. Visual perceptual functioning of the Chinese also appears to be related to learning the Chinese script. On the other hand, in longer term memory processes, there are distinctive manners in which words are remembered and the lexicon is organized. There are implications for the pattern of reading problems. Some aspects of cognitive style seem to be related to the manner of learning to read and write Chinese.

4.1 WORKING MEMORY

In working memory (see Baddeley, 1983, 1986; Baddeley & Hitch, 1974) temporary storage of information is carried out in connection with the performance of other cognitive functions such as language comprehension and problem solving. In Baddeley's model, there is a central executive with two main systems, an articulatory loop that stores and allows the manipulation of speech-based material and a visuo-spatial scratch-pad dealing with visual information. One important activity of the articulatory loop is the storage and manipulation of numbers in mental calculation and problem solving. There is now quite convincing evidence that the facility with which

Chinese people do their numerical manipulations has to do with the short duration of pronunciation of number names in Chinese, which allows a greater capacity for articulatory loop functions. Similarly, there are suggestions, perhaps not as strong, that the experience of learning the Chinese script, with its emphasis on the spatial layout of strokes, enhances visuospatial scratch-pad activity. Assuming that numerical and spatial reasoning is fundamental to mathematics, this means that the learning and use of the Chinese language could facilitate this important "nonverbal" activity.

4.1.1 Articulatory Loop and Number Names

Baddeley, Thomson, and Buchanan (1975) showed that short-term memory for words with shorter pronunciation duration (such as *wicket*) is better than those with longer duration (e.g., *coerce*). It should be noted that sound duration is not just a straightforward matter of syllabic length. The English *seven* with two syllables, for example, has a shorter sound duration than *six* with only one syllable (see later discussion). Baddeley also reasoned that because the phonological trace of items fades in about 2 seconds, rehearsal has to be completed in that amount of time to prevent forgetting items in temporary storage (e.g., Baddeley, 1983). Thus, the articulatory loop capacity or memory span works out to about 2 seconds worth of sounds.

Hoosain (1984a) compared the sound duration for number names, from one to nine, pronounced in the Cantonese dialect as well as in English. Respective native speakers pronounced these numbers in a natural manner at the rate of one number every second. Recordings of these pronunciations were processed with a mingograph, and length of sound durations was determined in terms of intensity above a baseline level. Table 4.1 shows that, overall, the durations were shorter for Chinese. The speed of rehearsing items in the articulatory loop, or manipulating numbers in one's head, is most likely to be faster than normal reading rates, and probably

TABLE 4.1
Pronunciation Durations (in msec.) for Numbers in Chinese and English

Numbers	1	2	3	4	5	6	7	8	9	Grand Mean
In English										
Mean	325	314	355	388	374	578	403	307	330	375
S.D.	126	73	59	193	86	105	55	81	54	
In Chinese										
Mean	247	342	458	478	302	198	264	257	285	314
S.D.	62	96	82	74	71	58	59	61	54	

From Hoosain (1984a).

closer to fast reading speed. To get a better estimate of such rehearsal times, Cantonese speakers were asked to read a list of 200 random numbers as fast as they could. They took an average of 265 milliseconds for each digit. In an earlier study by Ellis and Hennelly (1980), Welsh-English bilinguals, some reporting to be English dominant, were found to take an average of 321 milliseconds for English and an even longer 385 milliseconds for Welsh. K. S. Liu and Shen (1977) also reported that numbers were read more quickly in Mandarin than in German.

There are now a few studies comparing sound duration of number names and the corresponding digit spans in different languages (see Table 4.2). In forward digit span, or simply digit span, subjects are asked to repeat a sequence of orally presented digits in the given order. In backward digit span, they have to repeat the digits in reverse order. The maximum length at which subjects can do so correctly is taken as their span, and both forward and backward digit spans have been incorporated as part of many standard tests of intelligence. Although the various studies used slightly different procedures and strict comparison may be inappropriate, comparisons within each study and the overall pattern of the data quite clearly indicate that forward digit span in Chinese, whether in the Cantonese or the Putonghua (Mandarin) dialect, is distinctly larger than in the other languages. Also, the sound durations of digit names pronounced in Chinese are generally shorter. In Table 4.2, it can be seen that the product of the digit span and the average reading time for a digit ranges from 1.8 to 2.6 seconds in the various studies. These times are about the suggested 2 seconds worth of sounds stored in the articulatory loop.

Furthermore, in a group of 10 Chinese-English bilingual undergraduate students, Hoosain (1982) found that pronunciation speed for numbers was correlated with digit span. The students were asked to read a list of 200 random numbers as quickly as possible in Cantonese and in English and were then given a digit span test in Cantonese as well as in English. The correlation between reading time and digit span was -.66 for Cantonese and -.70 for English, indicating that faster reading speed was significantly associated with larger digit span. Typically, bilingual undergraduates in Hong Kong have an English digit span comparable to that reported for native English speakers, but their Chinese digit span would be a couple of digits larger. Hoosain (1979), for example, found a span of 9.9 for Chinese and 7.3 for English with a group of bilingual undergraduate students. Hoosain and Salili (1987), however, found a digit span of 6.6 for English with a similar group of subjects.[1]

---

[1] A noted decline in the level of command of the English language in the undergraduate population has been reported and the University of Hong Kong had proposed adding foundation courses to its curriculum, partly to improve the standard of English. English is the medium of instruction.

TABLE 4.2
Digit Span and Sound Duration in Different Languages

Reference	Language	Mean No. of Syllables per Digit Name	Digit Span			Rapid Sound Duration (msec/digit)	Normal Reading Duration (msec/digit)
Ellis & Hennelly (1980)[a]	Welsh	1.1	5.77			385	—
	English	1.1	6.55			321	—
Hoosain (1979, 1984a)[b]	Chinese (Cantonese)	1	9.9			265	314
	English	1.1	—			—	375
Naveh-Benjamin & Ayers (1986)[c]	English	1	7.21			256	—
	Spanish	1.625	6.37			287	—
	Hebrew	1.875	6.51			309	—
	Arabic	2.25	5.77			370	—
	Children		Kindergarten	1st grade	5th grade		
Stigler, Lee, & Stevenson (1986)	Chinese (Mandarin)	1	5.9	6.4	6.9	—	—
	Japanese		4.1	4.4	5.5	—	—
	English	1.1	4.6	5.1	5.9	—	—
	Adult						
	Chinese (Mandarin)	1	9.2			—	406
	English	1.1	7.2			—	527
			4 years old	5 years old	6 years old		
Chen & Stevenson (1988)[d]	Chinese (Putonghua)	1	4.6[d]	4.8	5.3	—	377
	English	1.1	3.4	4.4	4.5	—	471

Notes: [a]This study included digits 0 to 9. In rapid reading, subjects read 200 numerals at a time. [b]These studies included digits 1 to 9. In rapid reading, subjects read 200 numerals at a time. [c]This study excluded the digit 7, to avoid *seven* for English. In rapid reading, subjects read 100 numerals at a time. [d]These numbers are approximate, derived from Fig. 2, C. S. Chen and Stevenson (1988).

One might think that the difference between the span in the Chinese-English bilinguals' two languages only reflects the disadvantage of performing in a weaker second language. The Hong Kong bilingual undergraduates are generally still Chinese dominant, although they would all have studied English for more than 8 years, using it as the medium of instruction in high school and the university. In other reported studies comparing bilingual performance, no such big difference between digit spans in the respective languages has been found. After all, number names are always overlearned when one acquires a second language. For example, Glicksberg (1963), tested Spanish-English bilinguals who had to attend an intensive English course at a university and found a difference of only 0.8 of a digit between their performance in the two languages. Therefore, it is unlikely that the Chinese-English bilinguals' discrepancy of performance in their two languages was mainly due to second-language disadvantage. Inherent language differences would be more probable.

The Chinese subjects in the different studies of digit span included those in Hong Kong, Beijing, and Taiwan, and ranged in age from 4 years to adulthood. It is unlikely that such a diverse group of subjects could all have achieved bigger Chinese digit spans through common application of some strategy or sheer motivation. In fact, it has been shown that the Chinese superiority is diminished when backward digit span is compared instead (see Hoosain, 1984a; Stigler, Lee, & Stevenson, 1986). If Chinese subjects employed strategies or were more motivated, we would expect their superiority to be greater in the slightly more difficult backward span test, which is not the case.

There is some indication that forward digit span is a measure distinct from backward digit span. Paraskevopoulos and Kirk (1969) reported that intercorrelations of forward digit span with other subtests of the Illinois Test of Psycholinguistic Abilities ranged from .06 to .28 only, and suggested that forward digit span was an independent factor in the battery. When forward digit span was collapsed with backward digit span, such as in the Wechsler Adult Intellingence Scale, intercorrelations with other subtests increased to a range of .48 to .78 (Wechsler, 1955). Forward digit span involves only straightforward temporary storage and recall of the auditory items. Backward digit span requires some form of operation on the items. There is some suggestion that this includes some arrangement of the items and a "reading backward" of this arrangement. There is also a suggestion that such operations may involve the right hemisphere more, as contrasted with the primary involvement of the left hemisphere in forward digit span (see Costa, 1975; Rudel & Denckla, 1974).

In the case of word span, the advantage of short sound duration for number names does not apply. Whereas Chinese digit names are all monosyllabic, modern Chinese words tend to be bisyllabic and hence not necessarily of shorter length than English words. In fact, the sample of 60 Chinese words in the study by Hoosain and Osgood (1983), referred to in subsection 3.4.2, had longer pronunciation durations than their English translation equivalents. When syllabic length is matched word span for Chinese is comparable to that for English (see W. Zhang, Peng, & Sima, 1984). (Matching syllabic length is not exactly the same as matching actual sound durations, which is rarely done in memory research.)

Stevenson, Stigler, Lee, Lucker, Kitamura, and Hsu (1985) compared various cognitive performances of stratified random samples of children in three comparable cities in the United States, Japan, and Taiwan and found biggest differences in their digit span results. Over one-third of the first-grade and 68% of the fifth-grade Chinese students obtained perfect scores (with a maximum span of seven digits), whereas less than 5% of the American and Japanese first graders and 17% of the fifth graders could do so. However, the same Chinese children failed to show any advantage in a test of serial memory for words. If Chinese subjects have bigger digit span because of motivation or tendency to employ advantageous strategies, we would expect these factors to apply in other serial memory tasks, whether for words or numbers. This would be particularly the case if the same subjects are tested for the different tasks. The absence of Chinese advantage in word span, when the same subjects showed a superiority in digit span, indicates strongly that digit span differences have to be accounted for in terms of the nature of the stimulus. And it appears that it is the sound duration of number names in different languages that matters.

In testing and measurement of intellectual abilities, tasks dealing with numbers are usually classified as performance tests, in contrast with verbal tests like vocabulary. The implication is that language factors are irrelevant to the measurement. The preceding discussion would show that this is not at all the case. Digit span is also considered a more or less culture fair test (e.g., Jensen, 1970). This means that it is not supposed to be subject to variations in the cultural experience of the people being tested. Insofar as language can be considered as part of a culture, our notion of what is a culture fair test will have to be modified. Such considerations also apply to another type of measure of intellectual functioning traditionally taken to be a performance test—the measure of perceptual functioning, which we discuss in the next section.

4.1.2 Visuo–Spatial Scratch-Pad and Perceptual Abilities

The orthography of Chinese is based on the spatial organization of the components of characters. The learner is quickly expected to be familiar with dozens and then hundreds and eventually more than 3,000 visual configurations, relating them each to a sound and a meaning. In contrast, alphabetic words involve only sequences made up of elements from a pool of two dozen or so letters, the configuration of which is more or less tied to their pronunciation. One indication of the reliance of Chinese orthography on visual configuration is that most characters, except a few simplistic ones like those for 'one', 'two', and 'three' [1], cannot be described to a person who is not actually looking at them and who does not know the specific characters already. Just specifying their constituent strokes is insufficient; sometimes, one has to name their components, which are radicals or phonetics. With more complex characters, the locations and relative sizes of the various components cannot be conveyed in a straightforward manner orally, not even by naming the component radicals and phonetics. In contrast, in the case of alphabetic languages, one can describe a word to any literate person who is not looking at it by simply identifying its constituent letters in sequence. And even a child or someone who does not know the word can do it. This distinction illustrates the reliance of the Chinese script on visual configuration.

We now look at a number of differences in the performance of Chinese subjects in established psychometric tests involving perceptual functioning and see how visuo–spatial scratch–pad functioning is implicated in these tasks. Admittedly, it is simple to demonstrate a tendency for Chinese subjects to perform differently, but more difficult to demonstrate causal relations between having learned Chinese and performance on various tests. The tests involved include the coding test, the Bender Visual Gestalt Test, and Raven's Progressive Matrices. The coding test is a subtest, for example, of the Wechsler Intelligence Scale for Children (WISC). Slightly different tasks are given to children below 8 and to those 8 and above, but they both involve associating individual visual patterns to either certain geometric shapes or Arabic numerals and reproducing the appropriate pattern when presented one of the latter items. Correct reproduction of the patterns by the children depends on being able to temporarily store the visual shape required and drawing it as the answer.

In the Hong Kong Chinese version of the WISC, stratified random sampling was used to obtain locally standardized norms (The Psychological Corporation, 1981). There are three subscales that showed distinctively better performance by the Chinese standardization sample. These are the digit span, arithmetic, and coding subtests. We have already looked at digit span, and we turn to arithmetic in the following section. In the coding test, the Chinese norms are higher than the U.S. norms, and this is so for the youngest age level of 5 years to the oldest level of 15 years.

In another report, Stevenson (1984) compared American, Chinese, and Japanese children from Minneapolis, Taipei, and Sendai respectively and found that the Chinese children performed only nonsignificantly better on a coding test when compared with the Americans, although the Chinese did significantly better than the Japanese, and there was no significant difference between the Americans and the Japanese. This pattern was similar for both first- and fifth-graders.

In some ways, the Bender Visual Gestalt Test is similar to the coding test, although it is often used to assess visual-motor perceptual development. Children are asked to copy nine visual patterns onto a blank sheet of paper. The developmental scoring system by Koppitz (1963) is the one commonly used. As in the case of the coding test, success in this task requires the ability to temporarily store parts of the visual pattern to be copied. Pong-Leung (1983) tested a sample of 175 Chinese children in Hong Kong, aged 6 to 10 and with average scholastic achievement. She found significantly better performance in the Chinese sample in most age groups than in the U.S. normative sample. The greatest difference was found in the youngest age groups, and the mean score of the Chinese $6\frac{1}{2}$-year-old group was comparable to that of the U.S. 8-year-olds.

Tasks like the coding test and the Bender Visual Gestalt Test are applicable only to children because there is limited demand on temporary visual memory. There are no widely applied visual memory tasks comparable to the straightforward digit span test for auditory memory that are used for adults. In the latter case, within the range of a few digits, one is able to assess the limits of young children all the way up to the brightest adult. However, the Raven's Progressive Matrices, in the colored version for children as well as the advanced version, do provide a test involving perceptual reasoning if not simply perceptual memory. In each trial in the test, subjects are asked to look at a grouping of visual patterns, the last pattern of which is missing. They have to choose a pattern out of a few alternatives to complete the grouping. The relationship between visual patterns in a group has been described by Lynn (1987) as involving arithmetic or geometric progression coded in diagrammatic form. It would appear that in attempting to figure out the progression embodied in the visual patterns, it is necessary to store some of the visual characteristics temporarily. The actual arithmetic or geometric progression is usually quite straightforward (e.g., 1, 2, 3, 4). But the extraction of the progression requires keeping track of the visual patterns and their relationships. This, of course, is a visuo-spatial scratch-pad function.

J. Chan (1976) compared Chinese and native English speaking (mainly British) students in Hong Kong using the Raven's Progressive Matrices Test and found better performance in the former sample. In the earlier items of the test, which are easier, there were no differences between the two groups, but the Chinese scored significantly better in the later items. Lynn (1977) tested 13-year-old Chinese children in Singapore with the same test and reported a mean IQ of about 110 (a Malay sample tested in the same study had a mean score of 96). Whereas the Chinese did well in the Progressive Matrices Test, we ought to note that the test is considered by many people to be culture fair (e.g., Jensen, 1970). Similarly, Lynn, Hampson, and Lee (1988) tested 9-year-old Chinese children in Hong Kong with Cattell's Culture Fair Test and reported an adjusted mean IQ of 104.5. Items in this test consist of visual materials and include matrices problems.

There are also some studies of Chinese compared with other subjects in various tasks involving visual processes. Carlson (1962) compared the acquisition of form concepts with that of object concepts and number concepts among Chinese graduate students, American art students, American undergraduates, as well as other American youths and adults. The students learned nonsense-syllable names given to different instances of form, object, or number. The various groups did not differ in overall ability to learn the concepts. The Chinese students together with American art students found form concepts easier to learn than did the other students. There was not much group difference for object concept. For number concepts (actually, involving the association of the number 3, 4, or 6 to the various nonsense-syllable names), the Chinese were not significantly different from the other groups in most of the measurements, except that they were slower than American college students in terms of the trial in which the students began to give correct unprompted responses.

Lesser, Fifer, and Clark (1965) compared Chinese children with Jewish, Puerto Rican, and Black first-grade children. On verbal ability, Jewish children performed significantly better than the three other groups, and the Chinese ranked third. In reasoning tests, including picture analogies and picture arrangement, the Chinese children ranked first and the Jewish children second (both scoring significantly better than the others). In numerical ability, the Jewish children ranked first and Chinese children second (again, both performing significantly better than the others). In space conceptualization, the Chinese children ranked first (scoring significantly better than the bottom two groups), and the Jewish children second.

Although there is no direct evidence linking learning of Chinese and perceptual abilities, some indirect evidence is available from children of different levels of reading proficiency. Woo and Hoosain (1984) compared the performance of some weak readers and normal readers of Chinese in visual as well as auditory performance. The weak readers did significantly worse in subtests of the Frostig Developmental Test of Visual Perception measuring eye-motor coordination, figure-ground perception, constancy of shape, position in space, and spatial relations. The differences in their performance in auditory tests, including the auditory association test of the Illinois Test of Psycholinguistic Abilities and a digit span test, were much smaller. Furthermore, in a Chinese character recognition test, weak readers made much more visual distractor errors (when target characters were mixed with similar looking distractors) but not more phonological distractor errors (when targets were mixed with similar sounding distractors). In contrast, Liberman, Mann, Shankweiler, and Werfelman (1982) found that, for American subjects, good beginning readers of English did not do better than weak beginning readers in memory for abstract visual designs or for faces. However, they did do better in the use of phonetic representation.

Some further illumination of this contrast between Chinese and other scripts that primarily represent sounds is provided by a study of kanji and kana. Mann (1986) compared normal and weak Japanese readers and found a difference in their memory for abstract designs. The Japanese children's memory for abstract designs was not significantly related to their memory for kana, the syllabic script, but significantly related to memory for kanji, which is the script using borrowed Chinese characters. Such a study tends to reinforce the idea that among the alphabetic, syllabic, and "ideographic" scripts, it is the learning of the last type of orthography that is more related to visual-spatial performance. In contrast, more emphasis on phonological performance could be required for English (see Bryant & Bradley, 1985).

The close relationship between processing of Chinese and visual processes could perhaps be underscored by the more recent view in neurolinguistics that the occipito-parietal areas are more involved in processing Chinese, when compared with alphabetic languages (see subsection 5.4.2). It is also consistent with the conclusion of Paradis et al. (1985) that although Japanese aphasia studies all tend to report dissociation of performance for kana and kanji after left-hemisphere injury, there is a correlation of temporal lobe lesions with kana functions and occipito-parietal lobe lesions with kanji functions. This greater involvement of the occipito-parietal lobes does not have to mean that Chinese characters are represented as pictures (see O. J. L. Tzeng, Hung, Chen, Wu, & Hsi, 1986). The possibility we suggest is that the greater reliance of the Chinese script on visual-spatial relations could challenge the learner to become more attuned to such relations. The correlational data do appear to point to greater facility of Chinese subjects in intellectual tasks involving visual-spatial relations. Furthermore, the kinds of perceptual tests referred to earlier are traditionally considered nonverbal tests of intellectual abilities. It would now appear that even such nonverbal tests could be related to language functioning.

4.1.3 Mathematical Ability

There has long been a recognition that in cognitive performance there is a trade-off between storage and processing functions (e.g., Hunter, 1964). This would mean that the greater the amount of resources needed to maintain information in working memory, the less there is left to carry out operations on or manipulations of the information. In the last two sections we saw how Chinese language users could have a greater facility in holding numerical information in the articulatory loop as well as in handling visuo-spatial information in the scratch-pad. The implication would be that they are more capable of carrying out problem solving that involves such types of information. Mathematics is one subject that involves both types of materials, and one would be led to look for superior mathematics achievement in Chinese speakers. In fact, on the other side of the picture, Ellis and Hennelly (1980) made the suggestion that mental arithmetic was more difficult in Welsh than in English because of the longer digit sound duration and smaller digit span in Welsh.

Apart from the question of sound duration of numbers, the way in which language represents numerical values is also thought to relate to mathematics performance. Miura, Kim, Chang, and Okamoto (1988) pointed out that in Chinese, Japanese, and Korean, numerical names are organized in congruence with the traditional base 10 numeration system. For example, 12 is read as "ten-two," 14 as "ten-four" (not *fourteen*, reversing the order of the digits), and 20 as "two-ten(s)," with the spoken names corresponding exactly to the indicated quantities. In their study, children speaking these languages were compared with American children in a task asking them to read a number on a card and then show the number using commercially available toy blocks, which consisted of unit blocks as well as base 10 blocks. The Asian children preferred to use combinations of tens and ones to show the numbers, but the American children preferred to use collections of units. Also, more Asian than American children were able to construct the numbers both ways, which suggests flexibility of mental number manipulation. It appears that numerical language characteristics of the Chinese and Chinese-influenced languages affect the cognitive representation of numbers.

For the younger age groups, the WISC provides quite clear evidence of better mental arithmetic performance of Chinese children. Beginning with children aged 5 or 6, the norms showed that Chinese children performed better than the Americans. This difference peaked at the age of 13 years. Beyond that age level, the U.S. scores become generally higher, up to the oldest age tested of 15 years. There could be two explanations for the decline in performance of the older Chinese children. For one, in Hong Kong, most pupils switch from using Chinese as the medium of instruction in primary schools to using English in secondary schools. In the Hong Kong WISC standardization sample, 83% of the secondary school children were in this category, transferring to what are called Anglo-Chinese schools, whereas only 17% stayed on in Chinese schools using Chinese as the medium of instruction. Because the Hong Kong WISC is administered in the Cantonese dialect of Chinese, most of the older children would be tested in a language different from their medium of instruction for arithmetic at school. Furthermore, there is a tendency for the standard of arithmetic at the beginning of Anglo-Chinese schools to regress somewhat, so as to give pupils a chance to get adjusted to the new medium of instruction. A year or so after starting secondary schooling, Anglo-Chinese school pupils will cover more new ground in their mathematics, and they would suffer from being tested in a language different from their own medium of instruction.[2]

Second, in the arithmetic subtest of the WISC, the early items are more straightforward mental arithmetic questions, but the later items involve much longer verbal descriptions to get at the underlying arithmetic problem. Also, in the Hong Kong version of the arithmetic subtest, two extra questions are included, again of the verbal problem type. There are indications that the Chinese tend to perform weaker in tasks that require more elaborate verbal communication (see section 4.5). When the older children reach the verbal items of the subtest, it is likely that their weaker ability in verbal communciation results in the reversal in performance in the arithmetic subtest.

In the comparison of first graders and fifth graders, Stevenson et al. (1985) also looked at mathematics performance of the American, Japanese, and Chinese samples. The test was constructed after analyzing textbook contents in the three communities and identifying the concepts and skills introduced at each level. In an effort to avoid the possibility that failure in items could be due to poor reading ability, the descriptive problems were read to the children. Results showed that American children scored significantly lower than both the Japanese and Chinese children at both grade levels. The Chinese children scored slightly better than the Japanese children in grade 1, but the reverse was the case in grade 5. The authors also administered a large number of cognitive tasks to the children (see section 4.4). Regression analyses were conducted in which scores on these tasks were used to predict the mathematics scores. General information, coding, spatial realtions, verbal-spatial representation, and verbal memory appeared frequently in the equations.

An interesting study concerning the use of Chinese versus English in mathematics is that by J. Chan (1981a), who used what amounts to a longitudinal approach. He contrasted the achievement of a group of 240 Chinese school students with a comparable group of 193 Anglo-Chinese school students in Hong Kong. Anglo-Chinese schools are more popular in Hong Kong, and at the time of the study, there were more than five times

---

[2] This situation with junior secondary school pupils in Hong Kong has to be taken into consideration in looking at any cross-cultural comparison of mathematics achievement. Otherwise, a misleading picture could be derived from any otherwise merticulously planned study. This problem would not arise in places like Taiwan, where there is no switch in medium of instruction.

the number of students in these schools as compared with Chinese schools. A main difference between the two types of schools is that Chinese (Cantonese) is the medium of instruction in Chinese schools and English is the main medium of instruction in Anglo-Chinese schools, although English and Chinese as individual subjects are taught in both. The two groups of students came from a cross-section of government, government-aided, and private schools. The two groups used Chinese as the medium of instruction in primary school and did not differ significantly in their school achievement when they were twelve years old and all had to take the public Secondary School Entrance Examination in 1972. It was after this examination that individual pupils proceeded to Anglo-Chinese or Chinese secondary schools, mainly depending on parental choice. Five years later, all pupils took the public Certificate of Education Examination, which could be taken in either language.

English achievement cannot be directly compared, because the two groups took two separate examinations, and we can assume that the Anglo-Chinese school pupils had a higher level of achievement in their English. Otherwise, Chinese school pupils had lower grades in all school subjects except Chinese (which is understandable as this was their medium of instruction) and mathematics. The lower level of achievement by the Chinese school pupils in most of their subjects could reflect lower standards in the less popular Chinese schools, although attempts were made by the author to match such factors as teacher qualification, teaching facilities, school organization, and prestige. But the reversal of the achievement in mathematics is particularly meaningful in light of our present discussion.

If we think that Anglo-Chinese school pupils were handicapped because they had to work in a nonnative medium of instruction, we should note that such a handicap is usually considered to be more serious in school subjects involving a greater language component, such as history. As the most affected subject (apart from English itself) turned out to be mathematics, we would have to consider a language-related component in mathematics functioning that is not traditionally recognized. This has nothing to do with writing essays, learning loan words or technical terms adopted from foreign languages, or other verbal tasks, but has more to do with the facility in the functioning of both the articulatory loop and visuo–spatial scratch-pad.

Of course, the Anglo-Chinese school pupils were doing their mathematics in a second language, and it could be hard to think about numbers and their relationships in a foreign language. For example, McClain and Huang (1982) found a preferred language superiority even in the simple task of addition. They compared 10 Chinese-English bilinguals from Taiwan who were undergraduates at a U.S. university and who reported that Chinese was their preferred language with another 10 bilinguals who were born and/or received all their education in the United States and who reported that English was their preferred language. Both groups showed the preferred language superiority effect, for Chinese and English respectively. However, in addition, the response times for Chinese as preferred language for the first group were faster than the times for English as preferred language for the other group.

With regard to their relatively simple arithmetic task, McClain and Huang (1982) concluded that the difference between preferred and nonpreferred languages lay mainly in the encoding and/or response processes. Both would, of course, be related to phonological encoding times. At the one end, we have encoding the presented numbers for problem solving in working memory, and at the other end we have activating motor programs to articulate answers verbally (and pronunciation latencies for shorter sounding words are faster; see Eriksen, Pollack, & Montague, 1970). The students were asked to do sums that required one ($p + q = ?$), two ($p + q + r = ?$), or three ($p + q + r + s = ?$) operations. In the response time measures, the graphs for the preferred and nonpreferred languages had different intercepts but similar slopes. The intercept was taken to indicate time required to encode the given information as well as actually produce the answer, and the slope was taken to indicate time required to carry out the operations. Thus, the authors took the results to mean that once the numbers in each problem were encoded, computations proceeded at the same rate in both languages.

Thus, even in the simple task of mental addition there is a language-related difference. To return to J. Chan's (1981a) findings, it is more conventional to look for an answer to the better performance of Chinese school students in terms of things like curriculum or traditional emphasis on mathematics in Chinese schools. However, the preceding discussions suggest a more basic cognitive explanation. Although existing evidence is not conclusive in pointing at a direct causal role for a language-related information-processing difference, it is a distinct possibility that should be borne in mind.

Before we finish this section, there is a set of correlational data that indicates some association between digit span and mathematics performance. Hoosain and Salili (1987) tested 20 undergraduates at the University of Hong Kong for their English forward and backward digit spans. They were also asked to report their achieved grades in mathematics in the Certificate of Education Examination that was taken in English two or three years previously. The two sets of data had very limited variabilty. Both digit span and examination grades have a very small spread, particularly with the undergraduates who had all survived a very competitive screening system before gaining admission to the University. The mean forward and backward digit spans obtained were 6.6 and 5.7, respectively. The correlation between forward digit span and mathematics grade was .38

and that between backward digit span and mathematics grade was .42, both significant at the .05 level.

In this section, we have reviewed different kinds of evidence that suggest a connection between language characteristics and mathematics performance. The basis of this connection lies in working memory, with its dual mechanisms of articulatory loop and visuo–spatial scratch-pad. With the articulatory loop, shorter speech sounds for number names in Chinese provide an opportunity for increased capacity for numerical manipulation. With the visuo-spatial scratch-pad, experience of dealing with an orthography emphasizing visual configuration could facilitate visual operations.

4.2 MEMORY OF CHINESE WORDS

After the preceding discussions of the effects of learning and using Chinese on working memory functions, it is time to turn to the actual memory of Chinese words. We first look at the visual, phonological, as well as psycho-motor encoding of Chinese in memory. We then review some studies that look at what is a chunk in the case of Chinese items, taking us back to our earlier question of whether the character or the word is the salient unit in the Chinese language. Finally, we look at some long-term memory structure of the Chinese lexicon.

4.2.1 Visual Code

In the discussion of visuo–spatial scratch-pad functioning earlier in this chapter, we already touched on how visual configuration is significant in the identification of the Chinese character. Let us now proceed to the actual memory of Chinese characters and words and the role played by the visual code. In the absence of grapheme–phoneme conversion rules, the pronunciation of Chinese characters depends on a one-to-one association between a distinct visual configuration and a syllable. Thus, the entire visual configuration becomes the focus of attention. Furthermore, because of the prevalence of homophones, the visual form rather than pronunciation is the more disambiguating information concerning the identity of a character. This could mean a greater role for the visual code of words in Chinese than in English.

For English, there is a lot of evidence of acoustic encoding of language items in short-term memory, such as from confusion error patterns (e.g., Conrad, 1964). There is much less evidence of visual coding. In trying to memorize visually presented letters like c, confusion errors tend to be in the form of the similar sounding t rather than the similar looking o. At the word level, Baddeley (1966), for example, found that recall of visually similar but acoustically dissimilar words (like *rough*, *cough*, *dough*, and *bough*) was not significantly different from control words, but recall of acoustically similar though visually dissimilar words (like *bought*, *sort*, *caught*, and *wart*) was impaired. This means that the visual code plays a nonsignificant role compared to the phonological code, and confusion of shapes does not matter, whereas confusion of sounds causes interference.

Turnage and McGinnies (1973) compared the short-term memory of Chinese and English words presented to Chinese and American subjects, respectively. Words were presented at the rate of one per second, either orally or visually. Subjects were asked to indicate the serial order of the items presented by marking their order in a booklet printed with the words. Chinese subjects generally performed better than the American subjects. (However, the Chinese items were simply translated from the English, and no matching of their frequency of usage in the respective languages was made.) Furthermore, Chinese subjects performed better when the words were presented visually rather than orally. This was so for slow and average learners. The absence of the mode of language effect for fast Chinese learners was attributed to a ceiling effect. American subjects remembered their English words better when they were presented orally rather than visually, and this was so for the slow, average, or fast learners.

O. J. L. Tzeng (1982) reported on a serial learning study in which a list of nine Chinese words were presented either orally or visually to Chinese subjects and a list of nine English words were similarly presented to American subjects. In general, both lists showed the serial position effect, with the beginning few items as well as the last being recalled better than the middle items (known as the primacy and recency effects, respectively). Memory of the last couple of items on both lists was better if they were presented orally rather than visually. This recency effect is usually taken to indicate that the sound codes of the last items were still retained in short-term memory when recall took place. That such short-term memory tends to be in sound-related form is generally accepted in models of memory (e.g., Loftus & Loftus, 1976). However, for the earlier items of the lists — which had to be retained for relatively longer durations before recall — there was a difference between Chinese and English. Chinese words presented visually were remembered better than those presented orally. For English, there was no difference between memory for words presented in the two different modes. The distinctive Chinese phenomenon would suggest that there is a tendency for Chinese to be coded in visual form in certain situations, for reasons discussed later. Or at least, the visual code provides useful cues for the recall of items, which are not available in the phonological code. In such cases, therefore, words presented visually are recalled better.

Converging evidence for the view that the visual code plays a more distinct role in memory of Chinese words was provided by H. C. Chen and Juola (1982). Whereas graphemic and phonemic similarity tends to be correlated in English, this is not generally the case in Chinese. The authors made the commendable effort of controlling visual similarity and graphemic–phonemic confounding in the Chinese and English items. In a preliminary study, respective native Chinese- and English-speaking subjects were asked to rate pairs of characters or words in their language for visual similarity. This allowed the selection of item pairs that were highly similar visually and yet had clearly different pronunciations and meanings.

Pairs of characters and pairs of English words were prepared that either looked similar graphemically, were homophones, or had similar meanings. In the learning phase, subjects were presented one of each such pair in their native language only. They were asked to learn a list of such characters or English words for a subsequent memory test. In the test, subjects were asked to use a graphemic, phonemic, or semantic criterion to decide which item in a pair of presented items was similar to some character or word in the previously presented list. There was an immediate memory test and also a 24-hour delayed test.

For English, there were no significant differences in response time in trying to recognize whether the newer words looked or sounded similar or had a similar meaning to previously studied words, although there was some tendency for graphemic recognition tasks to be slower. For Chinese, the responses for graphemic decisions were faster and more accurate than both the phonemic and semantic decisions. The authors took the contrast between the two languages to mean that the scripts activate different coding and memory mechanisms. Chinese words produce more distinctive visual information, but English words result in a more integrated code.

In contrast to the visual code, one problem with the phonological code for single characters is that, with the prevalence of homophones in Chinese, a phonological code could be associated with quite a few different characters. This problem is compounded in the case of memory of unrelated sequences of single-character words. Support for this view has been provided by a study by W. Zhang, Peng, and Sima, (1984). In Experiment 4, they compared the learning of lists of high frequency single- and two-character words presented either visually or orally. The serial anticipation method was used. After one initial presentation of items of the whole list in sequence, subjects had to begin trying to anticipate which item followed which other item in subsequent presentations. The time required to be able to recall a criterion number of items was used as the basis for comparison. For two-character words, there was no difference between visual and oral presentation of items. But for single-character words, subjects required much less time to learn the lists presented visually. The better performance with visual presentation of single characters demonstrates that the sound code alone could be less useful, in view of the possibility of homophones. Because homophones of two-character words are rare, orally presented two-character words were recalled just as well as visually presented items.

This does not mean that the visual code for any type of Chinese item is always remembered better than other codes. For example, G. Zhang and Simon (1985) found that the span for radicals with no faimiliar pronounce-able names was only 2.71, much shorter than that for characters and words. Using longer exposure time, Yu, Jing, and Sima (1984) found a span of 4.55, still much smaller than the usual span for characters and words (see later discussion). Because these radicals have no simple names, it was assumed by G. Zhang and Simon (1985) that they were coded in a nonacoustic manner, either visually or semantically. In the former case, this would mean that the visual code has a smaller span than the acoustic. However, it might be noted that many radicals do have multisyllabic names [2]. In fact, names of radicals used as indices for listings are provided in some dictionaries, although nearly all these names are of three characters. Thus, radicals could still be coded acoustically, only these codes are multisyllabic and therefore take up more of the limited acoustic storage capacity compared with ordinary words.

4.2.2 Phonological Code

Let us now examine some more studies on the nature and role of the phonological code, as well as on the comparison of the role of the visual and phonological codes in encoding and retaining Chinese words. In general, the studies would show that the phonological code still plays an important role in remembering Chinese words, even though the visual code also serves some function. O. J. L. Tzeng et al. (1977) showed a target list of four characters to their subjects, at the rate of 1 second per character. As soon as the target list was removed, subjects had to shadow (repeat orally) a list of six interference characters presented to them orally. The target and interference lists of characters were obtained from three lists of characters, with items sharing either the same vowels, the same consonants, or both the same vowels and same consonants. In this manner, a 3 × 3 possible combination of target and interference lists was presented to subjects. They had to write down the characters on the target list.

Results showed that recall of the target characters was adversely affected by the similarity of the sound of the targets and the interference items, even though the targets were only visually presented. Vowel similarity had a greater effect than consonant similarity, in line with findings of studies with alphabetic languages (e.g., Crowder, 1971). The results were taken to mean that the memory of the target characters involved phonological recoding, so that the sound codes of the targets were subject to interference by the sounds of the interference items. This meant that it was not possible to memorize the targets solely in the visual code and that the phonological code was unavoidable.

Chu-Chang and Loritz (1977) compared the effects of visual, phonological, and semantic distractors in memory for visually presented lists of characters. Subjects saw lists of six characters for 4 seconds each and were then asked to circle target characters that were mixed with distractor items in a response booklet. The percentages of visual, phonological, and semantic errors were 34.7, 51.9, and 7.5, respectively. These numbers suggest the preponderance of the phonological code in memory. However, visual distractors only looked similar to the targets (although sometimes very closely similar), but phonological distractors had Cantonese pronunciations identical to the respective targets. This discrepancy prevents an unbiased comparison of the various codes in the study.

Wai (1978) compared visual and acoustic similarity of Chinese words in short-term memory and found evidence of both visual coding and phonological coding, although the effect of acoustic interference appeared to be greater. Four lists of character pairs were prepared, varying in high or low visual similarity as well as high or low acoustic similarity between members of a pair. High visual similarity character pairs share some common components, and they could either have identical or unrelated pronunciations. Low visual similarity pairs, in turn, could have similar or unrelated pronunciations. A pool of five pairs of characters, each pair sharing visual or acoustic similarity, was used to produce sequences of five characters, one character from each pair. Repeated sampling produced 20 such sequences that were used for presentation. Each character in a sequence was shown for 1 second, and subjects were asked to write down what they saw at the end of a five-character sequence, before the next sequence began.

The sequences sampled from homophone pairs produced significantly more substitution errors and less correct responses. Sequences from the visually similar pairs produced the same kind of results. However, there was some indication that visual encoding could be secondary to acoustic encoding. Recall of sequences from low visual–high acoustic similarity pairs was worse than from high visual–low acoustic similarity pairs. There was a significant interaction between visual and acoustic similarity in terms of number of correct sequences recalled, showing that the visual similarity effect was considerably reduced in the presence of strong acoustic similarity (which actually amounted to acoustic identity in most cases). It would appear that while the subjects still pretty much encoded words in acoustic form, they were quite capable of exploiting the visual code when the situation warranted.

A later study by Mou and Anderson (1981) compared the interference effects of graphemic similarity and phonemic similarity in memory for lists of four characters each. Graphemic similarity was created by using characters sharing the same radicals, and phonemic similarity created by characters sharing the same vowels as the target list. After looking at the target characters for 1 second each, subjects either went through visual interference by having to copy other characters or went through oral interference by having to shadow other characters presented through earphones. Results showed that both the same-vowel lists and same-radical lists produced more interference than different-vowel and different-radical lists, respectively. In addition, oral interference task produced a larger effect than visual interference task. Unfortunately though, in the shadowing interference task, characters were presented at the rate of one per second, but in the visual-interference task subjects were given 2 seconds to copy each character. It is not known how this time difference would have affected the relative strengths of the interference tasks. In any case, it can safely be concluded that both phonological and visual encoding had taken place in retention of the target characters.

Further evidence was provided by Yu et al. (1984). In their Experiment I, memory of lists of 12 single-character nouns with medium frequency was studied. One list had characters with same vowel sounds, another list had same consonant sounds, and a control list of characters of low similarity in their pronunciation as well as visual appearance was also included. Subjects looked at each list for 12 seconds and were then asked to write down from memory the characters in their correct order. The span for the control list was 5.68 characters, but the span for the same-vowel characters was only 4.80, and for the same-consonant characters 4.00. Furthermore, the errors made by the subjects tended to be characters that sounded similar to those presented (phonetic confusion errors) much more than characters that looked similar (morphological confusion errors). The finding of greater consonant interference than vowel interference is the opposite of what O. J. L. Tzeng et al. (1977) obtained, but the phonetic interference effect in general indicated again that phonological coding is unavoidable in memorizing visually presented Chinese words.

Homophone studies done by Zhang and Simon (1985) provided more evidence for the phonological code. In their Experiment 3, Chinese family names were used as it was possible to find enough family names with no homophones. A list of 24 characters that could be family names, with no homophones, was compared with a list of 12 pairs of homophonous family names. Sequences of characters of varying length were randomly sampled from the two lists to provide test materials. Subjects proceeded with the shortest sequence of three characters. They were asked to read presented characters aloud and then write down their recalls. The span for nonhomophone names was 7.00 and that for homophone names was only 5.33.

Nevertheless, if recalls that sounded identical to the originally presented names were all counted as correct, the respective spans became 7.67 and 7.92. This set of data was taken to mean that whereas the original visual information was recoded into an acoustical form, it was then decoded back to the corresponding visual code in recall.

Zhang and Simon (1985) also explored one implication of the prevalence of homophones in Chinese. It was thought that if a subject retained only acoustical information of a stimulus that had homophones, there would be a tendency for homophones of high frequency (referred to as dominant homophones) to be substituted for those of low frequency. The authors compared the memory span of three types of characters: those with no dominant homophones, those with only one dominant homophone, and those with more than four dominant homophones. They found that the short-term memory spans for the three types of characters were 5.50, 4.08, and 2.67, respectively, all significantly different from each other. When recalls that had the same pronunciation as the originals were counted, the spans became 7.25, 6.75, and 5.92, respectively (only the first and third spans were significantly different). The differences between the spans measured according to the two criteria were all significantly different. The authors took these results to mean that when only acoustical information can be retained, it might be coded in terms of the most frequently used grapheme in the homophone group. But, of course, it could also be that the sound code is neutral as to which grapheme it is attached to, and it is only at the time of response that the most dominant homophone tends to be produced as a result of response bias. In any case, it would be less likely for characters with more dominant homophones to be recalled correctly.

It seems quite clear that the phonological code for Chinese plays a pervasive and significant part in memory situations, just as for English. This is so in spite of the fact that the visual code also plays some role, perhaps more so than is the case with English words.

4.2.3 Psycho-motor Code

There are suggestions that memory for the visual configuration of Chinese characters is related to some motor engram for the whole or part of each character. We have already noted that the order of strokes for each character is emphasized in learning to write. The repetitive motor habits built up over the years might result in some psycho-motor code, such that partial activation of this code could trigger the whole sequence. Occasionally, one could see people engaged in finger tracing to remind them of forgotten characters. A more concrete indication of this has been provided by W. Zhang et al. (1984). In their Experiment 2, they tested the short-term memory for single-character words, two-character words, and idioms, comparing the use of written and oral responses in recall. For both types of words, written recall was superior to oral recall, although there was no difference for the idioms. They found some subjects reporting that if they were allowed to respond in writing, they could visualize the items so as to make the recall easier.

In aphasia studies, there are further indications of the role played by the motor engram. There appear to be more reports of facilitation of reading by finger tracing for Chinese than for alphabetic languages (see subsection 5.4.3).

The functioning of the psycho-motor code in memory for Chinese characters could be akin to that of "dynamic mental representation" in the work of Freyd (1987). She showed that in the perception and recognition of handwriting and other figures, the perceiver is sensitive to implicit information about movements that come to produce the final static forms. Reference was also made to Japanese master calligraphers and the appreciation of their brush movements (which could well apply to Chinese calligraphy). One difference between the psycho-motor code discussed here and Freyd's dynamic mental representation is that, in the latter case, movements implicit in a visual figure could be detached from the subject. In other words, they are in some sense perceived to be "out there." In the former case, the psycho-motor code is related to movements actually carried out by the subject's own muscles.

4.2.4 The Unit in Short-Term Memory

In our discussions of perceptual aspects of Chinese in the last chapter, one question we looked at was what constitutes the salient unit of perception in the language (see section 3.2)? Similarly, we can now ask what is the unit in short-term memory? Again, we would wish to know if it tends to be the character, a smaller unit like radicals within a character, or a larger unit like a word. A series of studies by Simon and his colleagues provided quite illuminating answers.

We noted in the last section that Yu et al. (1984) demonstrated that similarity in vowel or consonant sounds of characters produced interference for memory of a sequence of such items. In their Experiment 1, they further showed that partial identity of characters that shared common radicals did not produce similar interference. Subjects were shown a slide with 12 single-character nouns of medium frequency and an average of nine strokes. The characters all shared a common radical. Subjects were allowed 12 seconds and then asked to write down the words in their correct sequence. The mean number of single-character words recalled correctly was 5.53. This was about the same as the mean of 5.68 for a control list of characters and indicated that the similarity in the component radicals did not at all interfere with memory of the characters. In other words, the radicals appeared to have lost their individual identity within the respective characters. None of the subjects seemed to have even noticed that the stimulus items shared a common radical.

When noncharacter radicals are being presented for short-term memory, we have seen that they have a relatively small span of 2.71 or 4.55, depending on exposure time (Yu et al., 1984; Zhang & Simon, 1985). This means that the visual codes of these radicals are not very salient units in short-term memory. The authors of those studies did not seem to think that subjects coded the radicals in terms of their multisyllabic names, which would, in any case, not be efficient units of memory. The semantic codes for these radicals are also unlikely to be salient, because the radicals may not have clearly designated meanings. Their association with many diverse characters could render their own meanings less specific. For example, the radical derived from the pictograph for 'water' can be the component of characters meaning 'wine', 'sand', 'dirt', 'to cure', and 'hole' [3]. Often, the etymological connection of the radical with the characters of which it is a part could be lost to the ordinary reader. Given this situation, it can be difficult for some radicals to be coded in semantic form. In general, then, it would appear that it is unlikely for the radical in whatever code to be a contender for the natural unit of memory.

If the item smaller than the character is not the salient unit of memory, what about larger items? Yu et al. (1984) as well as Zhang and Simon (1985) showed that two-character words as well as four-character idioms behaved more like "loosely packed" units rather than "compact chunks." Against a baseline of a span of 5.68 for medium-frequency one-character words, Yu et al. (1984) found a span of 3.45 and 3.75, respectively, for low-frequency and high-frequency two-character words, and a span of 2.65 for four-character words (idioms). Using a different procedure, Zhang and Simon (1985) found a span of 6.58 for single characters, 4.58 for two-character words, and 3.00 for four-character idioms. In terms of chunks in the traditional sense (see Miller, 1956), a single-character word, a two-character word, as well as a four-character idiom should all be a chunk, so long as they are equally familiar. These results demonstrate that short-term memory capacity does not depend on the number of familiar chunks alone and that we have to take note of the number of syllabic units or perhaps length of sound duration within each chunk.

Although multicharacter words and idioms do not generally have spans equal to those of single-character words, there can be occasions when they become rather close. The serial presentation method used by Zhang et al. (1984) produced the smallest difference of 6.58 for single-character words and 5.92 for two-character words. It would apppear that whereas four-character idioms are probably too long to constitute single units in short-term memory, two-character words could amount to a unit, just as single-character words. The sequential presentation method allows the subject to consolidate the two-character word as a unit before the next item comes along, whereas simultaneous presentation does not facilitate this individual item consolidation.

To summarize this section, we have seen evidence that apart from the phonological code, the visual as well as the psycho-motor codes play some role in certain situations, perhaps more so than in the case of other languages. The unit of memory, when there is time for consolidation, is the word—if it is not more than two characters long.

4.3 MEMORY AND THE NATURE OF THE LEXICON

In short-term memory, number of chunks or sound duration plays a decisive part in determining capacity. However, in long-term memory and the organization of our lexicon it would be largely meaning and semantic relations that affect the way things are organized (e.g., Loftus & Loftus, 1976). There are some studies that indicated that memory structure for Chinese words is rather different from that of other languages, and it is possible to see how this might be related to the nature of how Chinese words are formed.

4.3.1 Association Network

Miron and Wolfe (1964) obtained word association data from subjects in 12 diverse language communities around the world, including Hong Kong Cantonese speakers. In each location, 100 male high-school subjects were asked to complete the frame *The* _____ *butterfly* or *The butterfly is* _____ . There were 100 such substantives acting as stimuli to elicit the subjects' qualifier associations. The data were analyzed to test the authors' hypothesis that the distributions should conform to a theoretical distribution of the lognormal form. For our present purpose, the relevant data are the number of types and tokens of responses produced by the Chinese subjects, compared with subjects using other languages. The number of tokens is simply the total number of actual responses that were admissible, that is, not obviously deviant from minimal usage standards. Out of a possible maximum total of 10,000 responses, 9,730 Chinese tokens were obtained, which was quite similar to the number for most other groups. However, the number of types of responses for the Chinese was high. Types of responses is the number of different kinds of answers provided by the subjects. For example, if there are a total of 10 responses and all are identical, we would have 10 tokens but only 1 type, while if all 10 are different, we would have 10 tokens and 10 types. The Chinese subjects produced 2,509 types of responses, which was by far higher than any of the other groups. The mean number of types for the remaining 11 groups of subjects was only 1,072, with a standard deviation of 414.

One likely explanation for this unique characteristic of Chinese word association pattern lies in the way in which Chinese words are constructed out of individual characters. We have seen that in modern Chinese, words tend to be bisyllabic. Their constituent characters are recombined in multifarious ways, producing many different words (see Fig. 2.6). As such, each bisyllabic or multisyllabic word can be indirectly linked to many other bisyllabic or multisyllabic words through some mutually shared characters somewhere along the way. The result of such a lexical structure for Chinese could be that in word associations, it is easier to elicit a wider range of responses. This would mean a greater number of types of responses in an association task like that of Miron and Wolfe (1964).

An alternative explanation for this pattern of results would be that, somehow, Chinese subjects wanted to avoid cliche qualifiers and tried to be unique. As a result, responses became more diverse across Chinese subjects. However, in other situations where Chinese subjects are given a chance to express themselves and produce a variety of verbal responses, they tend to be more reticent (see section 4.5). It is only in the more controlled situation of the word association response that we see a richer variety of verbal responses.

J. T. Huang (1979) provided evidence that component characters of two-character words play a significant part in associations elicited by the words. In support of his time-dependent separability hypothesis, he found that when there is sufficient time subjects would produce associates by responding to the first character and later to the second character of two-character words. One result of this separability would be that the correlation between word (as a whole) frequency and number of word associations elicited by multicharacter Chinese words becomes weaker than the corresponding correlation for English words (see J. T. Huang, 1979).

A study that was not directly concerned with word association provided further indication that a greater variety of words come to the mind of the Chinese speaker when he or she thinks about a word. O. C. S. Tzeng, Hoosain, and Osgood (1987) compared correlations between denotative codings of emotion terms in 23 languages and their affective meanings according to semantic differential ratings by the respective native speakers. Codings on 10 denotative components, such as *pleasantness, activation, control*, and *ego-orientation*, were used to correlate with subjective ratings of affective meanings of terms, such as *fear, devotion, laughter*, and so forth, in each language. The denotative codings for the emotion terms in each language were stable, but the affective meaning scores were subject to variation of each individual person's feelings at the time of the scoring. The correlations between denotative codings and affective meaning for the 23 language communities showed that the Hong Kong Chinese had one of the lowest goodness-of-fit between denotative codings and affective meanings. A likely explanation for this would be that when the Chinese subjects indicated their subjective feelings for a word, a greater variety of other words that share overlapping characters with the target word, such as indicated in Figure 2.6, could be aroused. This creates a situation that allows greater variability among subjects in the indicated affective meanings at the time of testing, depending on which associate words are aroused.

There is one other study of associations for Chinese words compared with English. McGinnies and Turnage (1968) looked at the free word associations of Chinese subjects in Taiwan and subjects in the United States. Thirty stimulus words, in their Chinese or English translation equivalent versions, were half high frequency items and half low frequency items. The subjects were presented the respective language items individually, either visually using test booklets or orally by the experimenter. They were asked to write down free association words that came to mind (in the same language). Stimulus words were presented repeatedly to elicit further associations before proceeding to the next word. American subjects produced more associations than Chinese subjects under all conditions. The number of association words produced would correspond to the number of tokens in the study by Miron and Wolfe (1964), in which case the Chinese produced as many tokens as the other groups. However, that was when the ceiling or expected number of tokens was pretty much predetermined, as subjects were asked to provide one response in each sentence frame. In the McGinnies and Turnage study, subjects were free to produce any number of word associations.

McGinnies and Turnage (1968) suspected that the relatively low number of Chinese association words produced could be related to characteristics such as differences in the actual number of verbal associations available in Chinese and in English, or in the "associative fluency" of the Chinese and American subjects. From the study by Miron and Wolfe (1964), it would seem that the former is not likely the case, because Chinese subjects produced the greatest number of variety of associations in 23 language groups. It is possible that there was a difference in cognitive style and Chinese subjects tend to be less forthcoming in verbal communication when they are not so induced (see section 4.5). In contrast, in the procedure used by Miron and Wolfe, subjects were presented the prearranged sentence frames and asked to produce the prescribed number of responses, which gave the Chinese subjects the opportunity to show their greater variety of available verbal associations.

4.3.2 Visual and Auditory Networks

McGinnies and Turnage (1968) found one other interesting difference in the pattern of Chinese and English associations. There was a greater tendency for the same association word to be produced using the two stimulus modes in English. For example, the word *village* in English, whether in the visual or oral mode, elicited *town* most often. In Chinese, the translation equivalent of *village* in the visual mode elicited the equivalent of *paddy field* most often, but the same word in the auditory mode elicited the equivalent of *farmers* most often. In fact, an identical word was the most frequent association word for both stimulus modes in English about three times more often than in Chinese. This reminds us of H. C. Chen and Juola's (1982) conclusion that English words produce a more integrated code in memory. The more distinct visual code in Chinese means that how things look could determine associations, not necessarily in the same way nor with the same results as how things sound. There is much less of a distinction with English, as the visual word still primarily represents the sound, and through this the same meaning as the spoken word. This again demonstrates the differential significance of the visual code in the perception of Chinese.

There was one other significant pattern of results, with Chinese subjects producing more associations to low .frequency words when they were presented visually than when presented orally. This was not found for English with the American subjects. The Chinese subjects also rated low frequency words as having been seen more often than heard, and high frequency words as having been heard more often than seen. The authors' explanation for this was that people tend to use less erudite language when speaking than when writing. American subjects rated both types of words as having been heard more often than seen (which is more likely if the written script primarily represents sounds and there is a lot of phonological recoding).

With English, when seeing an unfamiliar word it is still usually possible to give it a phonological reading and remember it in terms of this sound code. In the case of seeing an unfamiliar Chinese character, however, there is no such corresponding facility for arriving at a pronunciation (although, if it is a phonetic compound, one could guess according to the phonetic and be correct nearly 20% of the time). Such Chinese items would more likely be remembered in terms of their visual code. The net effect would be that low familiarity words in Chinese tend to be recognized as having been seen more often than heard.

To summarize this section, we have seen that associations produced by Chinese words tend to have a different pattern that could be related to the interlocking of component characters. Also, the absence of grapheme-to-phoneme conversion rules means that the visual word and the oral word could have greater detachment and produce different associations.

4.4 READING PROBLEMS

Quite obviously, reading problems have a perceptual as well as a memory dimension, and we have touched on the former in the last chapter. Here, we focus on memory aspects of reading. Given what we have discussed so far about the psycholinguistic properties of the Chinese language and orthography, would the nature of reading problems for Chinese be different from that for alphabetic languages? Dyslexia has been generally defined as a disorder marked by difficulty in learning to read despite a normal environmental or intellectual background. In England, for example, it is said that 3% to 5% of children have reading problems (Bryant & Bradley, 1985). Other estimates of reading disability for children in the West range from 5% to 15% of the population (see Reid & Hresko, 1981). Operationally, disability is often taken to be reading at two or more grades below a person's level.

As reading is the derivation of meaning from a string of graphic symbols, reading problems have been traced to one or more parts of this process, including: (a) analysis of the sequential visual structures, (b) linking of visual and auditory-linguistic structures, (c) establishment of regularities in grapheme-phoneme correspondences, and (d) grouping of words into larger units such as phrases and sentences (see Vernon, 1977). Stage (a) involves perceptual abilities we discussed in the section on visuo–spatial scratch-pad functioning. Woo and Hoosain (1984) showed that such abilities distinguish normal and weak Chinese readers (see subsection 4.1.2). The functioning of both stages (b) and (c) would be affected by the unique pattern of script-sound-meaning relations in the Chinese script. Because Chinese characters are monosyllables, the Chinese reader is spared the feat of mapping script and sound at the level of the phoneme. Awareness of the phoneme does not have to come naturally, and failure could be the basis of a lot of reading problems in the West (see Bryant & Bradley, 1985; Mann, 1988). But, in the absence of grapheme–phoneme rules, the association between each character and its pronunciation has to be learned individually, although there could be nonrule-governed clues from the phonetic.

Although the Chinese reader does not have to figure out grapheme-phoneme rules, he or she has the rather different burden of remembering a large number of individual script–sound associations (O. J. L. Tzeng & Hung, 1981). The advantage is the basis of the suggestion made occasionally that it could be easier for children with certain disabilities to learn

Chinese or their own language represented by Chinese characters (e.g., Rozin, Poritsky, & Sotsky, 1971). It could, of course, be easier if the number of items involved in a novel project is relatively small, and the novelty of it is still fun. The disadvantage is that it requires an effort those of us who have learned to read and write Chinese are thankful is over, although we are constantly reminded of the need for it when occasionally our memory fails. This script–sound association has two directions, one way when we have to read and the other way when we have to write. Chao (1968b) had these words to describe what it used to take to do the tasks: "the old style children were beaten by their parents or teachers for not learning their characters and after they learned how to read and write their characters, they beat *their* children for not learning the characters" (p. 112).

Corporal punishment may be out of fashion these days, but the discipline is still there. The truth, I suspect, is that there is some trade-off between the need for memorizing individual script–sound associations and the freedom from having to learn grapheme–phoneme rules. Some people might be better at one than the other, and this would be the distinction between the "Chinese" and the "Phoenicians," terms originally used to describe English readers who were good at whole-word pronunciations but poor in figuring out correspondences between letters and their sounds, or vice versa (see Baron & Strawson, 1976).

The last stage in reading (d), sorting words into larger units, has an extra twist in the case of Chinese. We have the preliminary task of grouping characters into words first, because there are no distinct boundaries for words. The task of grouping words into phrases in Chinese is also affected by the relative deemphasis of formal grammar and the reliance instead on the relative position of words in the sentence, as we noted in section 2.8.

With these differences in the task of reading, we should expect to see some variation in the manifestation of reading problems in Chinese. Over the years, it has often been thought that the incidence of reading disability amongst the Chinese is lower than in the West (e.g., Kuo, 1978). Of course, what one finds could depend on where and how one looks. If a crucial stage in reading Chinese is the memorization of script-sound association, rather than figuring out grapheme-phoneme conversion rules, failure to read could easily be taken as simply a failure to memorize something. A diagnosis of reading disability could be replaced with a verdict of not trying hard enough. When there are few rules to be mastered, failure to read or write becomes a simple failure of carrying out a mechanical task, which is seen as a motivational or disciplinary rather than cognitive problem. This reminds us of the use of corporal punishment to encourage learning to read and write, described by Chao (1968b).

A careful comparison of the incidence and nature of reading disability among Chinese, American, and Japanese children has been conducted by

Stevenson, Stigler, Lucker, Lee, Hsu, and Kitamura (1982). Fifth graders were tested in three cities judged to be comparable: Taipei, Minneapolis, and Sendai. Ten schools in Taipei were selected to constitute a stratified random sample, and 932 children were tested. Reading materials used in schools were consulted for the construction of tests to yield scores on sight reading of vocabulary, reading of meaningful textual material, and comprehension of the text. The tests were constructed to include a series of levels ranging from kindergarten, grades 1 to 5, and grade 6 to adult. In the vocabulary test, children were asked to sight-read single isolated words. Comparability of words in the three language communities were ensured by noting the grade level at which they first appeared as well as their respective frequencies of usage. The materials for reading and comprehending were clauses, sentences, and paragraphs, and children were asked to answer true-false and multiple-choice questions in connection with these passages. Besides the reading tests, 10 cognitive tasks were administered. They were thought to be related to reading ability and included coding, spatial relations, perceptual speed, auditory memory, serial memory for words, serial memory for numbers, verbal-spatial representation, verbal memory, vocabulary (giving definitions for presented words), and general information. A mathematics test was also included.

If we adopt the criterion of failing to read at the grade 4 level, 33% of the American children, 12% of the Chinese children, and 24% of the Japanese children were identified. If we adopt the common criterion for reading disability, that of reading at least two grade levels below their own grade, then there were 3% of the American children, 2% of the Chinese children, and 8% of the Japanese children. The children's reading level and their performance in the cognitive tasks were also compared. Children were identified who were both within the lowest 10% of the distribution of reading scores and who obtained an averaged standard score higher than one standard deviation below the mean for the cognitive tasks. These children had low reading ability as well as at least near-average intellectual performance. The percentages of children thus identfied were 6.3, 7.5, and 5.4, respectively, for the American, Japanese, and Chinese. Thus, although it depends on the criterion used, the incidence of reading disability in the Chinese sample was quite close to that for Americans.

There was, however, some indication that the weak Chinese readers had more general disability in learning, rather than specific reading problems, compared with the American or Japanese children. When the three reading test scores were correlated with the results of the mathematics test, there was no significant correlation for the Americans. For the Japanese, the only significant correlation was with the comprehension test. But for the Chinese, all three correlations with vocabulary, reading of text, and comprehension were significant.

Weak and normal readers in all three samples performed significantly differently in all 10 cognitive tasks. Further analyses to see which tasks were most effective in discriminating between the two groups in each sample revealed that general information was significant in all three samples. Verbal memory (ability to remember details of a brief story being read) was significant for both the Chinese and the Japanese, and serial memory for words was significant for the Chinese. Coding was significant for the Americans. Thus, it did not appear that perceptual features of stimuli played a more important role in reading Chinese or Japanese than in reading English. However, when only the weak readers were examined, verbal-spatial representation (requiring drawing figures that varied in their spatial arrangement on the basis of verbal directions) was significantly related to within-group differences in both the vocabulary and comprehension scores on the reading tests for the Chinese and Japanese, but not for the Americans.

A further aspect of the reading scores provided insight into the nature of Chinese children's reading problems. When we look at the reasons each child failed the fifth-grade test and had to take the fourth-grade test, we see that the American and Japanese children tended to do so because they had failed the vocabulary test, but the Chinese tended to do so more because they had failed the comprehension test. Of the Americans, 47% failed the vocabulary test, 22% failed the comprehension test, and 31% failed both. Of the Japanese, 40% failed the vocabulary test, 21% failed the comprehension test, and 39% failed both. But only 10% of the Chinese failed the vocabulary test, whereas 72% failed the comprehension test, and 18% failed both. Among those children having to take the fourth-grade tests, some failed again and had to further take the third-grade test. At this level, most failed the comprehension test rather than the vocabulary test, similarly so for the Americans, Japanese, and Chinese (the number of children involved was small). The vocabulary test involved sight reading of single words, and the Chinese children did not seem to have much of a problem. The task required only recalling the pronunciation of presented characters. The success of the Chinese with such a memorization task contrasted with their relative failure at answering comprehension questions, even though answers required only true–false or multiple-choice responses.

The finding that Chinese children with reading problems tended to fail comprehension rather than vocabulary (sight reading) tests echoes that of a report by Ai (1949). In this early study, pupils from grade 5 through junior high school were tested. In cases where incomplete knowledge of words was identified, the number of cases where the pupils only knew the pronunciation of words was about double that where they only knew their meanings, and this pattern was maintained at all the levels tested. Although details are not available, it can be assumed that pronunciation tests involved more straightforward answers than word meaning tests. An answer consisting of a single syllable is sufficient for a question about how to pronounce a character, but a more open-ended effort is required for questions about meaning.

Stevenson (1984) as well as Stevenson et al. (1985) reported additional results with first-grade children from the same three cities in the United States, China, and Japan. In addition to tests of reading ability (sight reading of vocabulary, reading of meaningful textual material, and comprehension of text), the children were also given the 10 cognitive tasks used in Stevenson et al. (1982), mentioned earlier. The largest cultural difference was in serial memory for numbers (digit span), with the Chinese children, both the first and fifth graders, doing significantly better. This better performance, however, was absent in the case of serial memory for words (word span). However, there were cognitive tasks on which the American children did better than the Chinese, and the Japanese also did better than the Chinese on a majority of the tasks. Among the 10 cognitive tasks and the mathematics test, the Chinese children did significantly better than the Americans only in memory for numbers (digit span) and mathematics. In all the other tests, the Americans performed either significantly better or there was no significant difference between the two groups of children. However, by fifth grade most of the cultural differences in these cognitive tests disappeared. Regression analyses were conducted in which scores on the cognitive tasks were used to predict the combined reading scores. The results showed high similarity for the three groups of first graders. General information and verbal-spatial representation entered significantly in the regression equations.

In the reading tests, the Chinese first graders scored higher on all three reading tests than the American and Japanese children. These included vocabulary (sight reading of words, as distinguished from the vocabulary test among the 10 cognitive tasks, which involved defining presented words), reading of text, and comprehension of text. Stevenson (1984) attributed the better reading performance of the Chinese first graders than the Americans at least partially to the fact that the Chinese spent more time in school, spent more time attending to their work while at school, and spent more time doing homework.

On the cognitive tasks, the Chinese first graders scored lower on the vocabulary test that required defining the presented words. Twenty-five comparable words in the three languages were used, and testing stopped when a child could not define four successive words. The Americans had a score of 14.88, the Japanese a score of 11.93, but the Chinese had a score of only 10.07. There were also more Chinese than American and Japanese first graders who were unable to define 13 of the first 15 words. The lower scores of the Chinese children on this task disappeared with the fifth graders. The authors thought that the poor performance of the Chinese first graders was due to their lack of experience in responding to adult questions.

To summarize this section, there are indications that younger Chinese children read better than American children, but then they work much harder at it. Much of the overall difference in various cognitive task performances appear to disappear as the children grow older, with digit span differences lingering on. However, the pattern of reading problems is somewhat different for the Chinese. They have less difficulty making specific script-sound associations when reading individual characters and more difficulty answering comprehension questions. Also, younger Chinese children had difficulty defining words. We look at this Chinese difficulty with verbal communication in the next section.

4.5 COGNITIVE STYLE

It is difficult to show conclusively that Chinese orthography learning experience is a cause of what could be characterized as Chinese cognitive style, but it is certainly part of the picture. Similarly, the sociocultural tradition of Chinese society itself is an important element.

Let us remind ourselves of the demands of learning to read and write Chinese. The price to pay for not having grapheme-to-phoneme conversion rules is that individual grapheme-to-phoneme associations have to be retained for reading, and phoneme-to-grapheme associations for writing. Small children who start learning to read and write would have to spend long periods of time engaged in repetitive oral as well as writing drills. In his comparison of reading abilities of first-grade Chinese and American children, Stevenson (1984) found that the Chinese children went to school an average of 240 days a year, compared to 178 days for Americans, spent less time on irrelevant activities during reading and math classes in school; and spent 77 minutes on weekdays, 66 minutes on Saturdays, and 42 minutes on Sundays on homework, compared with 14, 3, and 4 minutes, respectively, for the American children.

What is equally significant is the kind of tasks the children engage in during these long hours. One way to describe them would be that they are drills, either oral drills for script-to-sound associations or writing drills for sound-to-scirpt associations. Another way to look at all this work is that it requires specific answers that are labeled as either correct or wrong, rather than being open-ended, free expression of views or thoughts. It should be appreciated that carrying out such drills calls for a large measure of sustained discipline. Authoritarianism is thus tied to this system of learning discipline. Social and personality psychologists generally agree that authoritarianism is a significant element of Chinese socialization (e.g., Yang, 1986).

Appeal to authority and adherence to what is perceived to be correct does not end with the beginning learner of Chinese reading and writing. Memorization of any text that has to be learned may be considered an extension of memorization of specific script-sound-meaning associations in vocabulary learning. At higher levels in schools, particularly with the classical literature that secondary school pupils have to learn, memorization of entire passages of text is still practiced. Such learning habits eventually become an important element of cognitive style.

There are a few studies in the literature that touch on this aspect of Chinese cognitive style. Hoosain (1977) created a task that could be accomplished either by rote learning (memorizing a whole list of nonsense trigrams) or by meaningful concept learning (figuring out the common pattern of the trigrams, such as JMR, ADI, EHM, . . ., all with two letters missing between the first and second letters and four letters missing between the second and third letters). Subjects had to provide the third letter of each trigram when shown the first two letters. With an induced rote learning set, subjects who were undergraduates in Hong Kong quickly reverted to task accomplishment by rote learning as soon as the patterns in the trigrams became slightly more difficult to figure out. With a list like FHJ, TVX, NPR, . . ., where the common pattern stares one in the face, subjects all completed the task without resorting to rote memorization. Hoewever, with slightly more difficult patterns, such as JMR, ADI, EHM, . . ., such subjects all resorted to memorization rather than trying to find the pattern.

M. J. Chen, Braithwaite, and Huang (1982) compared how Taiwanese and Australian approach some cognitive tasks. The students were asked for their perceived relevance and perceived difficulty of different kinds of items on the Stanford-Binet intelligence test and the Wechsler Adult Intelligence Scale, as attributes of intelligent behavior. In the relevance ratings, both the Chinese and Australians produced an underlying three-factor structure comprising spatial–mechanical, verbal, and memory elements. They showed a basically common structure for the concept of intelligence. Both groups also agreed that the spatial–mechanical scales were most relevant to measuring intelligence. However, the two groups differed in their difficulty ratings. The Australians considered memory skills as more difficult than spatial–mechanical or verbal skills. But the Chinese judged memory skills as the easiest. Although this study only dealt with value judgments and perceived difficulty, it does provide some insight as to how the Chinese have become accustomed to the demands of memory tasks. It does not mean that the Chinese are necessarily better at memory tasks. We have seen that other factors play a crucial role in determining working memory capacity and, for example, the better performance of Chinese speakers on digit span is not matched by word span. Longer term memory processes, of course, are more subject to the influence of learning habits and strategies.

The corollary of a cognitive style that emphasizes adherence to what is taught to be right or wrong, and the tendency for verbatim learning, would be a reluctance to engage in open-ended and free expression of individual views of things. Stevenson et al. (1985) attributed the weaker performance of Chinese children on some verbal tasks to their lack of experience in responding to adult questions. This would be more so when the children perceived the task as involving some expression of themselves. This suggests that Chinese children can be disadvantaged by certain types of tests. Piagetian tests, for example, require open-ended questioning to discover what goes on in a child's mind to determine the level of cognitive development. Douglas and Wong (1977) compared Hong Kong Chinese and American high school pupils with Piagetian tests and reported that the Hong Kong sample scored lower on tests of the formal operation stage. The Hong Kong females also tended to perform lower than the males, and the authors observed that "Hong Kong females were timid and seldom verbalized" (p. 689).

In a somewhat related study, Wright et al. (1978) reported that Hong Kong Chinese, together with some other Asians, had a less differentiated view of uncertainty compared with British subjects. In one measure, for example, subjects were asked questions about factual matters that most people were not sure about (e.g., "Is the Suez Canal over 100 miles long?") and responses were classified into yes, no, don't know, catch-all responses (e.g., "I hope not.") and probability responses such as "rather unlikely." The numbers of types and tokens of probability responses were noted. The British subjects had a greater ability to adopt a probabilistic mind set, to discriminate uncertainty finely, and to express the uncertainty in words compared with the Chinese. The Hong Kong subjects, in fact, gave the lowest number of different probability word responses among the British, Indonesian, and Malay subjects, as well as the highest number of "don't know" responses (this could indicate an unwillingness to express probabilistic opinion rather than simple ignorance of facts).

In terms of relating cognitive functioning and childhood experience, J. Chan (1981b) demonstrated a significant correlation between parenting style and reading performance of the Chinese. He asked Hong Kong Chinese subjects aged 12 to 18 to answer a questionnaire that assessed their recollection of interaction with parents. The categories assessed included father's treatment of the child, mother's treatment, father's approach to teaching the child, mother's approach, father's attitude toward child discipline, and mother's attitude. Subjects were also administered a reading test that consisted of three parts: multiple-choice questions after reading a passage that would mainly test recognition of what was in the passage, short questions after reading a passage which was designed to test recall, and essay-type questions after reading a passage designed to test free expression.

Recognition scores in the multiple-choice test were not related to any parent–child interaction. However, performance with the short questions was found to be significantly related to less mother autocracy. Free expression with the essay type questions was significantly related to less father restriction. Combined reading test scores were significantly related to less father restriction and less mother demand. (Female subjects were also found to score higher than males on recognition, recall, and the combined score, but not on free expression.) What this pattern of results implies is that authoritarian upbringing tends to be related to difficulty in expressing oneself in verbal situations, although it is not related to ability for straightforward responses.

Other concepts that have been introduced in discussions of Chinese cognitive style and its relation to parenting variables are that of cognitive complexity and rigidity (see Boey, 1976). Cognitive complexity refers to the number of differentiated dimensions a person has in perceiving or construing the stimuli in a given domain. Greater cognitive complexity means that the person is able to see more aspects and relations in a cognitive situation. Rigidity refers to the persistence of a response or a response set when the demands of a task situation have already changed, and a different response is required. Boey investigated three different domains of situations: the interpersonal, the physical, and the numerical. In general, cognitive simplicity was related to rigidity. Parents' authoritarian attitudes tended to be related to cognitive rigidity. There was one particularly interesting finding. Cognitive rigidity in one domain was not always correlated with rigidity in other domains. This could mean that, for example, a person showing rigidity in the interpersonal domain can function with cognitive complexity and flexibility in the numerical domain. This possibility, of course, provides the hope that not all aspects of cognitive functioning are equally affected by authoritarian upbringing.

4.6 CONCLUSION

The one language effect that persistently shows up in a wide variety of cross-language reports is the larger digit span size for Chinese, most likely due to the shorter duration of sounds of digit names in Chinese. This, of course, is a good example of the result of bottom-up processes. We also have some indications that visual-spatial perceptual abilities are more involved in reading the Chinese script. Together they mean that in working memory functioning, the Chinese people could enjoy greater facility as a result of their language experience, and achievement in mathematics could well be a benefit of this facility. In such a case, we have verbal characteristics influencing what is traditionally regarded as non-verbal processes.

The manner in which Chinese words are stored in memory is also affected by characteristics of the orthography as well as morphology. Although words are usually coded phonologically, as in the case of English, the visual code as well as the psycho-motor code seem to play a greater role for Chinese than for English in comparable situations. Words are basically the unit of memory, although there are some ways in which constituents of multicharacter words function with greater independence. Association patterns for words in Chinese are different from those in English. Most of these characteristics of memory for Chinese words are largely determined by bottom-up processes.

The nature of reading problems is also determined by characteristics of the learning material. But some aspects of cognitive style should be more properly considered as involving top-down processes and are related to learning experience and the accompanying dose of authoritarian discipline. These include a willingness to adhere to designated goals but some reluctance to be forthcoming in open-ended situations. One manifestation of this is the propensity for memorization and reticence in open communication.

5 Neurolinguistic Aspects of the Chinese Language

Discussions of the neurolinguistic aspects of Chinese have been dominated by the possibility that cerebral localization of functioning in the language is different from that in other languages. Some suggestion has been made of a greater tendency for right hemisphere processing of Chinese, instead of the usual left hemisphere lateralization for other languages. But an alternative cerebral localization difference within the left hemisphere itself has also been suggested. Such possible differences would arise, of course, from characteristics of the Chinese language, such that it entails processing in different ways.

The two hemispheres of the brain are not symmetrical in the functions they perform (or indeed in their weight). Over 95% of right-handed people have their speech functions lateralized in the left hemisphere. However, left-handed people demonstrate a greater degree of bilateralization (see Beaumont, 1983). The greater involvement of one hemisphere is often demonstrated by better performance in experimental tasks in which information is initially conveyed to that hemisphere. It is also shown by differential language impairment as a result of brain damage.

The two cerebral hemispheres are usually thought to specialize in different manners of information processing, the left with analytic and sequential processing, whereas the right hemisphere is more concerned with spatial, global, or holistic processing (see Bryden, 1982). A fundamental aspect of language is its "duality of patterning" (Hockett, 1960), whereby a limited number of units, like the few dozen phonemes, are combined in an endless variety of sequences to make up the things we say. And such sound combinations are constituted very often within fractions of seconds. For instance, *cat* and *act* are made up of the same three sounds in different permutations, altogether lasting less than a second in normal speech. It falls on the left hemisphere to be mainly responsible for the monitoring of these quick and multifarious sound sequences in speech comprehension and production.

To illustrate the crucial difference in the functioning of the two hemispheres, as well as to demonstrate the visual hemifield presentation procedure used by many studies reviewed in this chapter, we look at the study by O. J. L. Tzeng and Wang (1984). In the hemifield presentation procedure, visual materials are shown for less than 180 milliseconds, which is about the time it takes a human's eyes to move from fixating at one thing to another. If subjects are instructed to fixate at a central location when such materials are presented to the right or left of the fixation point, the visual information is conveyed initially to the contralateral hemisphere as a result of the anatomy of the visual pathways to the brain. In the study by O. J. L. Tzeng and Wang, common three-letter words were presented in this manner, letter by letter. The temporal order of the letters formed one word, say *C-A-T*, with the entire sequence taking an average of less than 200 milliseconds. But, if somehow this quick temporal order was not monitored, the spatial locations alone would indicate a different word, such as *ACT*, simply by presenting the letter *C* first in the middle position, the letter *A* next in the first position, and the letter *T* last in the third position. Thus, temporally *CAT* was presented but spatially *ACT* was presented. Such letter sequences tended to be seen as *CAT* when presented in the right visual field and hence to the left hemisphere initially, but *ACT* in the left visual field and right hemisphere. This indicates quite clearly the distinction between temporal–sequential–analytic functioning of the left hemisphere and spatial–holistic functioning of the right hemisphere. The authors suggested that it is due to the location of a time keeping mechanism that the left hemisphere comes to specialize in the sequential processing of quick successions of speech sounds. Because of the importance of language functions to human beings, the left hemisphere comes to be referred to as the dominant hemisphere.

However, superimposed on this general scheme of things, variations due to language differences have been mooted. For example, Tsunoda (1985) postulated a subcortical switching mechanism that directs various sounds to cerebral hemispheres of Japanese and Polynesians in a different pattern compared to other peoples, because the Japanese and Polynesian languages use more vowel sounds. In the case of Chinese, possible differences are more related to orthographic characteristics of the language. In this chapter, discussions are centered on studies of hemifield presentation of Chinese words to normal subjects and on studies of the patterns of language impairment in aphasic patients. As a supplement to these discussions, the question of handedness among the Chinese and its relation to language lateralization, including bilingual language lateralization, are also reviewed.

5.1 EXPERIMENTAL STUDIES OF LATERALIZATION

Early indications that the lateralization of perception of Chinese words could be different from that of other languages came from reports on hemifield presentation of kanji compared with kana. Hatta (1977) reported that Japanese subjects tended to see single kanji characters better in the left visual field (LVF) showing a right-hemisphere (RH) advantage. For kana, his earlier studies reported a right visual field and therefore left hemisphere superiority (RVF-LH advantage). Sasanuma, Itoh, Mori, and Kobayashi (1977) reported a significant RVF-LH superiority for pairs of unrelated kana characters and no significant visual field difference for pairs of nonsense kanji characters. Incidentally, it should be noted that in the hemifield presentation literature in general, LVF-RH superiority for language items is less often obtained than RVF-LH advantage. This would be related to the overall lateralization of language functions in the left hemisphere (see Beaumont, 1982).

These two reports led to the view that hemisphere involvement differs in the processing of kanji and kana. Quite naturally, the most obvious contrast between the two scripts is assumed to account for the distinction (although their other distinctions, such as word length and part of speech, tend to be overlooked; see Paradis et al., 1985). This is the contrast between kanji being logographs/ideographs and kana being syllabaries. In the latter case, pronunciations are spelled out, just as with aphabetic languages. Also, by implication, it was thought that Chinese should behave similar to kanji and demonstrate a lateralization pattern different from alphabetic languages.

5.1.1 Kanji and Chinese Studies

Although a few years earlier, Kershner and Jeng (1972) found a RVF-LH advantage for two-character Chinese words, with Chinese subjects, the Japanese studies mentioned earlier attracted more attention because they raised the intriguing possibility of cross-linguistic differences. Early reports of selective impairment of kanji and kana in clinical aphasia studies (e.g., Yamadori, 1975) also added to the fascination. But, before we proceed, some caution against equating findings from kanji studies and Chinese studies has to be taken, although physically identical characters could be presented to the respective subjects.

For the Japanese, there are many significant factors differentiating kanji and kana other than orthography, including form class, frequency of usuage, and stroke complexity (see Paradis et al., 1985). It is very difficult to find kanji and kana items that are matched in these respects. Therefore, kanji to the Japanese subject has peculiarities that come with their unique role in the script, not comparable to the Chinese situation where the characters are the only script. It has been suggested that Japanese subjects might process kanji differently from how Chinese subjects process their characters (see Hasuike, Tzeng, & Hung, 1986).

As one indication of the dissimilarity, we can look at the report of Hatta (1977). He found a LVF-RH advantage for single- character kanji concrete nouns contrasted with RVF-LH advantage for two-character kanji words. His explanation was that single kanji characters can have multiple pronunciations, depending on their eventual combination with other characters to form words. In the absence of a definite phonological reading for single kanji characters, subjects coded the stimuli in some visual form and therefore showed RH superiority. With two-character kanji words, however, only one pronunciation is possible, and subjects used phonological coding, showing LH superiority. In the case of Chinese, a few characters can have a couple of pronunciations each, and their disambiguation depends on which other characters they are combined with to form multicharacter words. But the number of such characters (as distinguished from homophones, with different characters sharing the same pronunciation) and the prevalence of different possible pronunciations are nowhere near those for kanji. Therefore, Hatta's explanation would have much less weight if applied to Chinese. In view of such indications that properties of kanji might be different from those of Chinese, the present discussion of the lateralization of perception of characters focuses on Chinese studies.

In the following, we review the main hemifield presentation and related studies with Chinese subjects. Table 5.1 summarizes the main features of these studies.

5.1.2 Earlier Hemifield Presentation Studies

Kershner and Jeng (1972) tested Chinese-English bilingual Taiwanese graduate students in the United States. The stimuli shown included 60 each of high frequency two-character Chinese words, English words, and geometrical forms. Hemifield presentation as well as the simultaneous bilateral presentation procedures were used. In the latter, two distinct stimuli are shown simultaneously, one on each side of the fixation point. A particular visual field superiority is indicated if subjects tend to see the stimuli in that visual field better. The authors used an exposure time of 125 milliseconds. The two constituent characters of each Chinese word were presented vertically, one above the other, at an angular distance of about 6 degrees to either side of the fixation point, measured from the midpoint of the words. Immediately after the presentation of an item-pair, subjects were asked to write down or draw what was seen. Accuracy percentages for items shown in each visual field were analyzed.

For both hemifield presentation and bilateral presentation, English as well as Chinese words were seen better when shown in the right visual field. For geometric figures, on the other hand, there was a LVF-RH advantage with the hemifield presentation procedure but no visual field difference with the bilateral presentation procedure. Thus, a distinction between linguistic stimuli and visual–spatial stilumi was obtained. Furthermore, no difference was found in the lateralization patterns for the bilingual subjects' native and second languages.

According to Tsao, Wu, and Feustel (1981), Feustel and Tsao (1978) found faster response times for the pronunciation of two-character Chinese words presented in the RVF than in the LVF. No other details of the finding of RVF-LH advantage are available. Together with the study by Kershner and Jeng (1972), these two earlier studies would suggest that there is no difference in the lateralization pattern for Chinese words and English words, when respective native speakers were tested.

Hardyck, Tzeng, and Wang (1977, 1978) reported on two related series of experiments that used single-character Chinese words and their English translation equivalents. Pairs of Chinese-Chinese, Chinese-English, or English-English words were presented at a visual angle of 2.5 degrees or more from the fixation point. Right-handed bilingual subjects (except in Experiments 3 and 4, see later discussion) were asked to say "same/different" or push a same/different button to indicate if each pair of stimuli presented simultaneously had the same/different meaning or the same/different physical shape. The pairs of items were either both presented in the right hemisphere, both in the left hemisphere, or split up with each member of a pair on one side of the fixation point in a bilateral presentation. Response time or accuracy was monitored in different experiments.

No left/right visual field difference was found in these tasks, although responses were more accurate with the bilateral presentation procedure than with hemifield presentation. But in a recall test in Experiment 2 (Hardyck et al., 1978), held 5 minutes after the end of the experiment that measured response time, words originally shown in the RVF were better recalled, significantly so only for Chinese. In another approach (Hardyck et al., 1977, Experiments 3 and 4; Hardyck et al., 1978, Experiments 3 and 4), monolingual English speakers were shown pairs of Chinese-Chinese or English-English items. When there were 30 pairs of items in each language, with each word appearing only once (Experiment 3), there was again no

TABLE 5.1

Hemifield and Bilateral Presentaion Studies of Word Perception (Hemifield Presentation Used Unless Otherwise Stated)

Reference	Stimulus	Familiarity	Exposure Time	Visual Angle	Luminance	Subjects	Task	Response Measure	Result (Advantage)
Kershner & Jeng (1972)	(a) English words, (b) 2-character Chinese words, (c) geometric forms Hemifield and bilateral presentation	High frequency	125 msec.	6° to 6°39'	—	Right-handed Chinese graduate students in U.S.	Write down stimuli presented	Accuracy	RVF-LH for English and Chinese words for both hemifield and bilateral presentation; LVF-RH for geometric forms for hemifield presentation only
Hardyck, Tzeng, & Wang (1977)	*Exp. 1* Single-character words and English translation equivalents, shown together in one hemifield or bilaterally	Common	<150 msec.	2.5°	15 ftL.	Right-handed Chinese-English bilinguals	Say "yes/no" if pairs were translation equivalents or not	Response time	Not significant
	Exp. 2 Some of Exp. 1 words were shown in Chinese-Chinese, English-English, or Chinese-English pairs in hemifield or bilateral presentation	"	"	"	"	"	Manual response for same/different word/meaning	"	"

Study	Exp. / Stimuli		Exposure duration	Visual angle	Subjects	Task	Measure(s)	Results
	Exp. 3 English-English and Chiniese-Chinese pairs from Exp. 2	"	"	"	Monolingual English	"	"	"
	Exp. 4 English-English and Chinese-Chinese pairs made from 4 words and 4 characters	"	"	"	"	Same/different judgment	"	RVF-LH for English and LVF-RH fro Chinese
	Exp. 5 Pairs of figures from a spatial ability test; figures rotated	—	"	?	75 unspecified subjects	"	Accuracy	Not significant
	Exp. 6 6 pairs from Exp. 5	—	"	?	8 subjects	"	"	LVF-RH
Hardyck, Tzeng, & Wang (1978)	*Exp. 1* Single-character words and their English translation equivalents; Chinese-English pairs were presented together in one hemifield or bilaterally	Common	150 msec.	≥2.5°	Right-handed Chinese-English and English-Chinese bilinguals	Say "yes/no" if words had same meaning or not	Response time and accuracy	Not significant
	Exp. 2 Chinese-Chinese, Chinese-English, English-English pairs obtained from Exp. 1, in hemifield and bilateral presentation	"	"	9 ftL.	Mostly right-handed, Chinese-English and English-Chinese bilinguals	Push-button response for same/different meaning; unexpected recall test 5 minutes later	Response time and recall	RVF-LH for recall of Chinese words

(continued)

TABLE 5.1 (Continued)

Reference	Stimulus	Familiarity	Exposure Time	Visual Angle	Luminance	Subjects	Task	Response Measure	Result (Advantage)
	Exp. 3 Chinese-Chinese, English-English pairs from Exp. 2	"	"	"	"	Monolingual English speakers	Push-button for same/different physical shape	Response time	Not significant
	Exp. 4 4 Chinese-Chinese 4 English-English pairs.	"	"	"	"	"	"	"	RVF-LH for English and LVF-RH for Chinese
O.J.L. Tzeng, Hung, Cotton, & Wang (1979)	*Exp. 1* Single-character, phonetic compounds and pictograms	"	20–75 msec. (mean = 40 msec.)	—	—	Right-handed Chinese graduate students in U.S.	Naming	Accuracy	LVF-RH for both types of characters
	Exp. 2 2-character words	—	> 100 msec.	—	—	—	"	"	RVF-LH
	Exp. 3 2-character words and nonwords	—	—	—	—	Chinese graduate students	Push-button yes/no response if stimulus was a word or not	Response time	RVF-LH
Y.L. Huang & Jones (1980)	*Exp. 1* Single characters	Common	50 msec.	2.5°	—	Right-handed bilingual Chinese and monolingual U.S. subjects	Naming	Response time	Not significant

Exp. 2	A character in either hemifield, followed by 2 characters one on top of the other, both in center	"	30 msec. for Chinese, 50 msec. for American subjects	—	"	Say "top/bottom" indicating which character was presented previously	"	LVF-RH for both groups
Nguy, Allard, & Bryden (1980)	"Pictorial," "single," and "combination" single characters	Moderate to high frequency	30–80 msec.	2.5°	—	Right-handed Chinese undergraduates	Naming	Accuracy	Not significant for "pictorial," RVF-LH for "single" and "combination" characters
Tsao, Wu, & Feustel (1981)	4 single-character color names printed in various colors, and 4 patches of colors	HIgh	150 msec.	4°	—	Right-handed Chinese graduate students in U.S.	Read color names, name color of the ink of words and color of patches	Response time and accuracy	Accuracy not significant; for response time: RVF-LH for reading color names and naming ink color of words
Besner, Daniels, & Slade (1982)	Arabic numerals and Chinese number names (for 4, 5, . . . 9)	High	Variable, mean = 54 msec.	3.3°	—	Right-handed Japanese and Chinese university students in U.K.	Naming repeatedly shown items	Accuracy	RVF-LH for both sets of items

(continued)

TABLE 5.1 (Continued)

Reference	Stimulus	Familiarity	Exposure Time	Visual Angle	Luminance	Subjects	Task	Response Measure	Result (Advantage)
Ho & Hoosain (1984)	Pairs of single characters shown together in one hemifield forming (a) opposites; (b) homophone opposites, sounding like opposites only when pronounced; (c) unrelated nonopposites.	Common	170–190 msec.	3.34°	—	Right-handed bilingual undergraduates in Hong Kong.	Say "yes/no" to show if character pairs were opposites	Response time and accuracy	Accuracy not significant; for response time: RVF-LH for opposites, but not significant for other two types of items
Leong, Wong, Wong, & Hiscock (1985)	Single characters and pseudocharacters (mirror images of real characters)	Within-elementary school vocabulary	150 msec.	1° 50'	—	Right-handed Chinese university students	(a) Lexical decision, (b) phonological processing (sound like target?), (c) semantic processing (right category?)	Push button for yes/no; response time and accuracy measures	Response times not significant, accuracy shows: RVF-LH for phonological and semantic processing but no difference for lexical decision
Hoosain (1986b)	3-lettered English words and 2-character Chinese words	High frequency	150 msec.	3°	—	Right-handed Chinese-English bilingual undergraduates in Hong Kong	Translate word to opposite language	Response time and error	Response times not significant; error rates showed RVF advantage for both

Study	Stimuli	Frequency	Exposure duration	Visual angle	Luminance	Subjects	Task	Measure	Results
Lin (1986)	2-character Chinese words, nonsense syllables, latticed squares, Gestalt closure figures	High frequency	40 msec.	4°	—	Right-handed Chinese undergraduates in Taiwan	Immediately write down what was seen	Accuracy	Not significant for Chinese words and figures; RVF-LH for syllables and latticed squares
C.M. Cheng & Fu (1986)	*Exp. 1* Single characters, pseudocharacters, and noncharacters, each composed of two radicals	Half high, half low frequency	Variable, mean = 12.43 msec.	2.5°	—	Right-handed Chinese undergraduates in Taiwan	Pick out target item from 2-item choice.	Accuracy	Character advantage effect for LVF-RH
	Exp. 2 2-character words and nonword combinations	"	?	"	—	"	"	"	RVF-LH advantage for words; also, word advantage over nonwords only in RVF
Hoosain & Shiu (1989)	2-character words, 4-lettered English words, and 4-digit numbers, presented in pairs bilaterally	High frequency	120 msec.	2.86°	9.5 ftL.	Right-handed Chinese-English bilingual undergraduates in Hong Kong	Naming	Accuracy	RVF-LH for all items
Ho & Hoosain (1980)	2-character words and nonword combinations	Half high, half low frequency	12–21 msec.	3°	6.3 ftL.	Right-handed Hong Kong bilingual undergraduates	Lexical decision	Accuracy	LVF-RH for low frequency high stroke number words

(continued)

TABLE 5.1 (Continued)

Reference	Stimulus	Familiarity	Exposure Time	Visual Angle	Luminance	Subjects	Task	Response Measure	Result (Advantage)
C.M. Cheng & Yang (1989)	(Exp. 2) Single characters, pseudocharacters; 2-character words, pseudowords	High frequency	60 msec.	2.5°	—	Right-handed Chinese undergraduates in Taiwan	Pick out target item from 2-item choice.	Accuracy	LVF-RH for characters, RVF-LH for words
Hoosain (in press, b)	2-character Chinese words; 3-lettered English words	Common	57 msec. for Chinese; 74 msec. for English	2°50′	8.1 ftL.	Right-handed, left-handed, handedness switched Hong Kong bilingual undergraduates	Identification	Accuracy and response time	RVCF-LH for Chines and English for right-handers; nonsignificant for left-handers and handedness-switched subjects

significant left/right visual field difference in response time measures. However, when only a small subset of four Chinese words and four English words were repeatedly presented in different permutations to similar monolingual English speakers (Experiment 4) a LVF-RH advantage in response time was found for same/different physical shape judgments for Chinese word pairs and a RVF-LH advantage for English pairs.

In another contrast between showing a large number of items without repetition and showing a small subset of items repeatedly, the investigators used pairs of figures from the Thurstone Primary Mental Abilities Test. In Hardyck et al. (1977, Experiment 5), unspecified subjects were shown 72 pairs of the figures and asked if each pair was same/different (the researchers manipulated the extent of rotation of the figures relative to each other). Accuracy of response was measured and there was no significant visual field difference. However, when only six of these pairs of figures were repeatedly shown in Experiment 6 (Hardyck et al., 1977), for a total of 200 trials, there was a LVF-RH advantage when accuracy was compared.

The results led the authors to suggest that lateralization effects obtained only when memory processes were involved after subjects had learned all the stimuli being presented. This led to the better recognition of the small number of Chinese words presented in the LVF and English words in the RVF. Lateralization was not supposed to take place with active ongoing perceptual processes, when new items were presented in every trial, such as in the processing of the large sets of items in Experiments 3 and 5. The small target set size in the reduced experiments (Experiments 4 and 6) allowed the same/different push-button judgments to be made from memory, after subjects had learned the few stimuli to be presented, and this produced LVF-RH advantage for Chinese as well as visual forms but RVF-LH advantage for English.

What was suggested in terms of the contrast between memory processes and ongoing cognitive processes was assumed to apply to Chinese just as English, and indeed to visual figures. But there is little empirical support for this view — there are many hemifield presentation studies of ongoing cognitive processing, with large sample set size, that do produce visual field advantage (e.g., Beaumont, 1982). The absence of significant visual field effect for the perceptual tasks in the described experiments could have more to do with the length of time required to carry out the task called for, which was the judgment of same/different shape or meaning of two presented items rather than a simple report of what is seen. The response times found were all well over one second. In tasks taking such lengths of time, it would be most likely that whatever cognitive processes taking place would have involved both hemispheres as well as interhemispheric communication, such that the notion of behavioral measures of lateralization, whether comparing response time or accuracy, becomes rather meaningless. In contrast, in

Experiment 4 of Hardyck et al. (1977, 1978), with the reduced item set size of only four Chinese words and response times of well under one second, significant visual field effect was obtained.

To illustrate this point of lack of visual field effect with prolonged processing, we can look at a study by Ho and Hoosain (1984). They presented two-character items with constituents that were opposites, non-opposites, and homophone nonopposites that sounded like opposites when pronounced [1]. These item pairs were presented together in either visual field and subjects were asked to say "yes" or "no" to indicate if items were actually opposites or not. There was a significant RVF-LH advantage for the opposites, and the mean response time was 962 milliseconds for the RVF and 1,023 milliseconds for the LVF. However, the response times for the two types of nonopposites took an extra quarter of a second and no more visual field difference was found. Subjects had to dwell more on the constituent characters of nonopposites before ruling them out as nonopposites.

Returning to the finding by Hardyck et al. (1978) of the LVF-RH advantage for Chinese character pairs when shown to nonChinese speakers, this should be viewed as involving nonsense visual forms only, because these language items were meaningless to the subjects. The RH advantage found would therefore be consistent with other findings of RH advantage for visual–spatial processing and should not be lumped with the discussion of lateralization of perception of Chinese per se.

To summarize, it could be said that the earlier hemifield studies of Chinese actually gave a general picture of RVF-LH superiority for Chinese, similar to the situation in English.

5.1.3 One-Character and Two-Character Words

A study contrasting single characters and two-character words was carried out by O. J. L. Tzeng, Hung, Cotton, and Wang (1979). Rather than focusing on the logographic/ideographic versus alphabetic/syllabic distinction, they drew attention to the need to view the lateralization mechanism in terms of task-demand characteristics. In other words, their view was that lateralization was function specific rather than orthography specific. In their Experiment 1 they tested right-handed Chinese subjects with common single-character words. The items included both abstract and concrete terms and could be phonetic compounds or pictographs. They were presented in the right or left visual field for an exposure time adjusted for each individual so as to obtain a desirable level of accuracy for comparison. The actual exposure time averaged 40 milliseconds and ranged from 20 to 75 milliseconds. Measures of accuracy of identification of presented items showed a LVF-RH advantage, for both pictographs and phonetic compounds. It would appear that the presence of the phonetic in phonetic compounds did not matter to lateralization.

In their subsequent experiments, the authors used vertically arranged two-character words instead of single characters. In Experiment 2, similar procedures for the word identification task were used. The exposure times adjusted for this group of subjects were given in another article (Hasuike et al., 1986) as averaging 100 milliseconds or more. In this hemifield presentation procedure, the two-character words showed a RVF-LH advantage in accuracy of identification.

In Experiment 3, an attempt was made to eliminate the need to produce a verbal response in the word identification task. Two-character words were mixed with two-character nonwords created by mixing characters. Subjects were asked to push one button if the presented item was a meaningful word and another button if it was not meaningful. When response times for the meaningful words were analyzed, they were faster for items presented in the RVF. Thus, in both experiments for two-character words using somewhat different procedures, RVF-LH advantage was consistently found, in contrast with the LVF-RH advantage for single-character words.

The explanation given by the authors for this pattern of results was based on task differences in perception of single characters versus two-character words. In the former case, individual holistic patterns were involved, but with two-character words, sequential analysis was considered necessary to relate the stimuli and arrive at a single meaning for each presented pair of characters. Right-hemisphere advantage for the single characters and left-hemisphere advantage for two-character words were obtained in line with the general visual–holistic versus analytic–sequential differentiation of hemisphere specialization. It should be noted that such a view of two-character words is different from the discussion in section 2.6, that the components of two-character words form meaning wholes.

This account by O. J. L. Tzeng et al. (1979), based on functional differences in processing single- and two-character words, explained the findings reported up to that time in the literature. There appears to be scarcely any exception to the RVF-LH advantage for two-character words. We have seen reports of RVF-LH advantage for two-character presentations in Kershner and Jeng (1972), Feustel and Tsao (1978), O. J. L. Tzeng et al. (1979), as well as Ho and Hoosain (1984). There are occasional reports of no visual field difference for two-character words, but these could be due to the design of the studies.

For example, Lin (1986) found no visual field advantage for the writing down of presented high frequency two-character words. Taiwanese undergraduate subjects were shown the Chinese words, nonsense alphabetic syllables, latticed squares (each consisting of a 3 x 3 matrix with some combination of the constituent squares covered in black ink), and Gestalt closure figures. Exposure time for each item was uniformly 40 milliseconds. Subjects were asked to write down or draw immediately what was seen in each trial, and accuracy was analyzed. There was no visual field effect for the two-character Chinese words although a RVF-LH advantage was found for the nonsense syllables. There was also no visual field effect for the Gestalt closure figures but a RVF-LH advantage for the latticed squares. Looking at only the result for the Chinese words, there could be some artifact, as the manner of presentation used apparently produced a very easy task. The accuracy measurement showed a score of 92.07% for words in the RVF and 93.19% in the LVF. Too high a general accuracy level would preclude the possibility of significant visual field difference.

The finding of RVF-LH advantage for two-character presentations applies also to two-character words on each side of the fixation point in a bilateral presentation procedure. Hoosain and Shiu (1989), in their Experiment 2, showed two-character Chinese words paired with either another two-character Chinese word, a two-syllabled (four-lettered) English word, or a four-digit random number in bilateral presentation. Subjects were right-handed Chinese-English bilingual undergraduates in Hong Kong. Exposure time was 120 milliseconds and the items were presented at a visual angle of 2.86 degrees one on each side of the fixation point. Subjects were asked to report the words in whatever order they liked, and accuracy for items shown in the two visual fields was compared. Chinese words shown in the RVF were identified better and there was no significant difference whether the paired item was another Chinese word, an English word, or a number. However, when Chinese words were shown in the LVF, not only were errors higher but there were significant differences depending on what was the paired item. Performance was worst if the paired item in the RVF was an English word, next if it was another Chinese word, and then if it was a number. Both English words and numbers were also identified better when shown in the RVF.

In contrast to the consistency of the RVF-LH advantage for two-character presentations, single characters tend to show much greater variability in visual field advantage (see later discussion). In lateralization studies, the lack of clear-cut patterns in the results is sometimes found. The problem arises from the lack of strict comparability of studies that use different types of materials, procedures, and subjects. Therefore, comparison across studies in the same series done by the same author(s) are particularly valuable in clarifying issues, with comparable perceptual conditions, procedures, and subjects being used. Some of the single-character studies in the literature are reported as part of a series of experiments.

The experiments by O. J. L. Tzeng et al. (1979), for example, showed a contrast in the finding of LVF-RH advantage for naming single-character words with that of RVF-LH advantage for two-character words when factors such as visual field luminance were presumably constant. The only variable, apart from the single- versus two-character distinction, was the actual exposure time used. This was varied across subjects to maintain a desirable level of accuracy of identification and averaged 40 milliseconds for single-character words and 100 milliseconds or more for two-character words. This series of studies therefore alerts us to the role played by exposure time in lateralization.

There is another study of single characters that is a part of a series of comparisons, in the context of the word superiority effect (see subsection 3.2.2). C. M. Cheng and Fu (1986) presented single characters, single-character pseudo-characters (with components of characters being substituted with other similar looking components), and noncharacters (with components of characters placed in reversed positions) to Taiwanese undergraduates. The items were shown either in the left or the right visual field, at a visual angle of 2.5 degrees. Exposure time was adjusted for each subject so as to obtain an appropriate level of accuracy, and averaged 12.43 milliseconds. After each presentation, subjects were asked to pick out what they saw from a choice of two items, one of which was a distractor. The authors found that single characters were better identified in the LVF. But there was no visual field difference for the pseudo- and noncharacters. There was better accuracy performance on the characters than on the pseudo- and noncharacters, and the character superiority effect was bigger when all three types of items were shown in the LVF.

C. M. Cheng and Fu (1986) then repeated the same procedure with two-character Chinese words and two-character nonwords (with illegal combination of characters). The mean of the exposure times adjusted for individual subjects was not reported, although it probably could not be any lower than the 12.43 milliseconds for single characters. There was better recognition of two-character words than two-character nonword combinations, but the effect was significant only when items were presented in the RVF, not in the LVF. Furthermore, the two-character words were better recognized in the RVF than in the LVF. This finding of the word superiority effect in the RVF echoes that for English reported by Kreuger (1975). There was no visual field difference for the nonword combinations.

The contrast in the visual field effects for single characters and two-character words obtained in the cited study again means that lateralization is not a language-specific effect. C. M. Cheng and Yang (1989) reported a study using the same task and procedure as C. M. Cheng and Fu (1986). In their Experiment 2, four types of items were used: single characters, single pseudocharacters, two-character words, and two-character pseudowords (nonwords). Exposure time used was 60 milliseconds. Again, a LVH-RH advantage for single characters and RVF-LH advantage for two-character words were found, and there was no visual field advantage for pseudocharacters and pseudowords. To account for the contrast between single characters and two-character words, C. M. Cheng and Yang (1989) suggested that the right hemisphere is more efficient in lexical interpretation of the character, whereas the left is more efficient in lexical interpretation of words. The problem with such a view is that single characters can often function independently as words, such as the example character listed in C. M. Cheng and Yang (1989) [2], which means 'dead' in classical Chinese. We have noted that all educated Chinese have a fair knowledge of classical language and literature, and subjects in the study were students at one of the most prestigious universities in Taiwan.

To summarize, there seems to be a difference in the lateralization pattern of single characters and two-character words. This draws attention to function-specific characteristics and casts doubt on any proposal of a language-specific lateralization effect. Lateralization for two-character presentations appears to be quite stable, showing a RVF-LH advantage.

5.1.4 Lateralization for Single-Character Words

In the face of the consistent RVF-LH advantage reported for two-character words, it should be fruitful to see if there is the same consistency with single characters. It could help us identify factors other than the spatial–holistic and analytic–sequential distinctions. Nguy, Allard, and Bryden (1980) compared the distinction among "pictorial," "single," and "combination" characters, all of moderate to high familiarity. The first are intended to be stylized representations of the object they indicate, but from the examples given, it is difficult to see how some of the items fit the description. In section 2.3, we noted that a distinction should be made between having a pictographic etymology and having psychologically real pictographic function. The two appear to be confused in this particular classification of characters. Also, single characters are defined as "arbitrary symbols for words" and combination characters are "the synthesis of two characters into one." However, examples of single characters included a phonetic compound, and even a configuration of three component characters [3]. Considering such confusions in the classification of materials, it is safest to look at the results of this study as one simply of hemifield presentation of single-character words.

Subjects were right-handed Chinese undergraduates who were asked to identify orally each presented item. Exposure time was adjusted for individual subjects to obtain an accuracy level of about 70% and ranged from 30 to 80 milliseconds. Items were presented at a visual angle of 2.5 degrees. The accuracy results showed a RVF-LH advantage for all three types of items, but significantly so only for "single" and "combination" characters. In fact, the visual field difference for "pictorial" characters amounted to only 0.5%. The authors attributed the lack of lateralization for the last group of items to some right-hemisphere involvement in processing pictorial characters. However, if we do not accept the classification of "pictorial" characters, the main thrust of this experiment would be just a tendency for RVF-LH advantage for single-character words.

Y. L. Huang and Jones (l980) presented common single characters for 50 milliseconds each to right-handed Chinese subjects. Luminance level was not reported. Response time was measured in a naming task, and there was no visual field difference. A second experiment was carried out that consisted of two steps in each trial. First, one of the original 12 characters was again shown in either visual field at a visual angle of 2.5 degrees from the fixation point. Exposure time was 30 milliseconds for Chinese subjects and 50 milliseconds for a group of monolingual English speakers. After 4 seconds, two characters arranged vertically were presented in the middle of the visual field. One was identical to the one shown before and the other was randomly chosen from the remaining characters in the original sample of 12. The subject's task was to say whether it was the top or the bottom character that was the same as the one shown 4 seconds previously in either visual field. The non-Chinese speaking subjects were given 5 minutes prior to the experiment to look at the 12 characters on cards to become familiar with them.

Response time measures, for both the Chinese and non-Chinese subjects, showed that characters originally presented in the LVF were eventually identified faster 4 seconds later. Just as in the case of the study by Hardyck et al. (1977), we ought to treat the task by the non-Chinese speaking subjects as simply discrimination of meaningless visual forms, and a similar LVF-RH advantage was found. Again, lateralization effect was found in a task involving memory of relatively few presented items. But the RH advantage shown by the Chinese subjects would be inconsistent with the LH advantage found by Hardyck et al. (1978). This could be related to the different procedures used. Y. L. Huang and Jones (1980) used an exposure time of only 50 milliseconds and subjects had to retain the stimulus code for only 4 seconds. Hardyck et al. (1978) used an exposure time of 150 milliseconds and the incidental recall test was given 5 minutes later.

Tsao, Wu, and Feustel (1981) compared the Stroop effect (see subsection 3.4.1) when items were presented in the right versus the left visual field. They presented the Chinese for 'green', 'purple', 'yellow', and 'orange', which should all be single-character words, printed in black or any one of the alternative colors depicted, as well as square patches of one of the four colors. These were presented to right-handed Chinese graduate students in either visual field for 150 milliseconds, at a visual angle of 4 degrees from the fixation point. Three types of response times were obtained: a "reading time" for responses obtained when subjects had to read the characters for color names written in black ink, a "color naming time" for responses obtained when the color patches were presented and subjects had to name the colors, and an "interference time" for responses obtained when the color words were printed in an inconsistent ink color and subjects had to name their ink color.

No significant visual field differences were found when accuracy of responses was compared. There were also no visual field differences for response times in naming color patches. However, reading times were faster when the color names were presented in the RVF. An assessment of the amount of the Stroop effect was obtained by subtracting the reading times from the interference times. The effect was smaller for color names shown in the RVF. This finding of a smaller Stroop interference effect in the RVF for Chinese contrasts with an earlier finding of a greater effect in the RVF for English color names (Tsao, Feustel, & Soseos, 1979). The authors hypothesized that color information as well as Chinese characters could be competing for shared right-hemisphere perceptual capacities. But this would be difficult to maintain in the absence of any significant visual field effect for naming the color patches. In fact, the color naming times were marginally faster for patches presented in the RVF. The authors also noted the effect of exposure duration on lateralization. They attributed the faster reading times for the single-character color names in the RVF to the relatively long exposure time used, 150 milliseconds, as contrasted with the 20 to 75 milliseconds used by O. J. L. Tzeng et al. (1979) when the latter obtained a LVF superiority for single characters.

Besner, Daniels, and Slade (l982) presented Arabic numerals and Chinese number names (for the numbers 4 to 9 only) to Japanese and Chinese subjects. These few items were repeatedly presented, mixing Arabic numerals and Chinese number names, for three times for each item. Exposure time was adjusted for each subjects so as to obtain about 50% accuracy of identification. The average exposure time was 54 milliseconds, and items were presented at a visual angle of 3.3 degrees. Luminance was not reported. There was a RVF-LH advantage for both types of materials when accuracy rates for identification of the stimulus were compared. An earlier experiment was also reported in which English subjects also showed a RVF-LH advantage for Arabic numerals.

There are a number of unusual features of the study by Besner et al. (1982). The data were based on four male and four female subjects, one of each being Chinese and the rest Japanese. The procedure of repeated presentation of just a small number of items was unusual, although Hardyck et al. (1977, 1978) suggested that small target set size entailed precisely the kind of process that should reveal visual field advantage. The mean exposure time of 54 milliseconds was moderately high, but the obtained accuracy of identification was only about 30%. This suggested that the unreported luminance level must be extremely low. What was particularly unusual was that the stimulus size was huge, 10.6 x 10.6 degrees, which was by far the largest target size recorded for Chinese lateralization studies. Boles (1986) demonstrated, with both nonverbal and verbal indicators of number (dot clusters, bar graphs, dials, word names of numbers, and digits), that visual field differences for number depended largely on display format and that there was no evidence of lateralization for digits. In any case, Besner et al. (1982) found a RVF-LH advantage for the number names. The authors suggested that incidental stimulus characteristics, namely, the small number of strokes in the characters for numbers, could be related to the RVF-LH advantage found. They thought that other findings of LVF-RH advantage for single characters tended to involve items with more strokes and hence greater visual complexity.

Leong, Wong, Wong, and Hiscock (1985) used a very long exposure time of 150 milliseconds and a small visual angle of less than two degrees for presentation of single characters. The stimulus size was small, at about half a degree square. Three different tasks were given. In the lexical decision tasks, subjects had to decide if the presented item was a legitimate character or only a pseudocharacter (being mirror images of characters). In the phonological processing task, subjects had to decide if the presented character had a pronunciation like a target character pronounced by the experimenter. In the semantic processing task, subjects had to decide if the presented character belonged to a semantic category pronounced by the experimenter. No significant differences were found for response time scores. A RVF-LH advantage in terms of accuracy was obtained for the phonological processing and semantic processing tasks, but not for the task of lexical decision requiring less depth of processing.

The notion that lateralization could vary according to the depth of processing is an interesting one. However, the response times required for the three tasks did not appear to reflect the postulated levels of processing. It would be expected that lexical decision, phonological processing, and semantic processing require increasing amounts of cognitive activity that should be reflected in increasing processing times. The mean "yes" response times obtained in the three tasks of Leong et al. (1985) were 926 milliseconds (that a presented item was a character), 858 milliseconds (that a presented item was homophonous with a target character), and 907 milliseconds (that a presented item was a constituent of the semantic category of a target). These times by themselves did not appear to reflect an increasing need for cognitive processing. But a crucial factor to take into consideration when comparing these three mean times is that the same group of subjects was given the tasks, each separated from the next by 10-day intervals. The first task, that of lexical decision, actually required the longest response times. In fact, the average response time was close to one second, and the lack of visual field difference obtained could be related to the longer times, which could mean interhemispheric activities noted earlier in this chapter. The relatively faster times for the other two tasks could be the result of practice. The same group of subjects could become more adapted to the task situation, so that phonological and semantic processing did not require slower response times.

To summarize, perceptual condition as well as task demands affect lateralization for the single-character studies reviewed in this section. Particularly, variation in exposure duration as well as visual complexity seem to produce the discrepancies in visual field effect for single characters.

5.1.5 Perceptual Factors in Lateralization

Hasuike et al. (1986) emphasized the importance of the visual angle of the stimulus item, the exposure duration, as well as the luminance level in both the Chinese and Japanese literature on lateralization of perception of words. The role of the sensory input in visual hemifield studies in general has come to be appreciated (e.g., Sergent, 1983). The quality of the sensory input is significant in that the right hemisphere appears to be more adept than the left hemisphere in processing degraded sensory information. Hasuike et al. (1986) suggested that the general finding of RVF-LH advantage for two-character words and LVF-RH advantage for single characters in the Chinese and Japanese hemifield studies could be related to the tendency to use longer exposure times for two-character words and shorter exposure times for single characters.

However, if we look at only the Chinese studies, the picture appears to be RVF-LH advantage for two-character words and a variation of visual field advantage for single characters. We have findings of LVF-RH advantage for single characters (C. M. Cheng & Fu, 1986; Hardyck et al., 1977; Y. L. Huang & Jones, 1980; O. J. L. Tzeng et al., 1979;), no visual field advantage in some situations (Leong et al., 1985; Nguy et al., 1980), as well as those of RVF-LH advantage (Besner et al., 1982; Hardyck et al., 1978; Leong et al., 1985; Nguy et al., 1980; Tsao et al., 1981). One thing to be noted about single characters is that they do not seem to produce the general left-hemisphere advantage that is usually found for language items in alphabetic languages.

With two-character words, on the other hand, we have more of a one-sided finding of RVF-LH advantage. The procedures in studies of two-character words varied across a range of stimulus and task conditions, in: (a) exposure time, from 40 to 190 milliseconds (except for the study by Ho & Hoosain, 1989); (b) visual angle, from 2.5 to 6 degrees; (c) orientation of the component characters, both vertical and left to right; (d) nature of the task, from judgment of identity of physical shape of pairs of characters, straightforward naming, to judgment of whether pairs of characters were opposites or not; and (e) response measure, whether accuracy or response time. The scarcity of LVF-RH advantage in such tasks would suggest some built-in factor or artifact influencing lateralization.

In English, we do not have anything corresponding to this contrast between single characters and two-character words. From the perception of single letters to the perception of syllables, letter strings, and words, RVF-LH advantage is the norm (see Beaumont, 1982). Similarly, visual degradation tends to shift the visual field advantage from RVF to LVF for single letters (e.g., Murray, 1982) just as for words (Bradshaw, Hicks, & Rose, 1979). There are, of course, variations on the theme. For example, the RVF-LH advantage is less marked for concrete nouns than for abstract nouns, and there is some variation with imageability (see Beaumont, 1982). But the general pattern of left hemisphere superiority for all types of language items maintains.

To summarize, it would appear that the quality of the sensory signal, as determined by perceptual conditions, undoubtedly plays a role in lateralization. The invariance of the RVF-LH advantage for two-character presentations, in contrast with the fluctuation of hemifield advantage for single characters, suggests some built-in bias. In any case, it is worthwhile to see if it is possible to obtain any LVF-RH advantage for two-character words.

5.1.6 Right-Hemisphere Advantage for Two-Character Words

It is perhaps fair to say that none of the studies we have discussed so far specifically set out to demonstrate a LVF-RH advantage for two-character words. Ho and Hoosain (1989) managed to show such an effect in a rather extreme combination of conditions. Two-character words, of high/low frequency of usage and high/low number of strokes in each character, were presented to right-handed undergraduates in Hong Kong. They were mixed with two-character nonwords that were just random combinations of two characters. All two-character items were arranged vertically, subtending a visual angle of .87 by 2.15 degrees at a visual angle of 3 degrees from the fixation point. Exposure time was adjusted for individual subjects so as to be somewhat below each subject's perceptual threshold and ranged between 12 and 21 milliseconds. Accuracy rates obtained were lower than many found in the literature. Luminance was 6.3 footLamberts. Thus, the perceptual condition, with relatively short exposure time and low luminance, was generally created so that the sensory signal would be fairly degraded. In a lexical-decision task, subjects were asked to indicate as soon as possible whether each presented item was a word or nonword. They were told that half the items were words and half nonwords.

Fig. 5.1 shows the results in terms of accuracy of identification. In general, words with higher frequency of usage and words with lower stroke number were identified as words more accurately. The scores also showed that there was no visual field difference for high frequency words, whether they had high or low stroke number. But for the low frequency words, those with high stroke number were correctly identified as words significantly more often when they appeared in the LVF. Those with low stroke number showed a reversed trend that was not significant. In other words, it was possible to obtain a LVF-RH advantage for two-character words, with low frequency, high stroke number items presented at low luminance level and short exposure time.

Low stroke number generally means low spatial frequency, and there are suggestions that the right hemisphere is better tuned to the lower range of spatial frequencies (Sergent, 1987). This would appear to contradict our finding of a LVF-RH advantage for some of the high stroke number words. But, given the low luminance level in this study as well as the nonfoveal vision with the visual angle used, high stroke number could actually result in low perceptual output, given the modulation transfer functions of the human visual system (see Cornsweet, 1970). Subjectively, this means that high stroke number items tend to appear more blurred. The right hemisphere is more able to handle degraded sensory signal or low spatial frequency information (see Johnson & Hellige, 1986; Sergent, 1983, 1987).

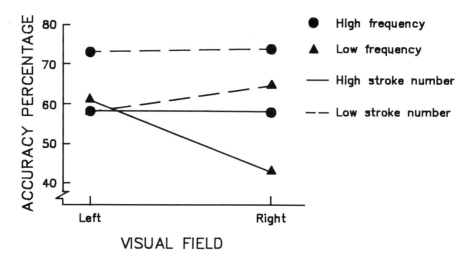

FIG. 5.1. Lexical-decision performance as a function of visual field, frequency of usage, and stroke number (from Ho & Hoosain, 1989).

The results of Ho and Hoosain (1989) further showed that the visual field difference between high and low stroke number words applied only to low familiarity items. For some time, we have known that familiarity enhances the prominence of the physical aspects of a stimulus (e.g., Pick, 1965). In the present study, greater prominence with higher familiarity reduced the effect of stroke number. Thus, we have an example of the interaction beatween state-limiting variables (such as exposure time, luminance, and visual angle affecting the quality of the sensory information) and the process-limiting variable of familiarity (cf., Sergent, 1983).

It is still necessary to look at the contrast in lateralization patterns for single characters and two-character words. The study by O. J. L. Tzeng et al. (1979) showed quite clearly that higher perceptual thresholds are needed for two-character words. Identical experimental conditions were used in hemifield presentation of single characters and two-character words, except that the authors required a much longer exposure time for the latter in order to obtain comparable levels of performance. In turn, longer exposure time tends to produce left hemisphere advantage (cf., Sergent, 1987). Thus, there is a built-in bias that differentiates two-character words and single characters.

However, whereas this bias accounts for the contrast between single characters and two-character words, it does not necessarily explain the greater fluctuation of hemifield advantage for single characters. The tendency to use shorter exposure time, in comparison with two-character words, does not explain the more frequent reports of right-hemisphere superiority for single characters than for alphabetic language items. Schmuller (1979), for example, used exposure times of only 4 to 9 milliseconds and still obtained a RVF-LH advantage for letters. In comparison, O. J. L. Tzeng et al. (1979) had a mean exposure time of 40 milliseconds when they found the LVF-RH advantage for single characters. The varying findings with single Chinese characters — sometimes LVF-RH and sometimes RVF-LH superiority — might have to do with either perceptual characteristics, such as their spatial frequency, or linguistic characteristics related to their status of being simultaneously visual, syllabic, and meaning units, or a combination of both perceptual and linguistic factors.

In footnote 7 of Chapter 3, we mentioned the greater spatial frequency of Chinese characters compared with English words, in terms of line density. Spatial frequency interacts with stimulus energy level to determine hemifield advantage. With higher energy levels, such as higher luminance or longer exposure time, the left hemisphere is more able to process high spatial frequencies (see Sergent, 1987). But in more visually degraded conditions, higher stroke number can actually produce lower spatial frequency output, leading to a LVF-RH advantage. Given the generally higher spatial frequency of Chinese characters and such interaction, there could be a greater tendency for hemifield superiority for single Chinese characters to fluctuate as a result of variation in stroke number and energy condition. And characters can vary from having a single stroke to more than 20. This affects two-character words less, because their requirement of longer exposure time provides generally higher stimulus energy levels. English items, on the other hand, with their generally lower line density (with longer words being spread out over a wider space), also tend to show a more stable left-hemisphere superiority.

The manner in which spatial frequency interacts with other factors determining the quality of the sensory signal may or may not be sufficient to account for all the fluctuations reported for single characters. Visual complexity, in terms of number of component strokes of characters, is very often not even reported in the Chinese hemifield perception literature. In any case, it is worthwhile to note the linguistic characteristics of the single character that could be related to its unusual lateralization pattern.

The characteristic of single characters as visual wholes — not requiring sequential processing, which could be the case for two-character or alphabetic words — is a relevant factor favoring the LVF-RH (see O. J. L. Tzeng et al., 1979). On the other hand, just being visual wholes may not be a sufficient condition. For example, no sequential analysis is required to identify individual English letters, but there is no tendency for LVF-RH advantage. An important difference between English letter and Chinese characters, apart from line density, is that the latter are meaningful. The character is not only a unit at the level of sensory integration but is the smallest unit of meaning. Letters, on the other hand, need to be combined in a sequence to represent meaning. Osgood and Hoosain (1974) demonstrated that, for English words, simultaneously being the unit at the meaningless sensory integration level as well as the smallest unit of meaning at the representational level provided perceptual salience. At this time, we cannot dismiss the possibility that perceptual salience of the character, based on the convergence of visual, syllabic, and meaning properties, is related to its lateralization pattern.

To summarize, the variables affecting lateralization in the perception of Chinese words interact, and it could well be that any obtained lateralization effect is "overdetermined" by a combination of factors, none of which is sufficient alone (see Sergent, 1987). We have affirmed the role played by perceptual factors in some situations, particularly the requirement of longer exposure time for two-character words and the variable but generally high visual–spatial frequency of Chinese characters. Single characters show a fluctuation in hemisphere lateralization in different situations. This could be related to their unique characteristic as the unit of visual integration, pronunciation, as well as meaning.

5.2 HANDEDNESS AND LATERALIZATION
OF BILINGUAL FUNCTIONS

Apart from the possibility of a different lateralization for the perception of Chinese words, there is a question of the likelihood of differential lateralization for languages of the bilingual. This could be particularly so if, as in the case of Chinese and English, the two languages are very different. The relationship between handedness and lateralization for language functions, plus the reported low incidence of left-handedness among the Chinese, raise the further question of what happens to the lateralization of the language functions of people with different kinds of handedness experience? These topics are discussed next.

5.2.1 Lateralization of Bilingual Functions

Although most people have their language functions lateralized in the left hemisphere, there are suggestions that bilinguals might have a somewhat different lateralization pattern, one possibility being a less strong lateralization than monolinguals (Albert & Obler, 1978). This particular view, however, has not received unanimous support (e.g., Galloway & Krashen, 1980; Vaid, 1983). It would appear that much of the contradictions in the findings have to do with variation in stimulus and task characteristics, as well as subject variables in the diverse studies reported. Most investigations of bilingual functions compared alphabetic languages, usually English and another European language. Even within this confine of European languages, linguistic differences have sometimes been used to account for diverse lateralization patterns. For example, Albanese (1985) tested English-French bilinguals with a dichotic listening test (an auditory version of the bilateral presentation procedure) and found that French-dominant subjects had a higher ambilaterality, that is, smaller right ear (LH) advantage[1] compared with English-dominant subjects. The author suggested that this is related to the greater salience of the French language, indicated by features like prevalence of accentuation and stress at the end of French words, which contribute to their prosodic stability and boundary definition.

    In the bilingual lateralization literature, there appears to be a trend for weaker lateralization or even right-hemisphere superiority for tasks in-

---

[1] In the auditory situation, somewhat different from the visual hemifield or bilateral presentation situation, sensory information entering a ear is largely transmitted to the contralateral hemisphere in the first instance, again as a result of the anatomy of neural connections (although there are some ipsilateral connections and some conduction of sound through the skull itself). A right-ear advantage would indicate a LH superiority in processing the auditory signal, and vice versa.

volving auditory processing in the second language when the bilingual's two languages are very different. The reported studies involved English contrasted, respectively, with Japanese, Crow Indian, and Cantonese Chinese. Miura (1983) tested Japanese-English bilinguals in an auditory discrimination task using English word lists and found a slight left ear (RH) advantage for the second language items. Vocate (1985) conducted an EEG study of Crow-English bilinguals while they listened to tapes in the two languages. There was a left-hemisphere lateralization for Crow but no general hemisphere difference for the corresponding processing of English, although lateralization varied in the course of the experiment.

With Chinese-English bilinguals, Hoosain (1984b) also found some indication of ambilaterality for a task involving auditory reception of the second language. Right-handed bilingual Hong Kong undergraduates were tested. They were given both forward and backward digit span tests in their native Cantonese and in English in a monaural listening procedure. Digits were recorded on tape and presented to subjects through headphones that transmitted the sounds to one ear only each time.

As can be seen in Table 5.2, there was a significant right-ear (LH) advantage for forward digit span in Cantonese, with a larger digit span when numbers were heard in the right ear. However, there was no significant difference for forward digit span in English, although there was a similar direction for right ear advantage. There was no significant ear advantage for backward digit span for either language. In subsection 4.1.1, we noted a suggestion that the backward digit span task might involve the right hemisphere more because of the operation needed to reverse the encoded numbers. This would explain the absence of right-ear advantage

TABLE 5.2
Digit Span with Monaural Presentation

	Chinese				English			
	Forward		Backward		Forward		Backward	
	Left ear	Right ear	Left ear	Right ear	Left ear	Right ear	Left ear	Right ear
Mean	9.3	9.8	7.1	7.1	7.5	7.8	6.6	6.2
t	2.54		0.00		1.36		1.65	
	($p < .02$)							
Individual subject performance ($n = 36$)								
Right-ear advantage	16		12		15		10	
No advantage	16		12		11		10	
Left-ear advantage	4		12		10		16	

From Hoosain (1984b). Reprinted with permission of the publisher.

for Chinese backward digit span, and, in fact, a marginal left-ear advantage for English backward digit span. The overall pattern shows a tendency for a reduced left-hemisphere lateralization for digit span performance in the second language of the Chinese-English bilinguals.

A study conducted by Neville and Tzeng (referred to in O. J. L. Tzeng, 1988) showed the reversed pattern for English-Chinese bilinguals, that is, greater right-hemisphere involvement for Chinese auditory processing. In an EEG study, American students who had learned Chinese as a second language showed greater right hemisphere evoked potential in a Chinese auditory discrimination task. This indicates greater right-hemisphere involvement in the second language. However, native Chinese speakers showed greater left-hemisphere evoked potential for the same task in Chinese.

In another study of Chinese-English bilinguals in Hong Kong, Hoosain (1990a) found evidence of greater right-hemisphere involvement for backward counting in English. Subjects first performed a finger-tapping task with their right and left index fingers, respectively. This assessed the number of quick taps that could be made within 20 seconds to obtain a baseline measure. The subjects were also asked to count backward by threes, starting with a high two-digit number (e.g., "97, 94, 91, 88, . . .") in both Cantonese and in English, again to obtain a baseline measure. They then performed a time-sharing task, tapping with their left or right index finger and counting backward in Chinese or in English simultaneously.

The rationale of this procedure (see Kinsbourne & Cook, 1971) is that because the contralateral hemisphere controls finger movement, if backward counting is also lateralized in the same hemisphere, time sharing of the tapping and counting tasks would lead to some change in performance compared with the respective baseline measures. In the baseline backward counting task, the bilingual subjects performed significantly better in Chinese than in English, indicating that they were not balanced bilinguals. In the simultaneous time-sharing trials, there was some increase in the backward counts performed but a decrease in the number of taps made compared with the respective baseline measures. Increase or decrease in performance could be a function of practice or fatigue, rather than a direct consequence of time-sharing. But the contrast suggested that subjects were diverting greater attention to counting when they performed the concurrent tasks. It should be noted that the possibility of one of the concurrent tasks being carried out better than baseline performance, due to arousal, has been acknowledged (e.g., Keele, 1968; Kinsbourne & Cook, 1971) although rarely reported.

The changes in tapping performance did not show any significant main or interaction effects. But, across all subjects (including right-handed, left-handed, and handedness switch subjects, see the following section) improvement in simultaneous Chinese counting was greater when subjects were tapping with their left hand, whereas improvement in English counting was greater when tapping with the right hand (see Table 5.3). It might be assumed that a smaller improvement in counting means that the hemisphere contralateral to the tapping hand was more involved in the counting task. Backward counting requires the subject to keep track of the last number arrived at, in the form of a sound code based on his or her own last response, before the next number can be figured out. The pattern of results obtained means that counting in Chinese involves the left hemisphere, but counting in English involves the right hemisphere more. However, in an earlier study (Hoosain & Shiu, 1989) no such language difference in lateralization was found. The subjects in the earlier study, though, performed nearly equally in their baseline counting in Chinese and English which suggests that they were less Chinese dominant. This would mean that lateralization of second language functions depends also on the stage of bilingual development (see Vaid, 1983).

In contrast to the reports of greater ambilaterality or right-hemisphere involvement in tasks requiring auditory processing of the second language that is very different from the native language, no such phenomenon is found in cases where the two languages are more similar. For example, no lateralization difference for the respective languages in auditory reception tasks was found when they involved Portugese and English bilinguals (Soares, 1984), English and French bilinguals (Albanese, 1985), as well as Dutch and English bilinguals (see Schouten, van Dalen, & Klein, 1985).

The ambilaterality or greater right-hemisphere advantage for auditory processing in the second language of Chinese-English bilinguals does not seem to extend to other functions. This was so even though there is some suggestion in the literature that greater dissimilarity in the bilingual's two languages and in the acquisition conditions for the two languages could lead to more dissimilar lateralization patterns (see Vaid, 1983). We have noted some ways in which the Chinese language is distinct from English in Chapter 2. The acquisition contexts for Chinese and for English are also very different for the Chinese-English bilinguals in Hong Kong. English is usually not used at home and is acquired in school in a formal learning

TABLE 5.3
Change in Performance on Concurrent Tasks

| | Chinese | | English | |
	Left Hand	Right Hand	Left Hand	Right Hand
Concurrent Counting	+15.65%[a]	+11.13%	+12.99%	+15.55%
Concurrent Tapping	−10.63%	−10.99%	−12.34%	−12.06%

[a]+ indicates improvement over baseline and − indicates deterioration. From Hoosain (1990a).

environment. If differences in linguistic characteristics and language acquisition contexts are conducive to differential lateralization patterns for the
bilingual's two languages, the situation in Hong Kong should provide quite
optimal opportunities for this to happen.

However, a couple of studies with Hong Kong Chinese-English bilinguals
did not find any evidence of differential lateralization of the two languages
when visual perceptual processing was involved. Hoosain (1986b) presented
three-lettered English words or two-character Chinese words to the bilingual speakers in a visual hemifield procedure. All items were high frequency, and subjects were asked to translate each presented word into the
opposite language as quickly as possible. Response times were faster when
both English and Chinese words were shown in the RVF, although they
were not statistically significant. However, error rates showed a significant
RVF advantage, and similarly so for English and Chinese words. Also,
Hoosain and Shiu (1989) did not find any lateralization difference for
Chinese and English among Hong Kong bilinguals in a bilateral visual
presentation task, and a RVF-LH advantage was found for both languages
(see subsection 5.1.3).

In contrast with visual tasks, the digit span and backward counting tasks
performed in the second language would involve what Carroll (1981)
referred to as phonetic coding ability in his study of foreign language
aptitude components. This is the ability to identify distinct sounds and
associate the sounds with the symbols that represent them. It has quite low
correlation with verbal ability itself and is suspected to have right-
hemisphere functioning in some people. Some support for this view was
provided by Schneiderman and Wesche (1986), who found that scores on
the Phonetic Script subtest (measuring phonetic coding) of the Modern
Language Aptitude Test correlated significantly with the number of correct
left-ear responses in a dichotic listening test. If differential lateralization for
auditory processing of a second language that is very distinct from the
native language stands up to further verification, it would mean that
discussions of bilingual lateralization should distinguish the nature of the
task, particularly auditory versus visual mode of functioning, in addition to
the nature of the languages involved.

5.2.2 Handedness Switch and Lateralization

We have already mentioned one connection between handedness and
lateralization of language functions: lateralization of language functions in
the left hemisphere is higher among right-handers. There are theories that
connect the development of handedness and cerebral lateralization (e.g.,
Annett, 1985). The incidence of left-handedness in the West appears to be
quite stable over the years, ranging from 5% to 10% depending on sampling

and the actual questionnaires used in different surveys. These usually list up to a dozen or so activities, such as writing and holding a knife, and ask the respondent to indicate strong or weak tendency to use one or the other hand to carry out the task. Suitable numerical scores are awarded, and a laterality quotient is derived from these scores, usually ranging from $+1$ or $+100$ (indicating exclusive use of the right hand for the entire range of activities) to 0 (complete ambidexterity) and -1 or -100 (exclusive use of the left hand). Some cut-off points are adopted to label the respondents as right-handed, ambidextrous, or left-handed.

The incidence of left-handedness appears to be much lower among the Chinese as well as among some other non-Western peoples. A survey of 10,314 Chinese in the People's Republic of China found only .26% left-handedness, but also 8.94% "ambidextrous" people (Guo, 1984). It is possible that the ambidextrous included native left-handers who had experienced forced handedness switch. Forced handedness switch, usually from using the left hand as the preferred hand to using the right as a result of social (mostly parental) coercion, is more common in authoritarian cultures, which results in a lower incidence of manifest left-handedness (see Binnie-Dawson, 1981). In an investigation in Taiwan with 4,143 subjects (Teng, Lee, Yang, & Chang, 1979), it was reported that for writing and using chopsticks, two activities that are more subject to social censure, the prevalence of exclusive left-hand use (about 1%) and either-hand use (2%–3%) was distinctly lower than that for other activities. For such activities as opening a door, hammering a nail, and throwing a ball, the incidence of preferred right-hand use for the Chinese was quite like that of an English sample, although the latter tended to show a higher incidence of left-hand use and a lower incidence of either-hand use. This pattern of results suggests that the incidence of native right/left handedness among the Chinese could be comparable to that of Westerners, although social pressure results in a significantly lower manifest left handedness in the more censored activities.

Handedness switch usually begins at the young age of 3 or 4, when children go to kindergarten and learn to write as well as start using chopsticks at home. There are indications that fine motor and finger movements are more relevant than gross motor arm movements in determining the relationship between hemisphere specialization and contralateral manual behavior (e.g., Young, 1977). It would appear therefore that the study of lateralization patterns of people who experienced forced handedness switch in childhood, particularly in writing, should provide interesting answers to the question of the effects of peripheral influences on hemispheric specialization. If handedness change influences the localization of language functions in the brain, we would expect that native left-handers who suffered handedness change should come to have a language laterali-zation pattern more like that of native right-handers. Otherwise, even though these people have come to use the right hand for writing and using chopsticks, they should display a lateralization pattern similar to other native left-handers. This latter situation is in line with the view that, ontogenetically, bias in hand usage could not produce changes in neuroa-natomical asymmetries (see Kinsbourne & Hiscock, 1977; Witelson, 1980).

Hoosain (in press, a) screened 556 Chinese-English bilingual undergrad-uates in Hong Kong, using a handedness questionnaire with items that included use of chopsticks in addition to writing; drawing; throwing; holding scissors, toothbrush, knife, match, hammer; and opening the door. The usual laterality quotient was computed and nine left handers (1.6%) were identified, with a mean preference for the left hand across the 10 activities and no switching to the right hand for writing or drawing. A group of 18 (3.2%) reported a preference for the right hand for writing and drawing but a general preference for the left hand for the other activities. Most of them also reported having experienced pressure to switch their preferred hand when they were small. These students were taken to be those who had experienced forced handedness switch, from the left hand to the right. It should be noted that there appeared to be more people who experienced forced handedness switch than straightforward left-handers in the Hong Kong Chinese population. Together, they constituted 4.9% of the sample screened and would appear to amount to a percentage comparable to the range of left-handedness in Western populations. A finger tapping test confirmed that the left- and right-handers could tap more times with their respective preferred hands. The forced handedness swtich group showed a more mixed performance in this tapping task.

Hoosain (in press, b) explored the lateralization patterns of these three groups of bilingual students. They were given a hemifield presentation task with common two-character Chinese words and three-lettered English words. Both the constituent characters of Chinese words and letters of English words were arranged in vertical orientation. Exposure time was adjusted for each student to produce about 75% accuracy rate in the identification task. Although both accuracy and response times were measured, only the former produced significant results. Analysis of vari-ance showed a significant main effect of visual field, with an overall accuracy rate of 78.3% for the right visual field and 73.7% for the left. Chi-square tests were made of the distribution of the individuals who identified more items in one visual field than the other or who identified an equal number of items in each. For the right-handers, the distribution was significant, showing a significantly greater number who identified more Chinese as well as English words in the right visual field. But for both the left-handers and the handedness switch groups, the distributions were not significant for either language, although in each case there were slightly more who identified more items in the right visual field (see Table 5.4).

Thus, there was no lateralization difference between Chinese and English in the visual task. The forced handedness switch group showed a pattern that was more like that of the left-handers than right-handers. It seems that forced handedness switch does not affect the development of language lateralization. Although fine motor movements in writing and drawing rather than gross arm movements such as opening doors were involved, this did not appreciably affect lateralization of language functions of either the native or the second language. The students had started learning English in school, which would be after the initiation of handedness switch at home. But the lateralization of visual processing functions for the second language did not appear to be affected.

To summarize this section, there is evidence from four communities of bilinguals, including Chinese-English bilinguals, that shows differential lateralization for auditory processing of the second language when it is unrelated to the native language. Such differentiation is not found in visual tasks. Switching of handedness during childhood does not seem to have any significant effect on lateralization of language functions.

5.3 CHINESE APHASIA STUDIES

A main topic of discussion in the Chinese aphasia literature is again the possibility of greater right-hemisphere involvement in using the language.

TABLE 5.4
Percentage of Subjects Showing Visual Field Advantage

Subjects	English	Chinese
Right-handed		
RVF Advantage	60.0	68.0
Equal	8.0	12.0
LVF Advantage	32.0	20.0
	$(p < .01)$	$(p < .005)$
Left-handed		
RVF Advantage	45.0	40.0
Equal	20.0	35.0
LVF Advantage	35.0	25.0
Handedness Switch		
RVF Advantage	41.7	37.5
Equal	29.2	41.7
LVF Advantage	29.2	20.8

From Hoosain (in press, b). Reprinted with permission of the publisher.

Of course, in the Japanese literature, there are corresponding discussions concerning kanji in contrast with kana. Although there used to be some inclination toward the view that kanji processing involves the right hemisphere more than kana, a revised view has more recently appeared, represented by the following conclusion of the comprehensive review by Paradis et al. (1985): "There is no clinically documented pattern of greater impairment for kanji with right hemisphere lesions and greater impairment for kana with left hemisphere lesions. Rather, the correlation seems to be with different regions within the left hemisphere—temporal for kana, occipito-parietal for kanji" (p. 196).

As the processing of kanji compared with that of kana has many peculiarities related to the difference in the roles of the two scripts in Japanese (see Paradis et al., 1985), we do not examine the Japanese literature but rather concentrate on the smaller literature on Chinese aphasia. In any case, our conclusion is similar to that of Paradis et al. (1985). The following are summaries of the principal available reports on Chinese aphasia, in chronological order. These include surveys done on quite large numbers of patients in the People's Republic, studies in Taiwan and in Hong Kong, as well as studies done elsewhere. Some are not published in easily available sources. The standard of reporting has been variable.

5.3.1 Lyman, Kwan, and Chao (1938)

This was the earliest reported case in English and concerned language impairment of a Chinese male as a result of a brain tumor. The patient was 42 years old and used to live in Shanghai but was treated in Peiping (Beijing). He was a well-educated and well-known financier, having studied naval architecture in Glasgow. He was thus a Chinese-English bilingual and was almost equally fluent in the two languages prior to his illness, but his Chinese dialects as well as his handedness were not reported.

His spontaneous speech was natural, and he had no difficulty expressing himself in Chinese or English. His memory appeared somewhat impaired. He had right hemianopsia but no left/right disorientation. When he could not read some presented English words, he would spell the letter aloud as an aid, thus managing to read 19 out of 20 words (the only error was reading *dry* instead of *day*). His Chinese reading was worse, managing to read only two highly familiar characters [4] out of a primary school passage. He finger traced the strokes of the characters to help him read Chinese. He could not understand the meaning of any part of the elementary Chinese text. In Chinese dictation, again, he could only write one character [5].

He was operated on and a large left occipito–parietal fibroblastoma was partially removed; parts of the overlying cortex in the region of the superior and inferior parietal lobes had to be excised. Postoperative tests were conducted 2 months after the operation. Except for the right hemianopsia, all performances showed improvement over preoperative tests. However, he was still poor in calculations, and his IQ was reported to be 70.

He still used letter reading to help in reading English and used finger tracing for Chinese. He could follow 7 out of 11 commands written in English but only 3 in Chinese. His written Chinese looked more tidy than his English. Characters with fewer strokes were copied better than those with more strokes, even though he might have known the meaning of the latter but not the former. Completing the blanks caused many difficulties. His Chinese errors were mainly substitutions with associated words and similar sounding words, and also characters sharing a component with the target. His copying errors in English included mostly letter substitutions, omissions, false starts, and occasionally additions, transpositions, and phonetic improvements (e.g., *nersing* for *nursing*). His difficulties in reading and writing contrasted with the fluency of his speech.

In general, this patient could read English much better than Chinese. Although his English writing had many spelling errors, he could express himself better in written English than in Chinese. Because of the scarcity of aphasia studies on Chinese, this report of greater impairment of Chinese than English with a left-hemisphere tumor had for a long time been a main source of the view that Chinese and English language functions are differentially lateralized.

5.3.2 April and Tse (1977)

The patient was a 54-year-old Chinese male laundry shop owner in New York who emigrated from China when he was 7. He was strongly right-handed with no history of family sinistrality and no evidence of early brain damage or seizure disorder. The patient usually spoke Chinese at home (probably Cantonese because he was born near Canton) and kept the accounts in well-written Chinese characters before his illness. He suffered sudden left hemiparesis and aphasia. A CT scan showed a large region of encephalomalacia in the distribution of the right middle cerebral artery, involving the frontal, temporal, and parietal lobes. There was no clinical, EEG, nor CT scan evidence of left cerebral hemisphere abnormality. The authors also excluded the possibility of bilateral representation of language because greater recovery of speech and language would be expected if this were the case.

The patient had greater preservation of English than Chinese, although Chinese was first learned and was the dominant language. Spontaneous aphasic utterances were made in English and not in Chinese. When addressed in Chinese, he responded in English first, then attempted

Chinese. The reponses were usually a mixture of English and Chinese speech. He also had some deficits in nonlanguage performance tasks. In English, he managed sparse, hesitant spontaneous speech, and verbal comprehension was relatively preserved. He could answer yes–no questions correctly, although he had difficulty following commands with more than three steps. Naming ability for colors and objects in pictures was relatively preserved, although reading simple sentences aloud was slow and erroneous, with omissions, hesitations, and repetitions. Writing numbers and letters from dictation was minimally impaired.

In Chinese, it was difficult for his family to understand his speech. Chinese utterances were always single words or short phrases, always accompanied by gestures. He could repeat single Chinese words correctly, but showed extreme impairment for sentence repetition. His speech was phonetically inaccurate and hardly intelligible. Writing was severely impaired and the patient made errors writing his own name. He wrote only some simple words from dictation and made many errors in sentence copying. He read 8 of 33 Chinese school words correctly but understood another 13 of those he could not read. When the 33 words were read to him in multiple-choice form, he chose 27 correctly.

The patient showed low nonlanguage performance scores in the Wechsler Adult Intelligence Scale and Raven's Coloured Progressive Matrices. There was impaired visual retention, showing left visual field neglect and also errors for figures in the right visual field.

The authors concluded that the patient had one right cerebral lesion responsible for aphasia and no left-hemisphere lesions. The patient had greater preservation of English than Chinese, and the suggested explanation was that early learning of Chinese, with its ideographic script based on visual-spatial relations, resulted in the establishment and maintenance of language dominance in the right hemisphere.

5.3.3 T'sou (1978)

This article reported on a 31-year-old female right-handed steno-typist in Hong Kong. She was a native Cantonese speaker but used English in her work. She was admitted a few hours after feeling dazed. She had no relevant past history. She was found to be well oriented, but her speech was grossly abnormal. CT scan showed a left posterior temporo-parietal hemorrhage. Her language performance was tested three times at 2-week intervals.

She was diagnosed as having conduction aphasia. She had little comprehension difficulties, but her speech was severely impaired. She had problems with confusion of frigatives in Cantonese but not in comprehension. She also had difficulty with the Cantonese tones, and exhaustive tests indicated particular difficulty with the low falling tone. In reading Chinese words consisting of one, two, three, or four characters, performance was inversely related to word length. She showed mirror-image inversion of sounds of some English words when asked to translate Chinese words (e.g., *god* became *dog*), but had no similar problem with Cantonese. The patient appeared to be aware of this and would attempt to correct herself. The absence of this difficulty for Chinese was attributed to two possibilities: (a) Cantonese syllables may begin with only a small class of consonants, and there is much less latitude for symmetry of combinations of sounds such as in English, so that both combinations are legitimate syllables and mirror images of each other. (b) The syllabic Chinese language does not have what corresponds to linearly arrranged phonemic or alphabetic representation of words. This linear representation provides a possibility for reversal.

By the third session, the problem with tones was over. Problems with frigatives subsided, and mirror-image inversion of English sounds also improved.

5.3.4 April and Han (1980)

This is a report of a case of persistent nonfluent aphasia. The patient was a Chinese man, aged 74. He was a bookkeeper in a New York Chinese restaurant. He was right handed with no history of family sinistrality. He had no history of prior brain damage or seizures. He was born in China and received 6 years of schooling in Cantonese. He emigrated to the United States when he was 20, before he started to learn English. He spoke and wrote Chinese at home and at work. CT scan showed that the patient had hemorrhagic infarction in the right frontotemporal region. But there was no clinical, EEG, or other indication of left cerebral dysfunction. Subsequent neuropathologic diagnosis was cystic encephalomalacia in the distribution of branch vessels of the right middle cerebral artery. There were no lesions in the left hemisphere.

The patient was initially mute and communicated by head-nodding and gesturing with the right hand. There was no marked difference between Chinese and English performance. He carried out three-step commands correctly. Reading comprehension for simple sentences was intact. Writing single words and simple sentences was grossly preserved. He started making verbal utterances 7 weeks after onset of illness. Verbal production of Chinese and English consisted of a few words with hesitation and perseveration. Verbal comprehension remained better than expression. His performance on Raven's Coloured Progressive Matrices was in the high range for aphasics.

Six months after the stroke the patient was readmitted to hospital with convulsions. His spontaneous Chinese conversation was less fragmented than English which consisted of one- or two-word responses, generally *yes* or *no*. He followed one-step commands but made errors with two-step commands. He wrote his own name in English even though he was told to do so in Chinese and required several requests before he could do it in Chinese. He could write his children's names only in English.

This is the second case of crossed aphasia reported by April, with aphasia resulting in right-hemisphere instead of left-hemisphere damage. The hypothesis of an altered cerebral dominance with the learning and use of the ideographic Chinese language, from the left to the right hemisphere, appeared to be supported by this and the earlier case (April & Tse, 1977). However, the authors referred to a survey of studies of an unspecified number of Chinese aphasics in New York and in Taiwan, showing that the incidence of crossed aphasia in Chinese patients was not higher than the 4% limit reported in the Western literature. These unspecified cases would not support the view that Chinese patients tend more to have their language functions lateralized in the right hemisphere, resulting in aphasia with right-hemisphere lesions.

5.3.5 Naeser and Chan (1980)

The patient was a 56-year old right-handed Chinese seamstress, who was born in China and who moved to the United States when she was 45. She did not speak English, and spoke three dialects of Chinese: Cantonese, Mandarin, and her native Jiangxi province dialect, which was not spoken by people around her any more. The patient suffered a left-hemisphere intracerebral bleed with two major lesion sites at the posterior portion of the middle temporal gyrus and in the anterior and superior portions of the parietal lobe. She was studied $1\frac{1}{2}$ as well as $2\frac{1}{2}$ years after the stroke using Mandarin, which was the dialect she responded to best at that time.

The patient was tested with a Mandarin version of the Boston Diagnostic Aphasia Examination. She had moderate to severe impairment of all modalities of language. Her conversational speech was mainly limited to yes–no responses, and most communication from the patient was through gestures. She was accurate in pointing at pictures when the tester pronounced their high frequency single-character and two-character names. But, in general, her language comprehension indicated moderate to severe deficit. She could repeat all the six monosyllabic words presented but only one of six bisyllabic words. Repetition errors included incorrect phonemes produced with a lot of articulatory difficulty, incorrect tones, verbal paraphasia, omissions, substitutions, and perseverations.

She could correctly read five out of six monosyllabic words shown but only one out of six bisyllabic words. Her best performance was in pointing out single characters pronounced by the tester from among five alternatives, yielding the highest score amongst all the subtests. Simple word–picture matching was also good. Her sentence reading and sentence comprehension were poor. She could write some single-character words but not two-character words. There was nonconformity to traditional stroke sequences in writing, but once a character was completed she would rewrite it in correct sequence. Writing performance was not directly related to number of strokes in a character. Tone perception was impaired.

In all modalities, there was only minimal language recovery over 2 years. There was overall similarity between this case and other severe cases of English-speaking aphasics. One notable difference was the isolated sparing for single-character recognition, and matching easier words to pictures.

5.3.6 X. Wang and Li (1981)

This article reported on a case of pure dysgraphia treated at Beijing Hospital. The patient was a 48-year-old right-handed male cadre with high school education. He had a left occipito- temporal infarct resulting in right hemianopsia. There was no left/right disorientation, aphasia, alexia, or acalculia. The patient performed well in pointing out words pronounced by the tester and did quite well in copying short phrases. His main difficulties were in copying dictation of characters shown to him for a while first, in dictation of characters, writing down answers to questions, and filling in blanks.

In copying dictation of characters seen for 1 minute, he correctly wrote four of the five presented similar sounding characters, also four of the five similar shaped characters, and three of the five characters with related meanings (which included antonyms as well as synonyms). Such performance alone might be attributed to failure of memory rather than dysgraphia as such, particularly if the subject was not well educated or if the characters were more difficult. However, in regular dictation, he failed to write four of the seven constituent characters of the full name of the People's Republic of China, which are highly familiar characters (and he was a cadre). The authors considered that his impairment mainly concerned memory for the visual code of characters, related to the left occipito-temporal infarct.

5.3.7 C. Y. Huang (1982)

This is a discussion of Chinese aphasia based on more than a dozen cases studied, but no detailed presentation of individual cases was given. The author's impression was that there was a high incidence of selective impairment of comprehension and reading abilities among Chinese patients (no actual figures were provided). A patient with a left-hemisphere hemorrhage could point out 14 of 20 characters when their meanings were given as prompts but not read any one of them. Another patient with transcortical sensory aphasia could read 16 of 20 characters, could complete all 20 incomplete characters, and scored 6 out of 10 on oral comprehension, but could not comprehend written commands and questions even though he could read them. A few similar cases were also referred to. It was suggested that the higher incidence of such selective impairment in Chinese could be related to its distinct script–sound–meaning relations, allowing more direct script–meaning associations. It could also be connected to the fact that lesions among Chinese patients tend to be more localized, resulting in more selective rather than global impairments.

Eleven patients did the character completion test, being presented with up to 20 characters with missing strokes and asked to complete them. There were dissociations of the form and the sound of characters, with patients being able to complete the characters without reading them. It was suggested that the right hemisphere retains memory of the form of characters without retaining other aspects of the script.

There was also a suggestion of greater involvement of the right hemisphere in Chinese. Reference was made to a right-handed university graduate with a right hemisphere hemorrhage who could complete only 14 of the 20 incomplete characters. The patient made phonological substitution errors in writing. He also failed to notice substituted homophones that created nonsense sentences.

5.3.8 Hughes, Chan, and Su (1983)

Aprosodia is the difficulty to comprehend or express emotional tone in speech and is usually connected with acute lesions of the right hemisphere. Patients with aprosodia often have no problems with word meaning or sentence structure.

Twelve Chinese patients in Taiwan, with right-hemisphere lesions, were compared with seven controls. The mean age of both groups was 55. Two of the patients were native left-handers forced to switch to the right hand for writing in early childhood. The rest were right-handed. All but two of the patients were studied in the first 2 months after the appearance of an acute lesion confirmed by CT scan. The other two showed no lesion in the CT scan, but clinical examination indicated supratentorial lesion. The control group was hospitalized for neurological conditions not involving cerebral lesions.

There were four tests for affective prosody: (a) a test of comprehension of neutral sentences recorded in Mandarin, with patients asked to indicate their emotional tone; (b) a test of discrimination with pairs of sentences read with the same or different emotional tone; patients were asked to indicate whether they were the same or different; (c) a test of repetition, with patients asked to repeat sentences with the original intonation; and (d) a test of execution, with patients presented sentences in a neutral tone and asked to repeat them in various specified emotional tones. There were two tests of emotional gestures, one requiring the patients to comprehend and identify gestures and the other to demonstrate gestures for emotional states. Finally, they were given a test for comprehension of semantic tonal difference. Two pictures were shown and the names of things depicted had identical phonemes but different tones. The tester announced one of the names and the patient had to point to the correct picture.

Aprosodia was found in 11 of the 12 patients, and the exceptional patient was tested 6 months post-onset. Some had sensory aprosodia, with relatively better expression of prosody than comprehension. Others had motor aprosodia, with more difficulties in expression than in comprehension. And others had global aprosodia. As a group, the patients with right hemisphere lesions performed significantly worse than the control group. On the other hand, in the test for detecting semantic tonal difference, many of the patients with lesions got perfect or near-perfect scores, and only 5 of the 12 showed mild deficit in the test. The scores in this test for the group as a whole were not significantly different from those of the control group.

The patients with cerebral lesions tended to perform better in comprehension and identification of emotional gestures than in the tests for affective prosody. But there was still evidence of impairment, and their performance was inferior to that of the control group. None of the patients with lesions showed aphasia when tested for simple naming, repetition, comprehension, or speech production. Aprosodia from right-hemisphere lesions appeared to be independent of propositional linguistic structure. Results were consistent with findings elsewhere with English speakers, showing that right-hemisphere lesions could produce deficit in comprehension and production of tonal change related to the affective component of prosody.

5.3.9 Rapport, Tan, and Whitaker (1983)

This article reported on seven cases of Chinese polyglots in Malaysia, all right-handed. Each patient underwent one or more of three types of tests: (a) Four patients had the Wada test, in which sodium amytal was injected into one of the carotid arteries, resulting in transient hemiplegia on the side of the body contralateral to the injection, indicating unilateral cortical suppression. Patients were then given an object-naming test and asked to name presented common objects in a specified language spoken by the patients, including English, Cantonese, Hokkien (another southern Chinese dialect), Mandarin, or Malay. Items were included only if the patient could name them in a prior test. The test was repeated with an injection into the other carotid artery to see the effects on the other hemisphere. (b) Three patients had cortical stimulation during awake craniotomy for surgical treatment of left-hemisphere lesions. Effects of cortical stimulation on the following were asessed: (i) object naming while looking at slides of line drawings and (ii) silent reading, using a pointer to identify which one of three objects in a picture was depicted by an accompanying word, with no verbal response required. (c) Four patients with left-brain CVAs were given periodical clinical tests to monitor the pattern of language loss and recovery after stroke.

. *Case 1.* A male mathematics teacher aged 32 who was exclusively right-handed (with a laterality quotient of +100). He was a native Cantonese speaker although he could not read or write Chinese. English was his dominant language, and he was also fluent in Malay. He had a left tentorial meningioma.

The Wada test was conducted in English and Cantonese. With right-sided injection, all responses were correct. With left-sided injection, English recovered before Cantonese. When errors were made in Cantonese, responses were almost always given in English.

Cortical stimulation at different locations interfered with speech in different manners. Simulation around the posterior sylvian fissure led to reproducible errors in English, which tended to be paraphasias (e.g., *egg* for *axe*). Some of these sites seemed relatively unrelated to Cantonese. Chinese errors were less reproducible and resulted from stimulation at scattered sites that tended to be more remote from the usually described posterior language regions. Errors were mostly failures to name objects, but there was a preserved ability to read the leading phrase [6] meaning 'This is a', used to elicit the naming response. However, as this patient was supposed to be unable to read Chinese, this ability to "read" the leading phrase would be actually nothing more than the recalling a set phrase.

. *Case 2.* A male small-businessman aged 41. His laterality quotient was also +100. He was fluent in spoken and written Chinese (Mandarin) and English, and he felt that his Mandarin was dominant. He could also speak Hokkien (his mother tongue), Cantonese, and Malay. He had a left frontal astrocytoma.

Wada test was conducted in Mandarin, Hokkien, and English. With right-sided injection, object naming was mostly correct, with only one error for each language. With left-sided injection, there were many incorrect or mute responses. Many of the incorrect responses requested in Mandarin were answered correctly in English. With recovery from the sodium amytal, use of English recovered first, followed by Hokkien and then Mandarin.

In cortical stimulation, Mandarin and English were tested. Mandarin errors following stimulation concentrated around the posterior sylvian fissure. English errors occurred at sites more peripheral and tended to be less reproducible.

In clinical tests, this patient had a preoperative minimal nonfluent nominal aphasia which he thought affected his Mandarin most. Postoperative local edema resulted in severe expressive aphasia, and he was unable to name in Mandarin, Hokkien, or English, although reading was unimpaired in Mandarin and English. There was more similarity in success and failure in naming tasks between Mandarin and Hokkien than between English and these dialects. This sugggested that locations associated with the two Chinese dialects were more closely related to each other than related to locations associated with English. The patient recovered within 1 month.

. *Case 3.* A male accountant aged 30 with a laterality quotient of +100. His mother tongue was Hokkien, but he was educated in English. He was also fluent in Cantonese and Malay but could not read or write Chinese. He had right temporal lobe hydrocephalus.

Wada test was conducted in English, Cantonese, and Hokkien. With right-sided injection, responses in all languages were correct. With left-sided injection, recovery occurred for English first, then Hokkien, and then Cantonese, corresponding to the order of his subjective fluency in the languages.

. *Case 4.* An unemployed female aged 24, with a laterality quotient of +75. Her mother tongue was Hokkien, but she was educated in Mandarin, which she felt to be her dominant language. She learned English in school and was also fluent in Cantonese. She had right anterior cerebral artery aneurysm and also had suffered a subarachnoid hemorrhage 3 years earlier.

Wada test was done in Mandarin, Hokkien, and English. With right-sided injection, 5 out of 48 responses were incorrect, 3 of these being requests made in Hokkien but correctly named in Mandarin. With left-sided injection, incorrect responses involved mostly objects properly named but not in the designated language. Responses requested in Mandarin and Hokkien were usually given correctly in English, suggesting that English was better preserved than Mandarin (the dominant language) or Hokkien. The apparent weaker lateralization of language functions could be related to weaker right-handedness or the sex of the patient.

. *Case 5.* A male clerk aged 23 with a laterality quotient of +100. He was fluent in spoken and written English and considered it his dominant language, although his mother tongue was Cantonese. From the description given, he did not appear to be able to read Chinese. He had a small left middle cerebral artery distribution arteriovenous malformation associated with a large left fronto–parietal intracerebral hematoma.

In the cortical stimulation tests, Broca's area could not be readily identified. There were only a few points strongly associated with language, and these were mainly located along the superior temporal gyrus. There were few errors in either language. English errors were more localized here, and Chinese errors were more scattered. Specific sites tended to be associated with either English or Chinese errors exclusively. All his errors were failures to name pictured objects.

In clinical tests, the patient was initially mute and obtunded. English and Cantonese comprehension returned within 24 hours. He recovered English functions faster than Cantonese and could read English throughout his hospitalization. He was quite well recovered by the time of surgery 13 days posthemorrhage.

Because the history of his arteriovenous malformation was unknown, the effect it had on development of his speech was uncertain. Together with findings of cortical stimulation, there is some possibility of mixed cerebral dominance related to congenital vascular anomaly.

. *Case 6.* A female housewife aged 45 with a laterality quotient of + 100. Hokkien was her mother tongue and dominant language. She was also fluent in Cantonese and English, which was her medium of instruction through secondary school. CT scan showed a left fronto–parietal intracerebral hematoma presumed to be secondary to a ruptured mycotic aneurysm.

She had a dense global aphasia for two weeks. By the fourth week, there was partial recovery of naming performance in all three languages/dialects. In 30 naming trials, many errors were common to two of her three languages/dialects. She was then lost to follow-up.

. *Case 7.* A male fish seller aged 39 with a laterality quotient of + 50. Hokkien was his mother tongue, but Mandarin was his dominant language. He understood simple English. He had a meningioma in the temporal horn of the left lateral ventricle.

His language performance was tested 1 week after surgery. He was not able to name any of the presented objects, either in Mandarin or in Hokkien. At 2 weeks, reading in Mandarin was unimpaired, and comprehension was good. His simple English was judged to be at the premorbid level. He was then lost to follow-up.

To summarize this series of studies, there was no support for the view that Chinese involves the right hemisphere more. There were two apparent exceptions. Case 4 seemed to show weaker lateralization, but the female patient had a lower laterality quotient. Also, Case 5 could have been afffected by the history of arteriovenous malformation. There was also no evidence of participation of more occipital cortex than for alphabetic languages. Instead, the cortical stimulation studies in particular indicated that different languages occupy different loci within the same hemisphere.

The loss and recovery of languages of the dysphasic polyglots showed that the most familiar language at the onset of illness recovered best (as indicated in the rule of Pitres). Languages that were both read and written as well as spoken recovered better than those that were only spoken. This applied, even though all languages of the four cerebral vascular accident patients were similarly affected initially. The dominant language recovered first or more completely, at least in the short run. When a patient spoke two Chinese dialects, they tended to recover in a similar way, and usually before English. Similar responses were more likely to occur between two Chinese dialects than between a dialect and English.

5.3.10 Guo (1984)

Reference was made to a survey of 159 cases of brain damage in the People's Republic of China. There were 150 right-handers, 81 of whom had left hemisphere damage. Of these, 75% were aphasic and 25% had no aphasia. Of the 69 with right-hemisphere damage, 19% were aphasic and 81% had no aphasia. These patients were most likely monolinguals. However, details of the nature and location of the lesions were not available. The sample of nine left-handers was small, but in any case, 5 of the 6 with left-hemisphere damage were aphasic. One of the three with right-hemisphere damage had aphasia.

Dichotic listening and visual hemifield studies conducted by the author on normal subjects found relatively low incidences of left hemisphere advantage. Again, no details were available. However, large proportions of the experimental subjects, sometimes over 50%, showed no visual field or ear advantage, a reflection perhaps of the experimental design.

5.3.11 C. Y. Huang (1984)

This article reviewed the features of morphological, phonological, and semantic errors in reading and writing disorders in Chinese, based on the author's own studies. It was considered uncommon for patients to produce entirely novel characters, and more common either not to respond or produce nonexistent characters with combination of existing radicals. Phonological errors might involve reading individual characters with vowel or consonant or tonal errors. Semantic errors included substitution with words having related meaning, partial substitution of component character of words, and syntagmatic type of response.

Dissociation of comprehension and pronunciation was thought to occur more often than in the case with alphabetic languages. Reference was made to a patient with severe Wernicke's aphasia. The score for matching pictures to words was 50 out of 61 correct, but there was complete inability to pronounce any of the words. With oral commands, the patient was able to find 27 out of 45 presented pictures, and 30 out of 61 printed words. He could correctly complete 35 out of 45 incomplete characters and made only minor morphological errors on 7 of the remaining 10. He could read only 18 of these 45 characters. Thus, recognition of the visual form and meaning of characters was independent of ability to pronounce them. It was suggested that the right hemisphere might be more involved in the recognition of visual form and meaning of Chinese.

5.3.12 X. T. Li, Hu, Zhu, and Sun (1984)

This is a report on a patient who was a 56-year-old right-handed male with a high school education. He was admitted to the hospital one day after experiencing a throbbing left-side headache and having difficulties reading and writing. He had normal oral comprehension and production. CT scan on the fifth day showed a high density zone in the left temporal–parietal cortical and subcortical areas, and that the hematoma had ruptured into the subarachnoid space.

The patient's reasoning and memory was good, with no acalculia or left–right disorientation. Sentence copying was good, but taking dictation and spontaneous writing were impaired. He was also good at picture naming (meaning to sound), picture identification from name (sound to meaning), and word-form matching (form to form). However, his performance was poor in word reading (form to sound), word identification from pronunciation (sound to form), and picture identification from printed word (form to meaning). The authors suggested that there was some breakdown in the interconnection among word shape, sound, and meaning, and that the left temporal-parietal area was the locus of the interconnection.

5.3.13 C. Y. Huang and Lau (1985)

The patient was a 79-year-old right-handed male high school graduate who had worked as a clerk before retirement. He was hospitalized with a sudden dense right hemiplegia and aphasia. CT scan showed an extensive left striatocapsular infarction. In the fifth week he had global aphasia but with preservation of reading. He wrote answers with his left hand.

He had little problem filling in incomplete characters. Copying from memory was moderately impaired for single characters and progressively worse for longer items. About one third of the dysgraphic errors were due to perseveration of previous responses or delayed responses to earlier stimuli. About one quarter were normal characters that bore no obvious relationship to the target. Morphological, phonological, and semantic errors were all found.

With neomorphic characters produced, most were combinations of normal components of characters. This indicated that characters were coded as combinations of subcomponents rather than as stroke sequences, spatially discrete units rather than temporarily sequential units. Some morphological errors had no resemblance to the targets in both initial strokes and subcomponents and only grossly resembled the target. These findings suggested a third route for retrieval of words, besides the lexical or phonological routes, which was a visual route employing holistic or macroscopic processes rather than sequential processes, possibly with right-hemisphere involvement.

5.3.14 X. Wang (1985)

This article reported a case of mirror writing. The patient was a 62-year-old right-handed male cadre who was admitted to the hospital with weakness of the right limbs and vomiting. He had logorrhea and paraphasia. His speech recovered within the same day as onset. CT scan showed that he had a left thalamic hemorrhage.

He was given a neurolinguistic examination 6 days later. He showed no aphasia, alexia, or apraxia. He had slight agraphia but marked mirror writing (it was not stated which hand was used). His writing of his name and address was all in mirror reversed characters, except for one character [7]. Copied dictation after seeing target characters for a minute also showed mirror writing, except for two characters [8], which are more or less left–right symmetrical. Copying of short phrases all resulted in mirror writing. Copied dictation of multicharacter words also showed mirror writing, except for three characters that were not written properly. Filling in of missing characters in multicharacter words resulted in six correctly written characters, as well as three characters in mirror image and three no responses. Subsequent testing two weeks as well as 1 month later also showed mirror writing and some agraphia.

The author referred to Russian studies that reported an incidence of about 8% of mirror writing when patients used the left hand. The author also referred to a series of 22 aphasic patients. Nine patients who could write with their right hand showed no mirror writing. But of the 13 who had to write with their left hand because of right hemiplegia, 1 showed mirror writing. Thus, the incidence of Chinese mirror writing appeared to occur only occasionally, and more likely when patients wrote with their left hand. It was suggested that in normal learning to write, graphic motor schemas in the left hemisphere as well as mirror-writing motor schemas in the right hemisphere are established. In normal writing, the former are dominant, although not as strongly for children. But when writing with the left hand, mirror writing schemas can be activated. With the present patient, the lesion of the thalamus itself or the thalamo–parietal pathway of the left cerebral hemisphere might give rise to dysfunction of graphic motor schemas in the left hemisphere as well as dominance of mirror writing motor schemas in the right hemisphere, resulting in mirror writing.

5.3.15 Hong, Cheng, and Hsi (1986)

This article was based on 20 cases of left-hemisphere subcortical putaminal lesions in Taiwan (43% of stroke cases in Taiwan were reported to involve hemorrhage at the putamen). Six of the patients had occlusive cerebral vascular accident and 14 had cerebral hemorrhage. The mean age of the patients was 47.5 years. All but one was studied in the first 1 or 2 months post-onset. CT scans were made of all patients. Their lesion sites were divided into five groups, and language behavior patterns of each group were summarized.

Group 1 (putamen and putaminal with deep frontal extension). Three patients in this group showed a slow, dysarthric, effortful, monotonous speech. Auditory comprehension was normal in three of the five cases. Writing showed mild impairment, with word finding difficulty. These patients were somewhat similar to cases of Broca's or transcortical motor aphasia in that they had right hemiplegia, effortful speech, and good comprehension. On the other hand, they were more fluent and could repeat more words than patients with Broca's aphasia.

Group 2 (putamen with posterior extension involving the auditory radiation in the temporal isthmas). Three out of the five in this group showed moderate comprehension deficits, with paraphasic and slightly dysprosodic speech. Two had effortful speech. Reading and writing were mildly impaired. All cases had difficulties with confrontation object naming.

Group 3 (putamen with wider extension anteriorly and posteriorly). Three of the five patients in this group underwent an operation because of the larger hematoma. One became mute initially and another had a choking problem. The majority in this group showed fast recovery in auditory comprehension but little recovery of speech.

Group 4 (internal capsule). There were three patients in this group. They tended to have only mild transient dysarthric speech. Language was otherwise normal.

Group 5 (putamen and thalamus). The two patients in this group generally showed fluent speech but somewhat confused behavior (e.g., a patient answered "twenty" when asked how many children he had). There was mild to moderate auditory comprehension impairment.

Eighteen of the these 20 cases had complete right hemiplegia and two had right hemiparesis. After rehabilitation, two of the patients had almost complete motor recovery, but the rest had lasting right hemiplegia. One pattern of lesions involving the putamen is that the precentral gyrus area tends to be involved and this controls motor functions of the face, lips, and tongue. Thus, patients tend to have dysarthric speech.

5.3.16 X. T. Li, Hu, Zhu, Song, and Y. Li (1986)

A total of 123 cases of acute cerebral vascular accidents admitted between 1980 and 1983 at Tian-Tan Hospital, Beijing, were reviewed. Of these, 87 were male and 36 female. Also, 117 of them were right-handed, 2 left-handed, and 4 ambidextrous. Fifty-seven of the cases with cortical lesions were reviewed in the article under discussion, and the rest with subcortical lesions were discussed in another (Y. L. Zhu, Song, Y. Li, X. T. Li, & Hu, 1986; discussed in the following subsection). Patients with ischemic or hemorrhagic lesions were included but not those with subarachnoid hemorrhage or brain stem lesions. Disorders were classified into seven types (see Table 5.5), as follows:

Nonverbal disorder. This type appeared to include simply those with no language abnormality. All 16 cases were right-handers, 11 had right-hemisphere lesions, and 5 left-hemisphere lesions.

Nonaphasic verbal disorder. There were 19 right-handers and one ambidextrous patient of this type. Patients were judged to be suffering consciousness impairment, memory and attentional deficits, and there was one case of hysterical mutism. It was judged that their language performance was not related to language impairment per se.

TABLE 5.5
Language Disorders and Cortical Lesion sites (Group Data)

Language Disorders	Cortical Lesions	
	Left Hemisphere	Right Hemisphere
Nonverbal disorders	5	11
Nonaphasic verbal disorders	16	3
Phonetic disorders	2	3
Mixed aphasia	4	0
Expressive aphasia	9	0
Receptive aphasia	2	0
Alexia, agraphia	2	0
Total	40	17

Source: X.T. Li et al. (1986).

Phonetic disorder. All five cases were right-handers. Three had right-hemisphere lesions and two had left-hemisphere lesions. One showed dysarthria and four showed dysprosody. They slurred their pronunciations and spoke with a nasal tone. This disappeared from 2 to 20 days after hospitalization.

Mixed aphasia. All four cases were right-handers with left-hemisphere lesions. They showed both receptive and expressive aphasia. However, they were alert. They passed a picture matching test.

Expressive aphasia. All nine were right-handers. They had intact auditory comprehension, although five of them initially had mixed aphasia. Symptoms were phonetic disorder (including phonemic paraphasia and perseveration), word-finding difficulty (with stammering and telegraphic speech), naming difficulty (with poor performance in an object-naming test, although patients were able to pick the right word from among alternatives), and lack of spontaneous speech.

Receptive aphasia. There were two cases, both right-handers with left-hemisphere lesions. They had impaired speech comprehension and gave irrelevant answers, with paraphasia but no dysarthria. However, there was some speech perserveration.

Alexia and agraphia. There were two cases, both with left-hemisphere lesions, but no details were provided.

In all of these classifications, there was a total of 40 patients with nonaphasic language disorders in which language performance was mainly affected by attentional and memory impairment rather than language impairment per se. Of these, 17 cases had right-hemisphere lesions. However, in all the 17 cases of genuine aphasic disorders, patients had left-hemisphere lesions.

5.3.17 Y. L. Zhu, Song, Y. Li, X. T. Li, and Hu, 1986.

This article reviewed 66 cases of subcortical lesions admitted to the Tian-Tan Hospital, Beijing, between 1980 and 1983. The subcortical structures involved included the corpus striatum, internal capsule, thalamus, and subcortical white matter near the lateral ventricle. Location of lesions were confirmed by CT scan. The patients were 47 males and 19 females, aged from 30 to over 70. There were 40 cases of cerebral hemorrhage and 26 cases of infarction. The disorders of these patients were classified into five types (see Table 5.6), as follows:

Nonverbal disorder. Fifteen cases, all right-handers, showed no speech abnormality. Twelve cases had right-hemisphere and three had left-hemisphere lesions.

Nonaphasic verbal disorder. There were 13 cases: 10 right-handers and 3

TABLE 5.6
Language Disorders and Subcortical Lesion Sites (Group Data)

	Subcortical Lesions	
Language Disorders	Left Hemisphere	Right Hemisphere
Nonverbal disorders	3	12
Nonaphasic verbal disorders	10	3
Phonetic disorders	18	10
Mixed aphasia	2	0
Expressive aphasia	7	1
Total	40	26

Source: Y.L. Zhu et al. (1986).

left-handers. Ten had left-hemisphere and 3 had right-hemisphere lesions (but the handedness of the 3 with right-hemisphere lesions was not identified). The language impairment of these patients was attributed to consciousness, memory, or attentional impairment.

Phonetic disorder. There were 28 cases, all right-handers, 18 of whom had left-hemisphere lesions and 10 with right-hemisphere lesions. All the patients were alert. There were 24 cases of dysprosody. Patients usually complained of a stiff and sluggish tongue. On examination it was found to be slightly deviated to the side contralateral to the lesion. The other 4 cases were of dysarthria. All 4 displayed pseudobulbar palsy due to the loss of muscles control of the speech organs. The 4 had bilateral subcortical lesions involving bilateral cortico-bulbar tracts.[2] Of those whose speech functions improved quickly, most had intracerebral hemorrhage, often with a small lesion and slight hemiparesis. But the morbidity of this group was 42.2%, compared with 8.8% for those with cortical lesions leading to phonetic disorders reported in X. T. Li et al. (1986).

Expressive aphasia. There were eight cases: seven right-handers with left-hemisphere lesions and one ambidextrous patient with a right-hemisphere lesion. The main symptoms were absence of spontaneous speech, dysnomia, word-finding difficulty, and difficulty in repeating sentences. Comprehension was mostly good. These subcortical cases of expressive aphasia were generally less severe than the cortical cases reported in X. T. Li et al. (1986). Four of these subcortical cases began as mixed aphasia.

Mixed aphasia. Two cases, both right-handers, had hemorrhagic lesions in the left hemisphere, and were hemiplegic. They did not speak fluently and had dysnomia. They also had poor comprehension.

---

[2] In those patients with multiple lesions, the lesion taken to be responsible for the clincial symptoms was considered as the major lesion. (It is not clear how this is actually done or whether it is valid.) This determined the general right/left-hemisphere lesion classification for each patient.

To summarize, only 1 out of 10 patients with aphasia had right-hemisphere lesion and that patient was ambidextrous. Most of the subcortical language disorders were phonetic disorders, which usually took less time to recover. A lesion in the thalamus generally caused nonaphasic verbal disorders. Subcortical aphasia was less severe than cortical aphasia. Phonetic disorders, mainly dysprosody, were not only caused by lesions in the hemisphere contralateral to the preferred hand, but also in the ipsilateral hemisphere. It was suggested that lateralization of language functions could begin at the subcortical level.

5.3.18 X. Wang (1986)

This article reported on mirror writing in samples of preschool children, school children, normal adults, and cerebral vascular disease patients with or without aphasia. Some mirror writing was found in a group of preschool children, aged from 5 to 7, consisting of 16 boys and 15 girls. The children were asked to write their names, Arabic numerals, and some characters. Instances of mirror writing were found in 8 of the children when they were asked to write with their right hand, and 16 of the children when asked to write with the left hand (the children's handedness was not reported). Sixteen of the children were also reported to show some left/right disorientation when asked to "raise up your left hand" and "touch your left ear with your right hand." Nine of these 16 showed mirror writing. (The incidence of left/right disorientation appears high, but no details of the condition in which the tests were carried out were available.)

Forty first-grade children were also tested: 23 boys and 17 girls, aged from 6 to 8 years. They were asked to write similar things as the preschoolers, with one and then the other hand. There was no mirror writing with the right hand, but 4 children showed partial mirror writing when asked to write with the left hand. Nine children were found to show some left/right disorientation, and 2 of these showed partial mirror writing.

Forty right-handed adults were also tested: 9 males and 31 females, aged from 22 to 51. They were asked to do dictation, spontaneous writing, copying, and filling in blanks with their left hands. None of the adults showed left/right disorientation, but one showed partial mirror writing.

Patients with cerebral vascular diseases, 27 with aphasia and 10 without, were similarly tested. Nine of the aphasic patients wrote with the right hand, but the rest could only write with the left hand due to right hemiplegia. None of the 9 showed any mirror writing. But among the 18 who had to write with their left hand, 6 showed partial mirror writing and 1 showed exclusive mirror writing. Six of the nonaphasic patients had left hemiplegia and wrote with their right hand, showing no mirror writing. The other 4 had right hemiplegia and wrote with their left hand (the handedness of these patients was not given). Two of these 4 writing with their left hand showed partial mirror writing.

Partial mirror writing included reversing the left–right, upper–lower location of components of characters, mirror writing of numerals, and reversing some stroke direction. Left/right disorientation is one of the causal factors of mirror writing but could not account for all the data. It was suggested that mirror-writing motor schemas are developed in the right cerebral hemisphere together with graphic motor schemas in the left hemisphere. The latter are usually more dominant than mirror writing motor schemas but might be less developed in children.

5.3.19 X. Wang and Cai (1986)

This article reviewed 25 patients with agraphia at Beijing Hospital. They were 23 males and 2 females, aged from 56 to 76, with a mean of 56.9 years. Seventeen had cerebral thrombosis and 8 had cerebral hemorrhage. However, there were no details concerning handedness and location of lesions. Patients were examined upon admission and twice more, in 1 month intervals. The following classification of agraphia was made.

Total agraphia. This was a severe form of agraphia, with patients being able to write strokes but not any character. Patients frequently had global aphasia or sensory aphasia.

Contructional disorder in writing. This was marked by producing extra strokes or having missing strokes in writing characters.

Repetitive writing phenomenon. A patient with a large low density area in the left hemisphere had global aphasia. Once he completed a character in copying, taking dictation, or writing from memory, he would persist in writing the same character.

Pictographic writing. When writing down names of pictures, patients drew pictures instead.

Writing overproduction. Patients overproduced characters when writing, such as during dictation. Many of the characters produced were improper and extra. A corresponding situation could take place with speech.

Mirror writing. A 62-year-old male patient had a left thalamic hemorrhage and right hemiplegia. He had a slight degree of agraphia and produced mirror writing.

In general, agraphia was more severe in patients with global or sensory aphasia and might be due to extensive lesion in the parieto–occipital region of the dominant hemisphere associated with contructional apraxia. Copying was relatively better, but more severe impairment was found in copying dictation, writing down names of pictures, and filling in blanks. In dictation, performance for characters with similar shapes was better than for those with similar pronunciations or meanings.

5.3.20 O. J. L. Tzeng, Hung, Chen, Wu, and Hsi (1986)

This article presented evidence from aphasia studies refuting the view that the right hemisphere is more involved with processing Chinese because of the visual-pictorial aspects of the script. In the first part of the article, the performance of two patients in Taiwan was compared. Their sex was not specified. CT scan showed that one had a central infarction in the left posterior parietal area (the LH patient), and the other a midline shift to the left side with compression of the right lateral ventricle, an area of increased attenuation at the right basal ganglia and also right deep parietal lobe (the RH patient). The LH patient was 55 years old, right-handed, and a mechanical engineer with 16 years of education. He or she spoke the native Taiwanese dialect and Mandarin. The patient had no hemiplegia and no hemianopsia, and was diagnosed as having conduction aphasia, agraphia, and alexia. The RH patient was 55 years old, right-handed, had 9 years of education, and was a driver. He or she had no hemiplegia, no hemianopsia, and no aphasia.

The two patients were given two types of tasks. One involved copying geometric figures, Chinese characters, pseudocharacters (not characters in use but formed with components in their conventional locations and therefore with permissible appearance), and noncharacters (orthographically not permissible). Items were presented one by one. It was reported that both patients copied the Chinese characters well, but it was not clear how many items were involved or whether they were copied onto a matrix. For the pseudocharacters and noncharacters, the patients were asked to copy items onto a matrix of 7 x 10 squares, starting from the top-left corner and copying the items one by one into each square in an orderly sequence. The other tasks included drawing pictures of 10 objects, writing down multi-character names of pictures, and constructing 10 sentences.

For copying geometric figures, the LH patient performed perfectly but the RH patient showed visual field neglect, omitting the left side of the figures. For copying pseudocharacters and noncharacters onto a matrix, the LH patient could do most of them, although there were occasional hesitations, erasing initial attempts, revising, as well as deleting. He or she copied items into the top-left square and onward in an orderly fashion, as instructed. The RH patient, on the other hand, started to copy the first item into the top-left square but then showed a tendency to put the following items on the right side of the matrix, leaving squares on the left side blank. Although the RH patient showed this general problem with the spatial framework of the matrix, he or she also showed a difference between copying pseudocharacters and noncharacters. Pseudocharacters conforming to orthgraphic conventions were copied correctly and without hesitation. But for noncharacters, not following orthographic constraints for character formation, there was a tendency to omit the left-side components, rather like the situation with drawing nonlinguistic figures. Thus, the RH patient performed well with regards to materials formed according to orthographic rules, but not quite so well with other visual-pictorial matters. The LH patient showed the reverse performance pattern, carrying out visual-pictorial tasks well.

In spontaneous drawing the LH patient had no difficulties, but the RH patient again showed visual neglect in the left visual field. In writing down names of pictures, the RH patient showed no difficulties, but the LH patient made errors of omission and commission, usually leaving out parts of characters while maintaining the overall relative locations of the rest of the characters. Thus, the two patients provided evidence that Chinese characters are not handled like pictures.

A visual gluing procedure was also adopted by the authors to test the ability of aphasic patients to maintain the sequential relations of components of characters presented separately, in order to identify characters. High frequency characters of up to nine strokes were used. They were divided into three to five fragments according to their stroke composition. These fragments were presented on separate cards and the patients had to identify the characters from the sequence of fragments presented. They were allowed to engage in finger tracing to help in the identification of half the items, but not for the other half. Six patients, all right handed males, speaking either their native Taiwanese or Mandarin, were tested. Two of the patients had right-hemisphere lesions, two had left-frontal lesions, and the remaining two had left-posterior lesions. The results quite clearly indicated the importance of the left hemisphere for the visual gluing task. Both the RH patients, with or without finger tracing, were almost perfect in identifying the fragmented characters in their mind's eye. The LH patients performed much worse, although finger tracing did help. The two anterior patients showed moderate impairment. With the two posterior patients, identification was a complete failure, although with finger tracing there was some improvement, particularly in one of them.

The authors suggested the possibility that somewhere in the parietal area and adjacent to the visual cortex is where graphomotoric schemas for integrating features into characters are formed. Patients who traced the strokes with their fingers, sometimes without even being aware of doing so, could be trying to evoke proprioceptive memory of writing characters.

5.3.21 Packard (1986)

This article compared tonal production of a group of aphasic patients in Taiwan with that of a control group from Taiwan as well as Beijing. The aphasic patients were six males and two females, aged from 21 to 66, all right-handed, and native Mandarin speakers. They were mild to moderate nonfluent aphasics but had no dysarthria. They all had unilateral left hemisphere damage. Four had infarction, one had hemorrhage, two had trauma, and one had a tumor. The eight controls were matched with the aphasics according to age, sex, and dialect area.

Sixteen monosyllabic words and 16 bisyllabic words were used. The monsyllables consisted of any one of four syllable-initial types, a vowel, and one of the four tones. The bisyllables were systematically varied to test for the possible effect of tonal environment on tonal error. All of the patients were given the items in a word-repetition task.

The aphasic group made many more errors than the control group, both for the consonants of words and tones. The number of tonal errors was not significantly different from the number of consonant errors. In the case of bisyllabic words, tone errors were not significantly influenced by syllable-initial consonant or by tonal environment. Substitution errors predominated, and their number was greater than those of distortions, omissions, and additions combined. Substitutions mostly involved responses that differed from the target on one distinctive feature only.

Although right-hemisphere lateralization for musical, tonal, and intonational stimuli has been generally reported in the literature, it was suggested that lexical specification of tones in the case of Chinese resulted in left-hemisphere lateralization. Tones in Chinese, like consonants, are listed in the lexicon as unit phonemes.

5.4 REVIEW OF THE APHASIA LITERATURE

From the small body of Chinese aphasia literature just summarized, we can extract the following possibilities that have been entertained concerning the way in which Chinese language functions might be handled differently, some of which eventually have been contradicted by evidence:

1. Chinese language functions could be more lateralized in the right hemisphere.
2. They could be localized more posteriorly, involving the parietal and occipital lobes.
3. Psycho-motor schemas could play a greater role in memory for Chinese words.
4. Tones in Chinese could entail a different localization pattern.

5.4.1 Right Hemisphere Involvement

Let us first look at the question of right-hemisphere involvement for Chinese (see Table 5.7 for a summary of studies of individuals with reported lesion sites and impairments). This possibility is suggested by some distinc-

TABLE 5.7
Lesion Sites and Language Disorder

Authors	Handedness	Site	Aphasia
Lyman et al. (1938)	?	L occi.-pari.	Alexia and agraphia
April & Tse (1977)	R	R mid. cere. arte.	Nonfluent aphasia
T'sou (1978)	R	L post. temp.-pari.	Conduction aphasia
April & Han (1980)	R	R mid. cere. arte.	Nonfluent aphasia
Naeser & Chan (1980)	R	L temp. & pari.	Mixed aphasia
Wang & Li (1981)	R	L occi. temp.	Dysgraphia
Rapport et al. (1983)	R	L temp.	—
	R	L mid. infe. front.	Min. nonf. nom. aph.
	R	R temp.	—
	R	R frontal	—
	R	L mid. cere. arte. & front.-pari.	Mute
	R	L front.-pari.	Dense global aphasia
	R	L temp.	(insufficient data)
X. T. Li et al. (1984)	R	L temp.-pari.	Alexia & agraphia
C. Y. Huang & Lau (1985)	R	L striatocapsular	Aphasia and dysgraphia
Hong et al. (1986)	R	L putamen w. ante.	Apraxia
	R	L putamen w. post.	Dysarthria & paraphasia
	R	L putamen w. wide	Global aphasia
	R	L internal capsule	Inappropriate rhythm
	R	L putamen w. thal.	Paraphasia with melody
Y. L. Zhu et al. (1986)	L	L thalamus	Nonaphasic verbal
	R	L putamen	Phonetic disorder
	R	L external capsule	Expressive aphasia
	L	L external capsule	Mixed aphasia
O. J. L. Tzeng et al. (1986)	R	L pari.	Conduction aphasia, alexia, agraphia
	R	R basal ganglia & deep pari.	—
	R	R basal ganglia	—
	R	R caudate	—
	R	L basal ganglia	Mild dysarthria
	R	L frontal	Broca's aphasia, apraxia
	R	L pari.	Conduction aphasia, agraphia, Gerstmann
	R	L pari. posterial temp.	Nom. aphasia, agraphia

occi. = occipital	nonf. = nonfluent
pari. = parietal	nom. = nominal
mid. = middle	aph. = aphasia
cere. arte. = cerebral artery	stari. = stariatocapsular
temp. = temporal	w. ante. = with anterior extension
infe. = inferior	w. post. = with posterior extension
front. = frontal	w. wide = with wider anterior & posterior extension
min. = minimal	w. thal. = with thalamus
	L/R = Left/Right

tive characteristics of the language. The orthography does not have sequential units of graphemes representing phonemes, but perceptual wholes representing syllables on their own. And one dichotomy taken to distinguish functions of the left and right hemispheres is sequential/holistic processing. Some earlier experimental studies also indicated a different lateralization pattern for Chinese characters. However, it would seem quite clear now, with much more evidence known, that the aphasia literature does not indicate greater involvement of the right hemisphere for Chinese.

Although April and Tse (1977) and April and Han (1980) found two individual cases of crossed aphasia, with right-handed subjects having right-hemisphere lesions showing language impairment, it became increasingly obvious that this was not going to be the general pattern. The survey of the larger samples of patients of unreported size, mentioned in April and Han (1980), did not find any incidence of crossed aphasia higher than the 4% upper limit cited in Western literature. Around 4% of right handed people have speech functions lateralized in the right hemisphere anyway. It is therefore doubtful if these occasional reports of crossed aphasia amount to anything, as far as the hypothesis of altered hemispheric dominance for nonalphabetic languages is concerned. Another point that should be noted is that many of the Chinese aphasic patients studied were bilinguals, and there are some reports of a higher incidence of crossed aphasia among bilinguals in general (see Albert & Obler, 1978).

There are now more reports that provide a clearer picture of the incidence of right- and left-hemisphere damage causing language impairment. C. Y. Huang (1982) referred to more than a dozen cases he had studied, with only one case of right hemisphere damage. Rapport et al. (1983) studied seven cases and found no evidence that Chinese involved the right hemisphere more. The report by Guo (1984) provided the highest incidence of crossed aphasia. In a survey of 150 cases of right-handed patients, Guo found that 75% of the 81 patients with left-hemisphere damage had aphasia, but only 19% of the 69 patients with right-hemisphere damage had aphasia. These figures still indicate a predominant left-hemisphere specialization, although the incidence does not appear to be as high as in some other reports. In their review of the polyglot aphasia literature, Albert and Obler (1978) noted up to a 17% incidence of crossed aphasia. Although it is unlikely that the patients in Guo's survey were bilinguals, they would quite probably speak more than one Chinese dialect.

The series of 123 cases reported by X. T. Li et al. (1986) and Y. L. Zhu et al. (1986) is probably most revealing. They covered one of the largest group of patients reported, and the authors are leading neurologists of the People's Republic of China. Of the 57 cases with cortical lesions, 17 out of the 40 cases with nonaphasic language disorders had right-hemisphere lesions, but none of the 17 cases of aphasic disorders had right-hemisphere lesions. In the 66 cases of subcortical lesions, 25 out of the 56 cases with nonaphasic language disorders had right-hemisphere lesions, but only one patient (who was ambidextrous) out of the 10 with aphasic disorder had right-hemisphere damage. It is quite clear from these studies that specialization for language tends to be in the left hemisphere for the Chinese, as for speakers of alphabetic languages. This conclusion is similar to that drawn by Paradis et al. (1985) after they surveyed 69 cases of Japanese aphasia and found only five with right-hemisphere damage.

Studies of people using American Sign Language (ASL) further provide us with some insight into the relationship between the nature of a language and lateralization of functions. ASL is a full-fledged language, autonomous and not just a mimicry of spoken language (Klima & Bellugi, 1979). However it is a language in the visual-spatial mode, based on the production and comprehension of hand configuration, location, and movement. Thus, meanings of signs are based on "ideographic" representation, just as Chinese words are.

There are indications that the left cerebral hemisphere subserves ASL, just as it does spoken languages. For example, A. Damasio, Bellugi, H. Damasio, Poizner, and Van Gilder (1986) reported on a right-handed hearing woman who was a native English speaker and also a skilled ASL user. The Wada test (see subsection 5.3.9) was performed prior to her operation for treatment of seizures. Injection of a barbiturate into the left carotid system resulted in aphasia in both English and ASL. Furthermore, after partial ablation of the right temporal lobe, ability to use English as well as produce and understand ASL was unchanged. Such studies with ASL users indicate that language lateralization in the left hemisphere is independent of the modality of language, whether auditory–vocal or visual–spatial.

5.4.2 Occipito-Parietal Involvement

There are some indications, although not overwhelming, that the occipito-parietal areas might be more involved in Chinese language functions. This, of course, echoes the conclusion of Paradis et al. (1985) for greater involvement of the occipito–parietal areas for Japanese kanji, in contrast to the temporal lobe for kana. In the earliest report, Lyman et al. (1938) found that a Chinese-English bilingual man with alexia and agraphia had an occipito-parietal tumor. There was greater impairment of reading and writing of Chinese compared with English, although the patient was supposed to be equally fluent in the two languages prior to his illness. But the seven patients of Rapport et al. (1983) showed no evidence indicating greater involvement of the occipital cortex than the usual language centers of the posterior sylvian fissure. However, in a cortical stimulation study of three of the patients, there was evidence indicating differential localization for Chinese and English within the left hemisphere. In two of the cases, errors in Chinese resulted from stimulation of scattered sites more remote from the usual posterior language areas. But the reverse was found in the third case.

In reports on agraphia, there are some indications of involvement of the occipital region. X. Wang and Li (1981), considered that impairment in the retention of the visual code of characters was the main cause of pure dysgraphia in their patient who had an occipito-temporal infarct. X. Wang and Cai (1986) also suggested that agraphia was more severe in cases with extensive lesion in the occipito–parietal region.

The findings concerning occipito–parietal lesions were only based on incidental observations. However, the study by O. J. L. Tzeng ct al. (1986) deliberately compared two right-hemisphere, two anterior left-hemisphere, and two posterior left-hemisphere patients. There was strong indication that more posterior lesions impaired identification of characters in the visual gluing task. This led to their suggestions that the parietal area and the adjacent visual cortex were more relevant for the formation of graphomotoric schemas, for integrating features of Chinese characters. This plays a role in reading and writing. However, in the absence of more evidence along this line, greater involvement of the occipito–pariental region for Chinese should remain an intriguing possibility to be kept in mind, rather than taken as conclusively demonstrated. The body of Chinese aphasia literature is much smaller than the Japanese, and it may be a little premature at the moment to make the same conclusion.

5.4.3 Pycho-Motor Schema

A number of reports have pointed to the relevance of psycho-motor schemas in reading and writing Chinese. The schema developed in writing characters appears to constitute a whole sequence of constituent movements. This is indicated by the patient of Naeser and Chan (1980) who managed to write some characters but not in the traditional stroke sequence. She would then rewrite them in the correct sequence. It was as if the psycho-motor sequence formed an integral whole that needed to be preserved. This patient had severe impairment to all language functions with minimal improvement after 2 years. Yet, recognition and writing of single characters (but not two-character words) were largely spared. This suggested that individual complete motor schemas, corresponding to visual Gestalt wholes, have a certain integrity that is absent in multicharacter schemas.

The independent existence of such motor schemas is suggested by the patients reported by C. Y. Huang (1982) who could complete high proportions of incomplete characters without being able to read them. Some investigators (Lyman et al., 1938; O. J. L. Tzeng et al., 1986) reported that their patients finger traced a sequence of character strokes which appeared to help in their attempt to read the characters. Sometimes they appeared to finger trace without being aware of doing so.

O. J. L. Tzeng et al. (1986) found that finger tracing helped the two patients with anterior damage only marginally, but helped one of the two posterior damage patients more, from 0% correct identification of characters to 25%. It is possible that in the long experience of character writing drills by Chinese children, the posterior parietal area is involved in handling proprioceptive cues built up in these repetitive psycho-motor sequences. This might turn out to be related to the possible greater involvement of the parietal lobe in Chinese.

There are references to the use of letter-tracing behavior in speakers of alphabetic languages to help in reading words (e.g., Benson & Geschwind, 1969, referred to such a patient of Charcot). This practice appears to be less common than letter-by-letter reading. In the latter case, patients who speak alphabetic languages find it necessary to spell out individual letters before they can read the word (cf., Beaumont, 1983). Nothing corresponding to letter-by-letter reading is reported in the Chinese aphasia literature. But finger tracing appears to play a greater role. This could also be related to the greater emphasis on handwriting in Chinese. An educated person is expected to be able to write with some finesse, and penmanship with the traditional brush and ink is still assigned homework through secondary school grades in Hong Kong. Works by accomplished calilgraphers are treated as fine art and bring in good sums. This might explain the report by Lyman et al. (1938) that their patient wrote more tidily in Chinese than in English, even though his Chinese was generally more impaired.

X. Wang (1985, 1986) suggested that at the same time as motor schemas are developed in the contralateral hemisphere during writing practice, mirror-writing motor schemas are developed in the ipsilateral hemisphere. This postulation accounts for the higher incidence of mirror writing when patients switch their writing hand when they have hemiplegia affecting the preferred hand. In such a case, the previously ipsilateral hemisphere assumes control of the writing hand. However, it might be possible to explain the higher incidence of mirror writing using the nonpreferred hand without postulating a mirror-writing motor schema. Switching hands itself involves some left-right shifts, for example, in the relative locations of the writing instrument and one's eyes. In any case, it is difficult to see what function a complementary mirror-writing motor schema might serve in the first place, developing side by side with the regular motor schema.

5.4.4 Tones

In addition to the orthography, another distinctive feature of Chinese is the use of tones. Aphasia studies indicate that the left hemisphere specializes in processing Chinese tones, even though the literature in general shows that the right hemisphere is more involved with musical, tonal, or intonational stimuli (e.g., Mazzucchi, Parma, & Cattelani, 1981, on the perception of synthesized tones). The report by Packard (1986), comparing eight aphasic subjects with left-hemisphere damage and eight control subjects, quite unambiguously showed that tone production in Chinese is lateralized in the left hemisphere. Packard (1986) suggested that this lateralization is the result of the lexical specification of tones in the Chinese language, that tones make a difference to lexical meaning.

However, impairment of processing of tones is to be contrasted with that of prosody. The former has a semantic function in Chinese, whereas the latter has an affective import. Hughes et al. (1983) showed that right hemisphere damage resulted in aprosodia in Chinese subjects, as in the case with English speakers. However, the same right-damaged Chinese subjects did not show much deficit in semantic tonal identification. Y. L. Zhu et al. (1986) also reported that sub-cortical lesions in the right hemisphere could cause aprosodia. It appears then that the perception of tones is specialized in the left hemisphere, even though other aspects of pitch variation that indicate the affective component of meaning might still be specialized in the right hemisphere.

In normal subjects, Tsang and Hoosain (1979) found that sentence pairs that differed in only a single character with different vowel sounds were distinguished better than those with characters differing in a tone. This could be explained by saying that tonal differences are due to pitch variations of degree, but segmental phonemes like vowels are categorized according to distinctive features. This nature of tonal differences, together with any disinclination to perceive tonal variations as having lexical implication (i.e., having meaning) could be one underlying reason why non-Chinese speakers find it difficult to master the tonal language. The finding of greater right hemisphere involvement in auditory discrimination of Chinese sounds by English-Chinese bilinguals (cf., O. J. L. Tzeng, 1988) could be related to some degree of failure to appreciate the lexical implication of tones in Chinese. In perception of musical material, there are reports that trained musicians and nonmusicians have different lateralization patterns. Bever and Chiarello (1974) found left-hemisphere advantage for musicians but right-hemisphere advantage for non-musicians. It could be that nonmusicians, just as nonnative speakers, tend to perceive sounds in a more disintegrated manner. It would be interesting if further work attempts to relate the two phenomena.

5.4.5 Other Suggestions

Whereas studies reviewed in section 3.2 on perceptual units quite clearly do not suggest perceptual salience for components of characters, a few reports in the aphasia literature indicate that components of characters are sometimes substituted. This was found, for example, with the patient of Lyman et al. (1938) who substituted characters sharing component radicals while filling in blanks [9]. Similar substitutions have been reported by C. Y. Huang (1984). C. Y. Huang and Lau (1985) reported a patient who produced new characters made up of recombination of components. In these examples, we are looking at functioning with impairment instead of normal functioning. Also, these were instances of writing instead of perception. The components involved can often function as characters on their own. With a breakdown in normal functioning, it could become possible that a dissociation "at the joint" occurred. A similar situation occurs when normal people have difficulty remembering how to write a character, and hesitation occurs at the junction of components. Sometimes, finger tracing helps to bridge the gap. In normal perceptual functioning, on the other hand, we have evidence that characters as wholes have perceptual salience.

A suggestion has been made that there is a greater tendency to dissociate the comprehension of word meaning and the pronunciation of their sounds in Chinese aphasia (C. Y. Huang 1982, 1984). This is attributed to the special script-sound-meaning relationship of Chinese orthography. However, in the absence of documented cases that allow cross-language comparison it is difficult to evaluate the suggestion. Nevertheless, it is a very plausible hypothesis and would be consistent with many of the other phenomena we have reviewed in this book, based on the direct script–sound and script–meaning relationships of the written word.

5.5 CONCLUSION

Neurolinguistic studies of Chinese are beginning to provide some answers to questions arising from the uniqueness of the Chinese orthography. In perceptual studies, the view that lateralization is function-specific rather than language-specific appears to be a generally sound one. There are indications that the same variables affect the lateralization of perception of Chinese and English words. Apart from single Chinese characters, with their own convergence of properties, Chinese words show similar perceptual lateralization patterns as units of other languages. Single characters tend to show a greater fluctuation of hemifield superiority because of a combination of perceptual and possibly linguistic factors.

In aphasia studies, there is again little evidence to suggest any overwhelming neurolinguistic effects of Chinese language uniqueness. It is now possible to say with some confidence that the right hemisphere is not more involved in handling Chinese in any significant sense, although early reports might lead to such a view. There is some suggestion that occipito–parietal areas might play a greater role in processing Chinese, but more investigation is needed to clarify the issue. Tones play a special role in Chinese and make a difference to meaning. But perhaps precisely because of this lexical function of tones, their processing is also lateralized in the left hemisphere, even though perception of musical tones and intonation is lateralized in the right hemisphere. There are indications, however, that the psycho-motor schema play a greater role in Chinese, largely due to the configuration of characters.

Despite the various suggestions of some difference in individual aspects of processing Chinese, there is no picture of a fundamentally different neurolinguistic mechanism in handling the language on the whole. Perhaps universal aspects of language are the overriding factor in the general neural mechanism for language processing.

6 Conclusion

The studies reviewed in this book do not point to any language effects that result in different conceptualizations of the world. Rather, they indicate some instances of different manners and facilitation of information processing. Many of these effects involve data-driven processes, and these do not appear to matter so much when leading to higher-up processes (see Hung & Tzeng, 1981). However, there are some important aspects of cognitive functioning with pervasive implications that are related to the use of the Chinese language and orthography. They include functions of working memory, including manipulation of numbers and perception of visual–spatial relations. They also include reading, as revealed by eye-movements and reading problems. Chinese language learning experience is also part of the picture of cognitive style in which the Chinese are more inclined to engage in tasks with well-defined goals and less in open-ended expression. Table 6.1 lists the more specific psycholinguistic characteristics of Chinese.

The language features that are related to much of these psycholinguistic properties include the convergence of script, sound, and meaning units in the Chinese character and the relationship among these three aspects of language. Pronunciation is not spelled out in Chinese, but each syllable is associated directly with the whole character. Meaning is also represented directly by each character. The manner in which the written character is constituted and the manner in which they in turn constitute different multisyllabic words and larger units of language lead to the many psycholinguistic characteristics of Chinese.

TABLE 6.1
Distinctive Chinese Psycholinguistic Characteristics
(Contrasted Primarily with English)

	Process Itself—Mainly[a]	Implications Higher Up?
Perceptual		
Visual acuity: no orientation difference	(b)	?
Directional scanning: preference depends on experience	(b)	?
Perceptual units: words; but characters, even as bound morphemes, retain some individuality	(b)	Could influence saccadic length particularly if reader attends
Phonological access: could be slower in some situations	(b)	to sound of individual characters.
Phonological recoding: less involved for individual words	(b)	Could be related to reports of smooth
Access to meaning: more direct for individual words	(b)	eye movements in reading (?)
Eye movements in reading: (i) saccadic movement shorter physically but comparable in terms of word units (ii) some unusual smooth movement	(a) & (b)	Reading habit
Memory		
Digit span: bigger	(b)	Greater working memory
Visual code of characters: plays greater role compared with English	(b)	facility: implication for mathematics
Psycho-motor code of characters: plays some role	(b)	?
Characters form different associative networks compared with English words	(a)	Affects semantic structure
Reading problems: script–sound associations require only memorization	(a) & (b)	(Correlated with cognitive style strong in memorization and weak in open-ended expression)
Neurolinguistic		
Experimental studies: differential lateralization of sigle-character and two-character words	(b)	?
Some indication of weaker lateralization of auditory functions of second language for Chinese-English bilinguals	(b)	?
Aphasia studies: No evidence of more right hemisphere involvement; some indication of more posterior involvement	(b)	?
General		
Bilingual carry-over effect from Chinese to second language (English)	(a?) & (b)	?

[a](a) = top-down   (b) = bottom-up

6.1 PERCEPTUAL ASPECTS

In visual perception, we have seen how the possibility of writing Chinese text horizontally as well as vertically affects both visual acuity and directional scanning. Chinese speakers do not share the native English speakers' better visual acuity for horizontal versus vertical arrays of linguistic items. Similarly, preferred direction of scan in visual perception is somewhat influenced by the extent of experience with horizontal or vertical texts. In perception of words, there are some indications that the character retains some individuality in multicharacter words, largely due to its property of being a sensory whole. Getting at the sound of characters could be slower, without grapheme–phoneme conversion rules, but getting at the meaning of individual words is in turn more direct.

On the other hand, when it comes to reading continuous text, the speed of getting at the meaning of individual words is not usually reflected in the speed of eye movements. Although Chinese texts are visually more dense than English, and fixation times for Chinese are comparable to those of native English speakers reading English text, saccadic lengths for reading Chinese are shorter. As a result, reading speed for Chinese and English texts become comparable. It is not entirely clear whether this compensating shorter saccadic length for reading Chinese is caused by bottom-up processes, such as related to the absence of space markers for word boundaries over and above those for morpheme (character) boundaries, or caused by a higher-up functioning limit, in terms of the amount of information represented by the sensory input that can be handled. In the latter case, eye-movement speed for Chinese has to be held back to accommodate universal limits in the cognitive mechanism. However, that this holding back is in terms of saccadic length rather than fixation time suggests that it has more to do with sensory information than a higher-up bottleneck. There is some possibility though that it has to do with the habit of pronouncing each character, overtly or covertly.

6.2 MEMORY ASPECTS

In memory aspects of the Chinese language, the shorter sound duration for number names in Chinese, with the corresponding larger digit span, offers the clearest example of how language difference could affect the facilitation of information processing (and this is not the result of the orthography as such). In terms of Baddeley's working memory model (e.g., Baddeley, 1983), shorter sound durations allow more numbers to be held in working memory or, alternately, provide more room for manipulation of a given set of numbers. There are quite convincing correlational data to indicate that such facilitation of information processing is related to mathematical performance.

On the other hand, the greater reliance of the Chinese script on visual configuration of strokes or other components of characters means that visual–spatial processing plays a more central role, compared with other languages. There is evidence that the visual code plays a greater role in memory of Chinese compared with English (H. C. Chen & Juola, 1982; Turnage & McGinnes, 1973; O. J. L. Tzeng, 1982). There is also indication that reading disability in Chinese is more related to visual rather than auditory functioning (Woo & Hoosain, 1984). Such evidence of the greater reliance of the Chinese script on visual–spatial processing is matched by indications that Chinese subjects often perform better in tasks involving visual–spatial coding, such as the coding subtest of the Wechsler Intelligence Scale for Children, the Bender Visual Gestalt Test (Pong-Leung, 1983), and the Raven's Progressive Matrices Test (J. Chan, 1976). The possibility that the user of the Chinese script is more adept at visual–spatial coding of information means facilitation in the functioning of the visuo-spatial scratch-pad, the other mechanism of working memory in Baddeley's model. This, of course, is also consistent with facilitation of mathematical functioning.

In longer term memory processes, the nature of the Chinese script could be related to a learning style that relies more on memorization. The underlying language characteristic is the unique script–sound–meaning relationship that can be described as character-as-a-whole to syllable-as-a-whole, as well as character-as-a-whole to meaning. The result is the need to memorize a large number of such associations, although this need is sometimes underestimated (as when the role of the phonetic in phonetic compounds is overemphasized), and other times overestimated (as when the need to learn a few thousand monomorphemic characters is confused with the need to know many more thousands of multimorphemic words made up of these characters). In any case, the discipline needed for memorization is entwined with the traditional authoritarian upbringing in Chinese society. The reliance on memorization comes to be extended to other situations of learning, and the Chinese have come to see memorization tasks as less demanding (M. J. Chen et al., 1982). A cognitive style more conducive to memorization of specific targets rather than engagement in open-ended communication is more typical of the Chinese student. In reading tests, this is characterized by the tendency for weak performance in tests for comprehension of text but not for ability to read characters.

It might be noted that high visual–spatial and low verbal performance has been considered to be the pattern of performance for orientals (Nagoshi, Johnson, & Honbo, 1989). The possibility that such a pattern of performance could be related to learning to read and write characters is supported by the fact that the Chinese script had been borrowed by the Japanese and Koreans, although a phonetic script is also being used in each case.

6.3 NEUROLINGUISTIC ASPECTS

In neurolinguistics, recent work clarifies a number of issues about differential lateralization for Chinese. Different results in hemifield studies between single-character and two-character words have been demonstrated to be largely a function of perceptual variables, although linguistic characteristics might well be relevant. There is no evidence for a greater right-hemisphere involvement for Chinese, although there is some indication of a greater right hemisphere involvement for second-language auditory functions of Chinese-English bilinguals (similar to other bilinguals when the languages concerned are unrelated). Within the left hemisphere, there is some suggestion that Chinese involves the posterior areas more, probably due to the greater role of visual–spatial processing. This is an interesting possibility; more evidence for this still has to be accrued and its implications assessed.

6.4 BILINGUAL CARRY-OVER EFFECTS

An interesting possiblity of top-down effects on cognitive functioning lies in the various reports that distinctive Chinese language behavior patterns were also found in the English performance of Chinese-English bilinguals. Freeman's (1980) Chinese-English bilingual speakers did not show significant horizontal–vertical acuity differences for English letters, as monolingual native English speakers would. Peng et al. (1983) found that the eye-movement patterns of Chinese-English bilinguals for English text resembled those of their patterns for Chinese, in terms of greater number of fixations per physical length of text. (However, in this particular case, there is some likelihood that these speakers' command of English might be responsible for the less than optimal performance.) O. J. L. Tzeng and Wang (1983) found the size incongruity effect for Chinese number names, and Chinese-English bilinguals also demonstrated the effect for English number names, although monolingual native English speakers did not. McClain and Huang (1982) reported that Chinese-English bilinguals could perform simple arithmetic in Chinese faster than English-Chinese bilinguals could perform in English. Furthermore, the Chinese-English bilinguals were also faster when tested in English, compared with English-Chinese bilinguals tested in English. These are the instances of a carry-over effect from native language to second language performance.

Among the few examples of carry-over effect from Chinese to a second language justed cited, it might be appropriate to distinguish between those involving more bottom-up processes, such as visual acuity and size incongruity, and those involving more long-term learning, such as eye movement in reading and arithmetic. The former appears to relate to more basic processes. The latter, however, could be more related to learning achievement or learning habits facilitated by the native language. We should ask whether these carry-over effects are induced within an experimental session or if they are more long term. In both the cases of visual acuity and size incongruity effect, the bilingual speakers were asked to perform in their native language and then, within the same experimental session, perform in the second language. If the order of language of the tasks was reversed and speakers still showed the carry-over effect with the second language task (which is now done prior to the native language version), it would mean that the effect is a more permanent one. Otherwise, this carry-over effect could be more a within-session habituation type of phenomenon. Visual acuity and the size incongruity effect involve quite dissimilar processes. If the carry-over language effect in such diverse situations is a more permanent phenomenon, its mechanism should be worth investigating.

6.5 LINGUISTIC RELATIVITY

According to Brown (1976), Whorf put forward two hypotheses:

1. Structural differences between language systems will, in general, be paralleled by nonlinguistic cognitive differences, of an unspecified sort, in the native speakers of the two languages.
2. The structure of anyone's native language strongly influences or fully determines the world-view acquired as the language is learned.

The area of cognitive experience that has been consistently investigated in relation to linguistic relativity over the last 30 years is that of color experience. The topic more recently investigated regarding Chinese is counterfactual reasoning. Both could provide evidence for language effects on world view, but we have noted that in both cases the weight of the evidence tends not to reinforce the Sapir–Whorf hypothesis (see Chapter 1). In fact, after witnessing attempts over the decades, many people have become less excited about the quest for language effects on world view.

In this book, we have concentrated on other than structure of language or world view. We looked at the script–sound–meaning aspects of the Chinese language (although not exclusively) and their effects on information processing. Quite often, it was not possible to show conclusively that language fully determines the nature of information processing (Hypothesis 2), although there are definite correlations between language characteristics and cognitive performance (Hypothesis 1).

Although we have seen that there are language and orthography differences in the manner and facility of information processing, such differences were not recognized in the original Sapir–Whorf hypothesis of linguistic relativity. The information processing approach in cognitive psychology began after the time of Sapir and Whorf, although the effect of mathematical notations in calculus, for example, on the ease of mental manipulation and problem solving (O. J. L. Tzeng & Hung, 1981) could have been noticeable to Sapir and Whorf. But, in fact, there was a deemphasis of "purely and simply symbolic systems" and their effects. Yet, such effects are an inherent aspect of linguistic relativity, and we might agree with Kay and Kempton (1984) that "The question of what [Sapir and Whorf] thought, although interesting, is after all less important than the issue of what is the case" (p. 77).

APPENDIX

Chapter 2

[1] The strokes are ﹑ , 一 , ｜ , ㇄ , ノ , ㇏ , ㇂ , ㇌ , labeled as 點, 橫, 直, 曲, 撇, 捺, 挑, 鉤 respectively.

[2] 兒

[3] The six characters are respectively 衣, 椅, 意, 兒, 耳, 二.

[4] 林

[5] 信 made up of 亻 meaning 'man' and 言 meaning 'word'.

[6] Such as 洗 'wash', 酒 'wine, and 河 'river'.

[7] 佛 has higher frequency of usage than 弗.

[8] 也 was pronounced as 他.

171

[9] 葡萄

[10] 蟋蟀 means 'cricket', but the second character alone has come to acquire the meaning of the entire two-character word in some usages, such as in 鬥蟀, meaning 'cricket fighting' (a kind of gambling event like cock fighting).

[11] Examples of the types of combination are: for (a) 富貴 , for (b) 動靜 , and for (c) 天堂.

[12] Contrast 出路 and 出新路. The latter loses the meaning of 'exit'.

[13] Contrast 長路 and 長柏油路. The latter retains the meaning of 'long road'.

[14] 的而且確 means 'most definitely' when the bimorphemic 的確 word has another two-character word inserted within its boundaries. The meaning of 的確 is not affected by this insertion, but no other insertions are allowed.

[15] 字 and 詞 for 'character' and 'word'.

[16] 師 and 老師 both mean 'teacher', in classical and modern Chinese, respectively.

[17] 完畢 and 鉛筆, 'finish' and 'pencil', respectively.

[18] 我俾個蘋果佢 and 我給他一個蘋果, 'I gave an apple (to) him' and 'I gave him an apple', respectively.

[19] 佢冇封利是 and 佢冇利是封, 'he/she has not given red packets' and 'he/she has no red packets', respectively.

[20] 故事 and 事故, 'story' and 'incident', respectively.

[21] 美國有所行動 and 美國所有行動, 'America has taken action' and 'all of America's action', respectively.

[22] 是 , 'is/are'.

Chapter 3

[1] With 陝 and 信 presented, subjects might report seeing 陰 instead.

[2] 苜 could be embedded in the character 寬, the pseudocharacter 廎 , or the noncharacter 屾苜.

[3] The radical 日 occurred in a character like 是 or a noncharacter like 景.

[4] The phonetics were 丙 and 廷 , and the phonetic compounds were 病 and 挺.

[5] 高 itself considered a nonphonetic compound, acutally acts as the phonetic in 橋 and 稿.

[6] The Chinese subjects would say 正 or 員 in Cantonese.

[7] 煤是一种植物 is a "homophone" sentence, and 铅是一种植物 is a control sentence.

Chapter 4

[1] 一, 二, and 三, 'one', 'two', and 'three', respectively.

[2] 氵 is labeled as 'three dots of water'.

[3] 氵 is the radical in 酒, 沙, 污, 治, and 洞, respectively.

Chapter 5

[1] 問答 are opposites, 冷華 are nonopposites, 得室 are homophone nonopposites.

[2] 设

[3] 貨 and 取.

[4] 一 and 哥.

[5] 哥

[6] 这個是.

[7] 上

[8] 英 and 芥.

[9] The patient wrote 請 instead of 話.

REFERENCES

Aaron, P. G., & Handley, A. C. (1975). Directional scanning and cerebral asymmetries in processing visual stimuli. *Perceptual and Motor Skills, 40*, 719-725.

Aaronson, D., & Ferres, S. (1986). Sentence processing in Chinese-American bilinguals. *Journal of Memory and Language, 25*, 136-162.

Ai, W. (1949). *Chinese writing.* Shanghai: Chunghwa. (In Chinese).

Albanese, J.-F. (1985). Language lateralization of English-French bilinguals. *Brain and Language, 24*, 284-296.

Albert, M. L., & Obler, L. K. (1978). *The bilingual brain.* New York: Academic.

Annett, M. (1985). *Left, right, hand and brain: The right shift theory.* London: Lawrence Erlbaum Associates.

April, R. S., & Han, M. (1980). Crossed aphasia in a right- handed bilingual Chinese man: A second case. *Archives of Neurology, 37*, 342-346.

April, R. S., & Tse, P. C. (1977). Crossed aphasia in a Chinese bilingual dextral. *Archives of Neurology, 34*, 766-770.

Au, T. K. F. (1984). Counterfactuals: In reply to Alfred Bloom. *Cognition, 17*, 289-302.

Baddeley, A. D. (1966). Short-term memory for word sequences as a function of acoustic, semantic, and formal similarity. *Quarterly Journal of Experimental Psychology, 18*, 362-365.

Baddeley, A. D. (1983). Working memory. *Philosophical Transactions of the Royal Society, London, B302*, 311-324.

Baddeley, A. D. (1986). *Working memory.* Oxford: Clarendon.

Baddeley, A. D., & Hitch, G. J. (1974). Working memory. In G. A. Bower (Ed.), *The psychology of learning and motivation: Advances in research and theory, Vol. 8* (pp. 47-90). New York: Academic.

Baddeley, A. D., Thomson, N., & Buchanan, M. (1975). Word length and the structure of short-term memory. *Journal of Verbal Learning and Verbal Behavior, 14*, 575-589.

Baron, J., & Strawson, C. (1976). Use of orthographic and word- specific knowledge in reading words aloud. *Journal of Experimental Psychology: Human Perception and Performance, 2*, 386-393.

Beaumont, J. G. (1982). Studies with verbal stimuli. In J. G. Beaumont (Ed.), *Divided visual field studies of cerebral organisation* (pp. 57-86). London: Academic. Beaumont, J. G.

(1983). *Introduction to neuropsychology.* Oxford: Blackwell.

Benson, D. F., & Geschwind, N. (1969). The alexias. In P. J. Vinken & G. W. Bruyn (Eds.), *Handbook of clinical neurology, Vol. 4. Disorders of speech, perception, and symbolic behaviour* (pp. 112-140). Amsterdam: North Holland.

Berlin, B., & Kay, P. (1969). *Basic color terms: Their universality and evolution.* Berkeley: University of California Press.

Bertelson, P., & de Gelder, B. (in press). The emergence of phonological awareness: comparative approaches. In I. G. Mattingly & M. Studdert-Kennedy (Eds.), *Modularity and the motor theory of speech perception..* Hillsdale, NJ: Lawrence Erlbaum Associates.

Besner, D., & Coltheart, M. (1979). Ideographic and alphabetic processing in skilled reading of English. *Neuropsychologia, 17,* 467-472.

Besner, D., Daniels, S., & Slade, C. (1982). Ideogram reading and right hemisphere language. *British Journal of Psychology, 73,* 21-28.

Bever, T. G., & Chiarello, R. J. (1974). Cerebral dominance in musicians and nonmusicians. *Science, 185,* 137-139.

Biederman, I., & Tsao, I. C. (1979). On processing Chinese ideographs and English words: Some implications from Stroop- test results. *Cognitive Psychology, 11,* 125-132.

Binnie-Dawson, J. L. M. (1981, August). *The cross-cultural aspects of the development of spaital ability: A bio-social approach.* Paper presented at the VIth ISSBD Conference, Toronto.

Bloom, A. (1981). *The linguistic shaping of thought: A study in the impact of language on thinking in China and the West.* Hillsdale, NJ: Lawrence Erlbaum Associates.

Blumenthal, A. L. (1977). *The process of cognition.* Englewood Cliffs, NJ: Prentice-Hall.

Boey, K. W. (1976). *Rigidity and cognitive complexity: an empirical investigation in the interpersonal, physical, and numerical domains under task-oriented and ego-involved conditions.* Unpublished doctoral dissertation, University of Hong Kong.

Boles, D. B. (1986). Hemispheric differences in the judgment of number. *Neuropsychologia, 24,* 511-519.

Boucher, J., & Osgood, C. E. (1969). The Pollyanna hypothesis. *Journal of Verbal Learning and Verbal Behavior, 8,* 1-8.

Bradshaw, G. J., Hicks, R. E., & Rose, B. (1979). Lexical discrimination and letter-string identificaton in the two visual fields. *Brain and Language, 8,* 10-18.

Braine, L. G. (1968). Asymmetries of pattern perception observed in Israelis. *Neuropsychologia, 6,* 73-88.

Brown, R. (1976). Reference: In memorial tribute to Eric Lenneberg. *Cognition, 4,* 125-153.

Bryant, P., & Bradley, L. (1985). *Children's reading problems.* Oxford: Blackwell.

Bryden, M. P. (1982). *Laterality: Functional asymmetry in the intact brain.* New York: Academic.

Carlson, E. R. (1962). Generality of order of concept attainment. *Psychological Reports, 10,* 375-380.

Carpenter, P. A., & Just, M. A. (1981). Cognitive processes in reading: Models based on readers' eye fixations. In A. M. Lesgold & C. A. Perfetti (Eds.), *Integrative processes in reading* (pp. 177-213). Hillsdale, NJ: Lawrence Erlbaum Associates.

Carroll, J. B. (1981). Twenty-five years of research on foreign language aptitude. In K. C. Diller (Ed.), *Individual differences and universals in language learning aptitude* (pp. 83-118). Rowley, MA: Newbury House.

Chan, J. (1976, July). *Is Raven's Progressive Matrices test culture- free or culture-fair? Some research findings in Hong Kong context.* Paper presented at the Third International Association for Cross-Cultural Psychology Congress, Tilburg, The Nethelands.

Chan, J. (1981a). A crossroads in language instruction. *Journal of Reading, 22,* 411-415.

Chan, J. (1981b). Parenting styles and children's reading abilities: A Hong Kong study. *Journal of Reading, 22,* 667-675.

Chan, M. Y. (1982). Statistics on the strokes of present-day Chinese script. *Chinese Linguistics, 1*, 299–305. (In Chinese).

Chao, Y. R. (1955). Notes on Chinese grammar and logic. *Philosophy East and West, 5*, 31–41.

Chao, Y. R. (1968a). *A grammar of spoken Chinese.* Berkeley: University of California Press.

Chao, Y. R. (1968b). *Language and symbolic systems.* London: Cambridge University Press.

Chen, C. S., & Stevenson, H. W. (1988). Cross-linguistic differences in digit span of preschool children. *Journal of Experimental Child Psychology, 46*, 150–158.

Chen, H. C. (1986). Component detection in reading Chinese characters. In H. S. R. Kao & R. Hoosain (Eds.), *Linguistics, psychology, and the Chinese language* (pp. 1–10). Hong Kong: University of Hong Kong Centre of Asian Studies.

Chen, H. C., & Chen, M. J. (1988). Directional scanning in Chinese reading. In I. M. Liu, H. C. Chen, & M. J. Chen (Eds.), *Cognitive aspects of the Chinese language* (pp. 15–26). Hong Kong: Asian Research Service.

Chen, H. C., & Juola, J. F. (1982). Dimensions of lexical coding in Chinese and English. *Memory and Cognition, 10*, 216–224.

Chen, L. K., & Carr, H. A. (1926). The ability of Chinese students to read in vertical and horizontal directions. *Journal of Experimental Psychology, 9*, 110–117.

Chen, M. J. (1981). Direction scanning of visual displays: A study of Chinese subjects. *Journal of Cross-Cultural Psychology, 12*, 252–271.

Chen, M. J., Braithwaite, V., & Huang, J. T. (1982). Attributes of intelligent behavior. *Journal of Cross-Cultural Psychology, 13*, 139–156.

Chen, M. J., Yung, Y. F., & Ng, T. W. (1988). The effect of context on the perception of Chinese characters. In I. M. Liu, H. C. Chen, & M. J. Chen (Eds.), *Cognitive aspects of the Chinese language* (pp. 27–39). Hong Kong: Asian Research Service.

Cheng, C. M. (1981). Perception of Chinese characters. *Acta Psychologica Taiwanica, 23*, 137–153.

Cheng, C. M. (1982). Analysis of present-day Mandarin. *Journal of Chinese Linguistics, 10*, 281–358.

Cheng, C. M., & Fu, G. L. (1986). The recognition of Chinese characters and words under divided visual field presentation. In H. S. R. Kao & R. Hoosain (Eds.), *Linguistics, psychology, and the Chinese language* (pp. 23–37). Hong Kong: University of Hong Kong Centre of Asian Studies.

Cheng, C. M., & Shih, S. I. (1988). The nature of lexical access in Chinese: Evidence from experiments on visual and phonological priming in lexical judgment. In I. M. Liu, H. C. Chen, & M. J. Chen (Eds.), *Cognitive aspects of the Chinese language* (pp. 1–14). Hong Kong: Asian Research Service.

Cheng, C. M., & Yang, M. J. (1989). Lateralization in the visual perception of Chinese characters and words. *Brain and Language, 36*, 669–689.

Cheng, R. L. (1985). Sub-syllabic morphemes in Taiwanese. *Journal of Chinese Linguistics, 13*, 12–42.

Ching, Y. C. T. (1988). Lexical tone perception by Cantonese deaf children. In I. M. Liu, H. C. Chen, & M. J. Chen (Eds.), *Cognitive aspects of the Chinese language* (pp. 93–102). Hong Kong: Asian Research Service.

Chu-Chang, M., & Loritz, D. J. (1977). Phonological encoding of Chinese ideographs in short-term memory. *Language Learning, 27*, 341–352.

Condry, S. M., McMahon-Rideout, M., & Levy, A. A. (1979). A developmental investigation of selective attention to graphic, phonetic, and semantic information in words. *Perception and Psychophysics, 25*, 88–94.

Conrad, R. (1964). Acoustic confusions in immediate memory. *British Journal of Psychology, 55*, 75–84.

Cornsweet, T. N. (1970). *Visual perception.* New York: Academic.

Costa, L. D. (1975). The relation of visuospatial dysfunction to digit span performance in patients with cerebral lesions. *Cortex, 11*, 31–36.

Crowder, R. G. (1971). The sounds of vowels and consonants in immediate memory. *Journal of Verbal Learning and Verbal Behavior, 10*, 587–596.

Damasio, A., Bellugi, U., Damasio, H., Poizner, H., & Van Gilder, J. (1986). Sign language aphasia during left-hemisphere amytal injection. *Nature, 322*, 363–365.

De Francis, J. F. (1950). *Nationalism and language reform in China*. Princeton: Princeton University Press.

Douglas, J. D., & Wong, A. C. (1977). Formal operations: Age and sex differences in Chinese and American children. *Child Development, 48*, 689–692.

Ellis, N. C., & Hennelly, R. A. (1980). A bilingual word-length effect: Implications for intelligence testing and the relative ease of mental calculation in Welsh and English. *British Journal of Psychology, 71*, 43–51.

Eriksen, C. W., Pollack, M. D., & Montague, W. (1970). Implicit speech: Mechanism in perceptual encoding. *Journal of Experimental Psychology, 84*, 502–507.

Fang, S. P., Horng, R. Y., & Tzeng, O. J. L. (1986). Consistency effects in the Chinese character and pseudo-character naming tasks. In H. S. R. Kao & R. Hoosain (Eds.), *Linguistics, psychology, and the Chinese language* (pp. 11–21). Hong Kong: University of Hong Kong Centre of Asian Studies.

Feldman, L. B., & Turvey, M. (1980). Words written in kana are named faster than the same words written in kanji. *Language and Speech, 23*, 141–147.

Feustel, T., & Tsao, Y. C. (1978, March). *Differences in reading latencies of Chinese characters in the right and left visual fields*. Paper presented at the meeting of the Eastern Psychological Association.

Freeman, R. D. (1980). Visual acuity is better for letters in rows than in columns. *Nature, 286*, 62–64.

Freyd, J. J. (1987). Dynamic mental representations. *Psychological Review, 94*, 427–438.

Frost, R., Katz, L., & Bentin, S. (1987). Strategies for visual word recognition and orthographical depth: A multilingual comparison. *Journal of Experimental Psychology: Human Perception and Performance, 13*, 104–115.

Galloway, L., & Krashen, S. D. (1980). Cerebral organization in bilingualism and second language. In R. C. Scarcella & S. D. Krashen (Eds.), *Research in second language acquisition* (pp. 74–80). Rowley, MA: Newbury House.

Glicksberg, D. H. (1963). *A study of the span of immediate memory among adult students of English as a foreign language*. Unpublished doctoral dissertation, University of Michigan.

Glushko, R. J. (1979). The organization and activation of orthographic knowledge in reading aloud. *Journal of Experimental Psychology: Human Perception and Performance, 5*, 674–691.

Greenberg, J. H. (1957). *Essays in linguistics*. Chicago: The University of Chicago Press.

Guo, N. F. (1984). Studies of lateralization in Chinese language functions. In H. S. R. Kao & R. Hoosain (Eds.), *Psychological studies of the Chinese language* (pp. 1–9). Hong Kong: Chinese Language Society of Hong Kong.

Haber, L. R., Haber, R. N., & Furlin, K. R. (1983). Word length and word shape as sources of information in reading. *Reading Research Quarterly, 18*, 165–189.

Hardyck, C., Tzeng, O. J. L., & Wang, W. S.-Y. (1977). Cerebral lateralization effects in visual half-field experiments. *Nature, 269*, 705–707.

Hardyck, C., Tzeng, O. J. L., & Wang, W. S.-Y. (1978). Cerebral lateralization of function and bilingual decision processes: Is thinking lateralized? *Brain and Language, 5*, 56–71.

Hasuike, R., Tzeng, O. J. L., & Hung, D. L. (1986). Script effects and cerebral lateralization: The case of Chinese characters. In J. Vaid (Ed.), *Language processing in bilinguals: Psycholinguistic and neuropsychological perspectives* (pp. 275–288). Hillsdale, NJ: Lawrence Erlbaum Associates.

Hatta, T. (1977). Recognition of Japanese kanji in the left and right visual fields. *Neuropsychologia, 15,* 685–688.

Healy, A. F. (1976). Detection errors on the word *the*: Evidence for reading units larger than letters. *Journal of Experimental Psychology: Human Perception and Performance, 2,* 235–242.

Healy, A. F., & Drewnowski, A. (1983). Investigating the boundaries of reading units: Letter detection in misspelled words. *Journal of Experimental Psychology: Human Perception and Performance, 9,* 413–426.

Healy, A. F., Oliver, W. L., & McNamara, T. P. (1987). Detecting letters in continuous text: Effects of display size. *Journal of Experimental Psychology: Human Perception and Performance, 13,* 279–290.

Ho, S. K., & Hoosain, R. (1984). Hemisphere differences in the perception of opposites. In H. S. R. Kao & R. Hoosain (Eds.), *Psychological studies of the Chinese language* (pp. 11–22). Hong Kong: The Chinese Language Society of Hong Kong.

Ho, S. K., & Hoosain, R. (1989). Right hemisphere advantage in lexical decision with two-character Chinese words. *Brain and Language, 37,* 606–615.

Hockett, C. F. (1960). The origin of speech. *Scientific American, 203,* 89–96.

Hong, M. M. P., Cheng, P. T., & Hsi, M. S. (1986). The language/motor aspect of subcortical putaminal lesions in the left hemisphere. In H. S. R. Kao & R. Hoosain (Eds.), *Linguistics, psychology, and the Chinese language* (pp. 297- 307). Hong Kong: University of Hong Kong Centre of Asian Studies.

Hoosain, R. (1977). Rote or concept learning as a function of set and difficulty. *Psychologia, 20,* 237–240.

Hoosain, R. (1979). Forward and backward digit span in the languages of the bilingual. *The Journal of Genetic Psychology, 135,* 263–268.

Hoosain, R. (1982). Correlation between pronunciation speed and digit span size. *Perceptual and Motor Skills, 55,* 1128.

Hoosain, R. (1984a). Experiments on digit spans in the Chinese and English languages. In H. S. R. Kao & R. Hoosain (Eds.), *Psychological studies of the Chinese language* (pp. 23–38). Hong Kong: The Chinese Language Society of Hong Kong.

Hoosain, R. (1984b). Lateralization of bilingual digit span functions. *Perceptual and Motor Skills, 58,* 21–22.

Hoosain, R. (1986a). Language, orthography, and cognitive processes: Chinese perspectives for the Sapir-Whorf hypothesis. *International Journal of Behavioural Development, 9,* 507–525.

Hoosain, R. (1986b). Psychological and orthographic variables for translation asymmetry. In H. S. R. Kao & R. Hoosain (Eds.), *Linguistics, psychology, and the Chinese language* (pp. 203- 216). Hong Kong: University of Hong Kong Centre of Asian Studies.

Hoosain, R. (1990a, August). *Cerebral lateralization of bilingual vocal-auditory functioning.* Paper presented at the Annual Convention of the American Psychological Association, Boston.

Hoosain, R. (in press, a). Left handedness and handedness switch amongst the Chinese. *Cortex.*

Hoosain, R. (in press, b). Cerebral lateralization of bilingual functions after handedness switch in childhood. *Journal of Genetic Psychology.*

Hoosain, R., & Osgood, C. E. (1983). Information processing times for English and Chinese words. *Perception and Psychophysics, 34,* 573–577.

Hoosain, R., & Salili, F. (1987). Language differences in pronunciation speed for numbers, digit span, and mathematical ability. *Psychologia, 30,* 34–38.

Hoosain, R., & Shiu, L. P. (1989). Cerebral lateralization of Chinese-English bilingual functions. *Neuropsychologia, 27,* 705- 712.

Hsieh, N. M. (1982). *Reading of Chinese characters and words and phonological recoding.* Unpublished master's thesis, National Taiwan University.

Huang, C. Y. (1982) Aphasia in Chinese. In H. S. R. Kao & C. M. Cheng (Eds.), *Psychological research on the Chinese language* (pp. 183–190). Taipei: Wenhe. (In Chinese.)

Huang, C. Y. (1984). Reading and writing disorders in Chinese: Some theoretical issues. In H. S. R. Kao & R. Hoosain (Eds.), *Psychological studies of the Chinese language* (pp. 39–56). Hong Kong: The Chinese Language Society of Hong Kong.

Huang, C. Y., & Lau, W. K. (1985, July). *Dysgraphia in subcortical infarction.* Paper presented at the Second International Symposium on the Neural and Motor Aspects of Handwriting, Hong Kong.

Huang, J. T. (1979). Time-dependent separability hypothesis of Chinese words association. *Acta Psychologica Taiwanica, 21*, 41–48.

Huang, S. F. (1978). Historical change of prepositions and emergence of SOV order. *Journal of Chinese Linguistics, 6*, 212- 242.

Huang, Y. L., & Jones, B. (1980). Naming and discrimination of Chinese ideograms presented in the right and left visual fields. *Neuropsychologia, 18*, 703–706.

Hughes, C. P., Chan, J. L., & Su, M. S. (1983). Aprosodia in Chinese patients with right cerebral hemisphere lesions. *Archives of Neurology, 40*, 732–736.

Hung, D. L., & Tzeng, O. J. L. (1981). Orthographic variations and visual information processing. *Psychological Bulletin, 90*, 377–414.

Hung, D. L., Tzeng, O. J. L., Salzman, B., & Dreher, J. (1984). A critical evaluation of the horse-racing model of skilled reading. In H. S. R. Kao & R. Hoosain (Eds.), *Psychological studies of the Chinese language* (pp. 75-101). Hong Kong: The Chinese Language Society of Hong Kong.

Hunter, I. M. L. (1964). *Memory.* Baltimore: Penguin.

Hurvich, L. M., & Jameson, D. (1974). Opponent processes as a model of neural organization. *American Psychologist, 29*, 88- 102.

Jensen, A. R. (1970). Hierachical theories of mental ability. In B. Dockrell (Ed.), *On intelligence* (pp. 119–190). Toronto: Ontario Institute for Studies in Education.

Johnson, J. E., & Hellige, J. B. (1986). Lateralized effects of blurring: A test of the visual spatial frequency model of cerebral hemisphere asymmetry. *Neuropsychologia, 24*, 351–362.

Kalgren, B. (1949). *The Chinese language.* New York: Ronald.

Kay, P., & Kempton, W. (1984). What is the Sapir-Whorf hypothesis? *American Anthropologist, 86*, 65–79.

Kay, P., & McDaniel, C. (1978). The linguistic significance of the meanings of basic color terms. *Language, 54*, 610–646.

Keatley, C. W. (1988). *Facilitation effects in the primed lexical decision task within and across languages.* Unpublished doctoral dissertation, University of Hong Kong.

Keele, S. W. (1968). Movement control in skilled motor performance. *Psychological Bulletin, 70*, 387–403.

Kershner, J. R., & Jeng, G. R. (1972). Dual functional hemispheric asymmetry in visual perception: Effects of ocular dominance and post-exposural processes. *Neuropsychologia, 10*, 437–445.

Kinsbourne, M., & Cook, J. (1971). Generalized and lateralized effects of concurrent verbalization on a unimanual skill. *The Quarterly Journal of Experimental Psychology, 23*, 341–345.

Kinsbourne, M., & Hiscock, M. (1977). Does cerebral dominance develop? In S. J. Segalowitz & F. A. Gruber (Eds.), *Language development and neurological theory* (pp. 171-191). New York: Academic.

Klima, E. S., & Bellugi, U. (1979). *The signs of language.* Cambridge, MA: Harvard University Press.

Koppitz, E. M. (1963). *The Bender gestalt test for young children.* New York: Gruene & Stratton.

Kreuger, L. E. (1975). The word superiority effect: Is its locus visual-spatial or verbal? *Bulletin of the Psychonomic Society, 6*, 465-468.

Kucera, H., & Francis, W. N. (1967). *Computational analysis of present-day American English*. Providence, RI: Brown University Press.

Kugelmass, S., & Lieblich, A. (1970). Perceptual exploration in Israeli children. *Child Development, 41*, 1125-1131.

Kuo, W. F. (1978). A preliminary study of reading disability in the Republic of China. *Collected Papers* (National Taiwan Normal University), *20*, 57-78.

Lai, C., & Huang, J. T. (1988). Component migration in Chinese characters: Effects of priming and context on illusory conjunction. In I. M. Liu, H. C. Chen, & M. J. Chen (Eds.), *Cognitive aspects of the Chinese language* (pp. 57-67). Hong Kong: Asian Research Service.

Lee, K. F. (1976). Polysyllabicity in the modern Chinese verb: An attempt to quantify a linguistic shift. *Journal of Chinese Linguistics, 4*, 24-46.

Leong, C. K. (1986). What does accessing a morphemic script tell us about reading and reading disorders in an alphabetic script? *Annals of Dyslexia, 36*, 82-102.

Leong, C. K., Wong, S., Wong, A., & Hiscock, M. (1985). Differential cortical involvement in perceiving Chinese characters—levels of processing approach. *Brain and Language, 26*, 131-145.

Lesser, G. S., Fifer, G., & Clark, D. H. (1965). Mental abilities of children from different social class and cultural groups. *Monograph of the Society for Research in Child Development, 30*(4), 1-115.

Li, C. N., & Thompson, S. A. (1974). An explanation of word order change: SVO—SOV. *Foundations of Language, 12*, 201-214.

Li, C. N., & Thompson, S. A. (1977). The acquisition of tone in Mandarin-speaking children. *Journal of Child Language, 4*, 185- 200.

Li, X. T., Hu, C. Q., Zhu, Y. L., Song, Z. W., & Li, Y. (1986). Language disorders in patients with cerebral vascular accidents. In H. S. R. Kao & R. Hoosain (Eds.), *Linguistics, psychology, and the Chinese language* (pp. 265-277). Hong Kong: University of Hong Kong Centre of Asian Studies.

Li, X. T., Hu, C. Q., Zhu, Y. L., & Sun, B. (1984). Neurolinguistic analysis of Chinese alexia and agraphia. In H. S. R. Kao & R. Hoosain (Eds.), *Psychological studies of the Chinese language* (pp. 151-165). Hong Kong: The Chinese Language Society of Hong Kong.

Liberman, I. Y., Mann, V. A., Shankweiler, D., & Werfelman, M. (1982). Children's memory for recurring linguistic and non- linguistic material in relation to reading ability. *Cortex, 18*, 367-375.

Light, T. (1979). Word order and word order change in Mandarin Chinese. *Journal of Chinese Linguistics, 7*, 149-180.

Lin, C. S. (1986). An experiment on the hemispheric difference in the perception of visual stimuli and the validation of tests and scales hypothetically measuring cerebral laterality. *Bulletin of Educational Psychology, Taiwan Normal University, 19*, 37-54.

Lindsay, P. H., & Norman, D. A. (1977). *Human information processing: An introduction to psychology*. New York: Academic.

Liu, I. M. (1983). Cueing function of fragments of Chinese characters in reading. *Acta Psychologica Taiwanica, 25*, 85-90.

Liu, I. M. (1988). Context effects on word/character naming: Alphabetic versus logographic languages. In I. M. Liu, H. C. Chen, & M. J. Chen (Eds.), *Cognitive aspects of the Chinese language* (pp. 81-92). Hong Kong: Asian Research Service.

Liu, I. M., Chuang, C. J., & Wang, S. C. (1975). *Frequency count of 40,000 Chinese words*. Taipei: Lucky Books.

Liu, I. M., Yeh, J. S., Wang, L. H., & Chang, Y. K. (1974). Effects of arranging Chinese words as units on reading efficiency. *Acta Psychologica Taiwanica, 16*, 25-32.

Liu, K. S., & Shen, H. M. (1977). Effects of language structure and intertrial interval on the speed of silent reading. *Acta Psychologica Taiwanica, 19,* 57–59.

Liu, L. G. (1985). Reasoning in counterfactuals in Chinese: Are there any obstacles? *Cognition, 21,* 239–270.

Loftus, G. R., & Loftus, E. F. (1976). *Human memory: The processing of information.* Hillsdale, NJ: Lawrence Erlbaum Associates.

Lyman, R. S., Kwan, S. T., & Chao, W. H. (1938). Left occipital- parietal brain tumour with observations on alexia and agraphia in Chinese and in English. *The Chinese Medical Journal, 54,* 491–515.

Lynn, R. (1977). The intelligence of the Chinese and Malays in Singapore. *Mankind Quarterly, 18,* 125–128.

Lynn, R. (1987). Japan: Land of the rising IQ. A reply to Flynn. *Bulletin of the British Psychological Society, 40,* 464–468.

Lynn, R., Hampson, S., & Lee, M. (1988). The intelligence of Chinese children in Hong Kong. *School Psychology International, 9,* 29–32.

Ma, M. (1970). *An anatomy of written Chinese.* (An inaugaural lecture.) University of Hong Kong Supplement to the Gazette, vol. 17, no. 6.

MacNichol, E. F. (1964). Three-pigment color vision. *Scientific American, 211,* 48–56.

Mandelbaum, D. G. (Ed.). (1951). *Selected writings of Edward Sapir on language, culture and personality.* Berkeley: University of California Press.

Mann, V. A. (1986). Temporary memory for linguistic and nonlinguistic material in relation to the acquisition of Japanese kana and kanji. In H. S. R. Kao & R. Hoosain (Eds.), *Linguistics, psychology, and the Chinese language* (pp. 155- 167). Hong Kong: University of Hong Kong Centre of Asian Studies.

Mann, V. A. (1988). Phonological awareness: A critical skill for beginning readers of alphabetic systems. In I. M. Liu, H. C. Chen, & M. J. Chen (Eds.), *Cognitive aspects of the Chinese language* (pp. 109–118). Hong Kong: Asian Research Service.

Mason, M. (1978). From print to sound in mature readers as a function of reading ability and two forms of orthographic regularity. *Memory and Cognition, 6,* 568–581.

Mazzucchi, A., Parma, M., & Cattelani, R. (1981). Hemispheric dominance in the perception of tonal sequences in relation to sex, musical competence and handedness. *Cortex, 17,* 291–302.

McClain, L., & Huang, J. Y. S. (1982). Speed of simple arithmetic in bilinguals. *Memory and Cognition, 10,* 591–596.

McConkie, G. W., & Rayner, K. (1975). The span of the effective stimulus during a fixation in reading. *Perception and Psychophysics, 17,* 578–586.

McCusker, L. X., Hillinger, M. L., & Bias, R. G. (1981). Phonological recoding and reading. *Psychological Bulletin, 89,* 217–245.

McGinnies, E., & Turnage, T. W. (1968). Verbal association by Chinese and American students as a function of word frequency and mode of presentation. *Psychological Reports, 23,* 1051–1060.

Meyer, D. E., Schvaneveldt, R. W., & Ruddy, M. G. (1974). Functions of graphemic codes in visual word recognition. *Memory and Cognition, 2,* 309–321.

Miller, G. A. (1956). The magical number seven, plus or minus two: Some limits on our capacity for processing information. *Psychological Review, 63,* 81–97.

Miron, M. S., & Wolfe, S. (1964). A cross-linguistic analysis of the response distributions of restricted word associations. *Journal of Verbal Learning and Verbal Behavior, 3,* 376–384.

Miura, I. (1983). Which is more effective, monaural or binaural listening? *Bulletin of the Phonetic Society of Japan, 174,* 3- 11.

Miura, I. T., Kim, C. C., Chang, C. M., & Okamoto, Y. (1988). Effects of language characteristics on children's cognitive representation of numbers: Cross-national comparisons. *Child Development, 59,* 1445–1450.

Morikawa, Y. (1981). Stroop phenomena in the Japanese language. *Perceptual and Motor Skills, 53,* 67–77.

Morikawa, Y. (1986). Stroop phenomena in the Japanese language (II): Effects of character-usage frequency and number of strokes. In H. S. R. Kao & R. Hoosain (Eds.), *Linguistics, psychology, and the Chinese language* (pp. 73–80). Hong Kong: University of Hong Kong Centre of Asian Studies.

Mou, L. C., & Anderson, N. S. (1981). Graphemic and phonemic codings of Chinese characters in short-term retention. *Bulletin of the Psychonomic Society, 17*, 255–258.

Murphy, G. L. (1988). Comprehending complex concepts. *Cognitive Science, 12*, 529–562.

Murphy, G. L. (in press). Noun phrase interpretation and conceptual combination. *Journal of Memory and Language.*

Murray, J. E. (1982). *The effects of exposure duration on visual field differences in letter identification.* Unpublished master's thesis, University of Waterloo.

Naeser, M. A., & Chan, S. W. C. (1980). Case study of Chinese aphasia with the Boston Diagnostic Aphasia Examination. *Neuropsychologia, 18*, 389–410.

Nagoshi, C. T., Johnson, R. C., & Honbo, K. A. A. (1989). Familial resemblances for cognitive abilities profiles of Caucasian and Japanese Americans. *Personality and Individual Differences, 10*, 127–129.

Naveh-Benjamin, M., & Ayers, T. J. (1986). Digit span, reading rate, and linguistic relativity. *The Quarterly Journal of Experimental Psychology, 38A*, 739–751.

Nguy, T. V. H., Allard, F. A., & Bryden, M. P. (1980). Laterality effects for Chinese characters: Differences between pictorial and nonpictorial characters. *Canadian Journal of Psychology, 34*, 270–273.

Novotna, Z. (1967). Linguistic factors of the low adaptability of loan-words to the lexical system of modern Chinese. *Monumenta Serica, 26*, 103–118.

Osgood, C. E., & Hoosain, R. (1974). Salience of the word as a unit in the perception of language. *Perception & Psychophysics, 15*, 168–192.

Osgood, C. E., & Hoosain, R. (1983). Pollyanna II: Two types of negativity. *The Journal of Psychology, 113*, 151–160.

Osgood, C. E., May, W. H., & Miron, M. S. (1975). *Cross-cultural universals of affective meaning.* Urbana: University of Illinois Press.

Paap, K. R., Newsome, S. L., & Noel, R. W. (1984). Word shape's in poor shape for the race to the lexicon. *Journal of Experimental Psychology: Human Perception and Performance, 10*, 413–428.

Packard, J. L. (1986). Tone production deficits in nonfluent aphasic Chinese speech. *Brain and Language, 29*, 212–223.

Paradis, M., Hagiwara, H., & Hildebrandt, N. (1985). *Neurolinguistic aspects of the Japanese writing system.* New York: Academic.

Paraskevopoulos, J. N., & Kirk, S. A. (1969). *The development and psychometric characteristics of the Revised Illinois Test of Psycholinguistic Abilities.* Urbana: University of Illinois Press.

Peng, D. L., Orchard, L. N., & Stern, J. A. (1983). Evaluation of eye movement variables of Chinese and American readers. *Pavlovian Journal of Biological Sciences, 18*, 94–102.

Peng, R. X. (1982). A preliminary report on statistical analysis of the structure of Chinese characters. *Acta Psychologica Sinica, 14*, 385–390.

Pick, A. D. (1965). Improvement of visual and tactual form discrimination. *Journal of Experimental Psychology, 69*, 331–339.

Pong-Leung, S. W. (1983). *Performance of Hong Kong Chinese children on the Bender Visual Gestalt Test.* Unpublished master's thesis, University of Hong Kong.

Posner, M. I. (1978). *Chronometric explorations of mind.* Hillsdale, NJ: Lawrence Erlbaum Associates.

Prinzmetal, W., Treiman, R., & Rho, S. H. (1986). How to see a reading unit. *Memory and Language, 25*, 461–475.

Psychological Corporation, The. (1981). *Hong Kong Wechsler Intelligence Scale for Children Manual.* New York: Author.

Rapport, R. L., Tan, C. T., & Whitaker, H. A. (l983). Language function and dysfunction among Chinese- and English-speaking polyglots: Cortical stimulation, Wada testing, and clinical studies. *Brain and Language, 18*, 342–366.

Rayner, K. (1975). The perceptual span and peripheral cues in reading. *Cognitive Psychology, 7*, 65–81.

Read, C., Zhang, Y.F., Nie, H.Y., & Ding, B.Q. (1986). The ability to manipulate speech sounds depends on knowing alphabetic writing. *Cognition, 24*, 31–44.

Reicher, G. (1969). Perceptual recognition as a function of meaningfulness of stimulus material. *Journal of Experimental Psychology, 81*, 275–280.

Reid, D. K. & Hresko, W. P. (1981). *A cognitive approach to learning disabilities.* New York: McGraw-Hill.

Rosch, E. (1974). Linguistic relativity. In A. Silverstein (Ed.), *Human communication: Theoretical perspectives.* New York: Halsted.

Rozin, P., & Gleitman, L. R. (l977). The structure and acquisition of reading II: The reading process and the acquisition of the alphabetic principle. In A. S. Reber & D. L. Scarborough (Eds.), *Toward a psychology of reading: The proceedings of the CUNY conference* (pp. 55–141). Hillsdale, NJ: Lawrence Erlbaum Associates.

Rozin, P., Poritsky, S., & Sotsky, R. (1971). American children with reading problems can easily learn to read English represented in Chinese characters. *Science, 171*, 1264–1267.

Rudel, R. G., & Denckla, M. B. (1974). Relation of forward and backward digit repetition to neurological impairment in children with learning disabilities. *Neuropsychologia, 12*, 109–118.

Sasanuma, S., Itoh, M., Mori, K., & Kobayashi, Y. (1977). Tachistoscopic recognition of kana and kanji words. *Neuropsychologia, 15*, 547–553.

Schmuller, J. (1979). Hemispheric asymmetry for alphabetic identification: Scaling analysis. *Brain and Language, 8*, 263- 274.

Schneiderman, E. I., & Wesche, M. B. (1986). Right hemisphere processing and foreign language aptitude. *Review of Applied Linguistics, 71*, 43–64.

Schouten, M. E. H., van Dalen, T. E., & Klein, A. J. J. (1985). Ear advantage and second language proficiency. *Journal of Phonetics, 13*, 53–60.

Seidenberg, M. S. (1985). The time course of phonological code activation in two writing systems. *Cognition, 19*, 1–30.

Sergent, J. (1983). Role of input in visual hemispheric asymmetries. *Psychological Bulletin, 93*, 481–512.

Sergent, J. (1987). Failures to confirm the spatial-frequency hypothesis: Fatal blow or healthy complication? *Canadian Journal of Psychology, 41*, 412–428.

Shen, E. (l927). An analysis of eye movements in the reading of Chinese. *Journal of Experimental Psychology, l0*, 158-183.

So, K. F., Potter, M. C., & Friedman, R. B. (1978). *Reading in Chinese and English: Naming versus understanding.* Unpublished manuscript, Massachusetts Institute of Technology.

So, P. Y. C. (1979). *An evaluation of character simplification in contemporary China from a linguistic and psychological point of view.* Unpublished master's thesis, University of Hong Kong.

Soares, C. (1984). Left-hemisphere language lateralization in bilinguals: Use of the concurrent activities paradigm. *Brain and Language, 23*, 86–96.

Stern, J. A. (l978). Eye movements, reading, and cognition. In J. W. Senders, D. F. Fisher, & R. A. Monty (Eds.), *Eye movements and the higher psychological functions* (pp. 145–155). Hillsdale, NJ: Lawrence Erlbaum Associates.

Stevenson, H. W. (1984). Learning to read Chinese. In H. W. Stevenson & Q. Jing (Eds.), *Issues in cognition* (pp. 163- 177). Washington, DC: National Academy of Sciences and American Psychological Association.

Stevenson, H. W., Stigler, J. W., Lee, S. Y., Lucker, G. W., Kitamura, S., & Hsu, C. C.

(1985). Achievement of Japanese, Chinese, and American Children. *Child Development*, *56*, 718- 734.

Stevenson, H. W., Stigler, G. W., Lucker, G. W., Lee, S. Y., Hsu, C. C., & Kitamura, S. (1982). Reading disabilities: The case of Chinese, Japanese, and English. *Child Development*, *53*, 1164–1181.

Stigler, J. W., Lee, S. Y., & Stevenson, H. W. (1986). Digit memory in Chinese and English: Evidence for a temporally limited store. *Cognition*, *24*, 1–20.

Stroop, J. R. (1935). Studies of interference in serial verbal reactions. *Journal of Experimental Psychology*, *18*, 643–662.

Sun, F. C., Morita, M., & Stark, L. W. (1985). Comparative patterns of reading eye movement in Chinese and English. *Perception and Psychophysics*, *37*, 502–506.

Sun, F. C., & Stark, L. W. (1986, April). *The analysis of reading eye movements in Chinese and English – an approach to study information processing in the central nervous system.* Paper presented at the Shanghai Symposium on Neuroscience, Shanghai.

Suen, C. Y. (1986). *Computional studies of the most frequent Chinese words and sounds.* Singapore: World Scientific.

Taylor, I., & Taylor, M. M. (1983). *The psychology of reading.* New York: Academic.

Teng, E. L., Lee, P. H., Yang, K. S., & Chang, P. C. (1979). Lateral preferences for hand, foot and eye, and their lack of association with scholastic achievement, in 4,143 Chinese. *Neuropsychologia*, *17*, 41–48.

Treiman, R. A., Baron, J., & Luk, K. (1981). Speech recoding in silent reading: A comparison of Chinese and English. *Journal of Chinese Linguistics*, *9*, 116–125.

Tsang, K. K., & Hoosain, R. (1979). Segmental phonemes and tonal phonemes in comprehension of Cantonese. *Psychologia*, *22*, 222- 224.

Tsao, Y. C., Feustel, T., & Soseos, C. (1979). Stroop interference in the left and right visual fields. *Brain and Language*, *8*, 367–371.

Tsao, Y. C., Wu, M. F., & Feustel, T. (1981). Stroop interference: Hemispheric difference in Chinese speakers. *Brain and Language*, *13*, 372–378.

Tse, J. K. P. (1978). Tone acquisition in Cantonese: A longitudinal case study. *Journal of Child Language*, *5*, 191–204.

T'sou, B. K. (1978). Some preliminary observations on aphasia in a Chinese bilingual. *Acta Psychologica Taiwanica*, *20*, 57–64.

Tsunoda, T. (1985). *The Japanese brain.* Tokyo: Taishukan.

Tu, H. T. C. (1930). The effects of different arrangements of the Chinese language upon speed and comprehension of silent reading. *Journal of Genetic Psychology*, *38*, 321–327.

Turnage, T. W., & McGinnies, E. (1973). A cross-cultural comparison of the effects of presentation mode and meaningfulness on short-term recall. *American Journal of Psychology*, *86*, 369–381.

Tzeng, O. C. S., Hoosain, R., & Osgood, C. E. (1987). Cross- cultural componential analysis on affect attribution of emotion terms. *Journal of Psycholinguistic Research*, *16*, 443- 465.

Tzeng, O. J. L. (1982). On orthography and the relation between reading process and recognition. In H. S. R. Kao & C. M. Cheng (Eds.), *Psychological research on the Chinese language* (pp. 85–101). Taipei: Wenhe. (In Chinese).

Tzeng, O. J. L. (1988, December). *Pioneering new grounds for Chinese language research.* Paper presented at the Conference on Chinese Psychology, University of Hong Kong.

Tzeng, O. J. L., & Hung, D. L. (1978). Reading the Chinese character: Some basic research. *Acta Psychologica Taiwanica*, *20*, 45–49. (In Chinese.)

Tzeng, O. J. L., & Hung, D. L. (1981). Linguistic determinism: A written language perspective. In O. J. L. Tzeng & H. Singer (Eds.), *Perception of print: Reading research in experimental psychology* (pp. 237–255). Hillsdale, NJ: Lawrence Erlbaum Associates.

Tzeng, O. J., Hung, D. L., Chen, S., Wu, J., & Hsi, M. S. (1986). Processing Chinese logographs by Chinese brain damaged patients. In H. S. R. Kao, G. P. Galen, & R. Hoosain

(Eds.), *Graphonomics: Contemporary research in handwriting* (pp. 357- 374). Amsterdam: North Holland.

Tzeng, O. J. L., Hung, D. L., Cotton, B., & Wang, W. S.-Y. (1979). Visual lateralization effect in reading Chinese characters. *Nature, 282,* 499–501.

Tzeng, O. J. L., Hung, D. L., & Wang, W. S.-Y. (1977). Speech recoding in reading Chinese characters. *Journal of Experimental Psychology: Human Memory and Learning, 3,* 621–630.

Tzeng, O. J. L., & Wang, W. S.-Y. (1983). The first two R's. *American Scientist, 71,* 238–243.

Tzeng, O. J. L., & Wang, W. S.-Y. (1984). Search for a common neurocognitive mechanism for language and movements. *American Journal of Physiology, 246,* R904-R911.

Vaid, J. (1983). Bilingualism and brain lateralization. In S. J. Segalowitz (Ed.), *Language functions and brain organization* (pp. 315–339). New York: Academic.

Vernon, M. D. (1977). Varieties of deficiency in the reading process. *Harvard Educational Review, 47,* 396–410.

Vocate, D. R. (1985). Lateralization of auditory language: An EEG study of bilingual Crow Indian adolescents. *Communication Research Reports, 2,* 46–52.

Wai, F. Y. (1978). The effect of visual and acoustic similarity on short-term memory for Chinese words. *The Quarterly Journal of Experimental Psychology, 30,* 487–494.

Wang, L. (1959). *Modern Chinese grammar.* Hong Kong: Chung Hua. (In Chinese).

Wang, W. S.-Y. (1973). The Chinese language. *Scientific American, 228,* 50–60.

Wang, X. (1985). Mirror writing. *Chinese Journal of Neurology and Psychiatry, 18,* 108–110. (In Chinese.)

Wang, X. (1986). Mirror writing and the development of Chinese written language. In H. S. R. Kao, G. P. van Galen, & R. Hoosain (Eds.), *Graphonomics: Contemporary research in handwriting* (pp. 321–328). Amsterdam: North Holland.

Wang, X., & Cai, X. (1986). Agraphia in Chinese aphasic patients. In H. S. R. Kao & R. Hoosain (Eds.), *Linguistics, psychology, and the Chinese language* (pp. 245–254). Hong Kong: University of Hong Kong Centre of Asian Studies.

Wang, X., & Li, J. (1981). Dysgraphia. *Chinese Journal of Neurology and Psychiatry, 14,* 148–151. (In Chinese).

Wang, Y., & Taylor, I. (1990). *The use of pinyin in reading instruction in China.* Unpublished manuscript, University of Toronto.

Wechsler, D. (1955). *Manual for the Wechsler adult intelligence scale.* New York: The Psychological Corporation.

Weinreich, U. (1966). Explorations in semantic theory. In T. A. Sebeok (Ed.), *Current trends in linguistics. Volume III* (pp. 393–477). The Hague: Mouton.

Whorf, B. L. (1956). *Language, thought, and reality. Seclected writings of Benjamin Lee Whorf.* Cambridge, MA: MIT Press.

Witelson, S. F. (1980). Neuroanatomical asymmetry in left-handedness: A review and implications for functional asymmetry. In J. Herron (Ed.), *Neuropsychology of left-handedness* (pp. 79- 113). New York: Academic.

Woo, E. Y. C., & Hoosain, R. (1984). Visual and auditory functions of Chinese dyslexics. *Psychologia, 27,* 164–170.

Woodworth, R. S. (1938). *Experimental psychology.* New York: Holt.

Wright, G. N., Phillips, L. D., Whalley, P. C., Choo, G. T., Ng, K. O., Tan, I., & Wishuda, A. (1978). Cultural differences in probabilistic thinking. *Journal of Cross-Cultural Psychology, 9,* 285–299.

Wu, J. T., & Liu, I. M. (1988). A data base system about the psychological features of Chinese characters and words. In I. M. Liu, H. C. Chen, & M. J. Chen (Eds.), *Cognitive aspects of the Chinese language* (pp. 171–186). Hong Kong: Asian Research Service.

Yamadori, A. (1975). Ideogram reading in alexia. *Brain, 98,* 231–238.

Yang, K. S. (1986). Chinese personality and its change. In M. H. Bond (Ed.), *The psychology of the Chinese people* (pp. 106–170). Hong Kong: Oxford University Press.

Yau, S. C. (1982, July). *Linguistic analysis of archaic Chinese ideograms*. Paper presented at the XV International Conference on Sino-Tibetan Languages and Linguistics, Beijing.

Yeung, N. C. (1989). *Pre-lexical phonological activation in silent reading of Chinese.* Unpublished master's thesis, University of Hong Kong.

Young, G. (1977). Manual specialization in infancy: Implications for lateralization of brain function. In S. J. Segalowitz & F. A. Gruber (Eds.), *Language development and neurological theory* (pp. 290–311). New York: Academic.

Yu, B., Jing, Q., & Sima, H. (1984). STM capacity for Chinese words and phrases under simultaneous presentation. In H. W. Stevenson & Q. Jing (Eds.), *Issues in cognitions* (pp. 317- 329). Washington, DC: National Academy of Sciences and American Psychological Association.

Zhang, G., & Simon, H. A. (1985). STM capacity for Chinese words and idioms: Chunking and acoustical loop hypotheses. *Memory and Cognition, 13*, 193–201.

Zhang, W., Peng, R., & Sima, H. (1984). STM capacity for Chinese words and idioms with visual and auditory presentations. In H. W. Stevenson & Q. Jing (Eds.), *Issues in cognition* (pp. 331- 344). Washington, DC: National Academy of Sciences and American Psychological Association.

Zhu, Y. L., Song, Z. W., Li, Y., Li, X. T., & Hu, C. Q. (1986). Language functions of subcortical structures. In H. S. R. Kao & R. Hoosain (Eds.), *Linguistics, psychology, and the Chinese language* (pp. 279-295). Hong Kong: University of Hong Kong Centre of Asian Studies.

Zhu, Y. P. (1987). *Analysis of cueing functions of the phonetic in modern Chinese.* Unpublished paper, East China Normal University. (In Chinese).

Zipf, G. K. (1949). *Human behavior and the principle of least effort.* Cambridge, MA: Addison-Wesley.

Author Index

Subject Index

A

Affective meaning, 46–48, 86
Agraphia, 146, 149, 152, 156, 158
Alexia, 149, 158
Alphabetic language, 6, 12–13, 20, 28–29, 34, 37, 39, 45, 68, 83, 89, 112, 123, 125, 160
Ambidexterous, 130, 148, 151
American sign language, 158
American subjects, 72–73, 77, 87–88, 90–94
Aphasia, 83, 132–162, 165
  Broca's, 147
  conduction, 135, 153
  crossed, 137–157
  global, 143, 145
  transcortical sensory, 139
  Wernicke's, 145
Apraxia, 152
Aprosodia, 139–140
Arabic numeral, 3, 9, 25, 46, 50, 68, 118
Arithmetic, 68–69, 72–74
Articulatory loop, 62–64, 72, 74, 76
Auditory processing, 126

B

Bender Visual Gestalt Test, 68–69
Bilingual,
  balanced, 46
  carry-over effect, 165, 168–169
  Chinese-English, 30, 46, 51, 59, 64, 66, 74, 102, 126–128, 131–133, 168
  English-Chinese, 127, 168
Boston Diagnostic Aphasia Examination, 137
Bottom-up process, 3, 28, 35, 52, 54, 57, 60, 97–98, 164–166, 168
British subjects, 96
Broca's area, 143

C

Calculus, 3
Cantonese, 8, 21, 48, 63–64, 72, 74, 80, 85, 127, 135, 140–143
Categorization (of information), 3
Cattell's Culture Fair Test, 70
Cerebral hemisphere, 66, 71, 99
Character, 5–7, 13, 16, 18–19, 20, 22, 27, 31, 38, 76, 84, 164, 166
Chunk (of information), 76, 84, 185
Classical Chinese, 1, 12, 14, 18–19, 21, 116
Coding test, 68–69, 91–92
Cognitive rigidity, 97
Cognitive style, 87, 94–98, 164
Colloquial style Chinese, 18
Color term, 2
Comprehension (of language), 4, 26, 62, 138, 145, 162
  test, 91–93
Conceptually-driven process (see top-down process)